Dimensions of Mind

Dimensions
of
Mind

Tarthang Tulku

 Dharma Publishing

UNDERSTANDING SELF AND MIND

Knowledge of Freedom: Time to Change
Revelations of Mind
Dimensions of Mind

ISBN 978-0-89800-087-0
Library of Congress Control Number: 2016946589

Printed in the USA by Dharma Mangalam Press,
Ratna Ling, 35755 Hauser Bridge Road, Cazadero, CA 95421

10   9   8   7   6   5   4   3   2   1

Dedicated to
Leslie Bradburn

Contents

Part Two: Making our Way on the Path

Part Three: Self-Liberation

Part Four: In the Center

CONTENTS

List of Exercises

Foreword

For more than 40 years, I have lived in America, and during that time I have had many opportunities to engage people from all walks of life. Although I do not interact much with the public at large, I do regularly see the members of our small community as well as some of the short-term volunteers who come to Odiyan, which has been my home for the past twenty years.

It will surprise no one if I say that I have observed in the people I meet many signs of dissatisfaction and a tendency to fall into a wide range of negative emotions. This holds for everyone, across different age groups, different levels of education, and different professions. Different people have different concerns, different psychological patterns, different neuroses, but at this level, people are more the same than different.

Although some of the patterns I encounter may relate to specific aspects of the Western mindset or the present historical situation, at a deeper level, the people I meet here in the West suffer from a way of engaging the world that holds for everyone, everywhere. Because it so fundamental, it can be difficult to recognize or describe. Yet that is what I want to do in this book.

In the past few decades, Westerners have increasingly grown interested in Buddhism. Apart from the fairly small numbers who follow a traditional path, they typically pursue one of two approaches. One group looks to Buddhist teachings and practices for relief from their own discomfort and suffering. They do not care so much for religious practices and prayers. Instead, they are drawn to different forms of yoga, such as the Kum Nye Tibetan Yoga we teach in our centers, or to meditation. Right now the practice of mindfulness—often cut off from its Buddhist roots—is especially popular.

The second, much smaller group takes a more intellectual or conceptual approach. They are interested in such concepts as shunyata, enlightenment, transcendental wisdom (Prajnaparamita), and the many different levels of doctrine in which Buddhism is so rich. Their sense is that Buddhist thinkers and scholars developed ideas that are unknown in the West, and this produces a certain fascination. Western academics for the most part take this approach, and following it, they have produced numerous translations and studies.

There is nothing new in this. Even in Tibet, students of the Dharma tended to follow one of these two approaches, though the path of ritual and prayer was perhaps the most widely practiced of all. Those who pursued conceptual studies faced the same limitations that confront Western scholars. Although they might learn a great deal at the intellectual level, including the complex distinctions among different philosophical schools, their approach left them with no direct experience of the truth of the teachings. Those who followed the path of practice, on the other hand, faced the potential risk of misunderstanding the teachings. Even if they considered that they had gone beyond the conceptual level, their experience might be shaped almost completely by their own projections, without their realizing that this was so.

Of course, the great masters of the tradition were able to move beyond such limits. The twenty-five disciples of Padmasambhava manifested the highest realization. The same is true of the great Nyingma teachers, such as Rongzom, Longchenpa, and Jigme Lingpa, to name just a few, as well as the great masters of each of the other schools of the Tibetan tradition. The teachers with whom I studied had likewise attained the highest levels of understanding. My sense is that accomplished practitioners could be found more frequently in earlier centuries than in recent times, but it remains true that the path to realization has remained open in the Tibetan tradition since the time of the great Dharma kings.

In the West, this path of realization has not yet been traveled. Instead, it has been the intellectual approach and the fascination with Buddhism that has set the framework for the study of the Dharma, while meditative approaches are still evolving.

Buddhism today generally has a positive image. Well-known teachers are widely respected, and there is a sense that Buddhism as a religion is grounded in kindness and compassion, with little evidence of the violence that can be found in other religious traditions. Still, when we look deeper, the fundamental issue remains. Without a grounding in deep and sustained practice, it is easy for even dedicated Dharma students to stay on a superficial level. The practice of mindfulness, compassion, and fundamental kindness are positive, but as long as they are centered on the needs and wishes of the self, on what will benefit me as an individual, they will not be that meaningful.

For many years, I have been looking for ways to introduce in a preliminary way teachings, ideas, and practices that could take interested students to a deeper level. In 1977, I published the first in a series of books presenting the Time, Space, and Knowledge Vision, intended as one step in this direction. In 2013, I published *Revelations of Mind*, which offered a different approach, one that I took further in *OK Mantra*, a book that has not yet been released to the general public. I intend to continue to explore this approach in other titles as well.

In developing these approaches, I found it best not to present ideas in traditional Buddhist terms. The West is a new world, and a new language may be required to take understanding to a deeper level. Of course, I have not set aside my Buddhist training. Still, there seems no harm in trying different styles of communication. The point is not to present 'accurate' accounts of what Buddhism has to say, but rather to benefit those who come in contact with these teachings.

In the present book, I follow out themes I have been reflecting on for some time. Here I will mention just one. The suffering and unhappiness that constitute samsara can be traced to four foundations: 'I', 'me', 'mine', and mind. In what follows, I refer to these as the gateways to samsara, but it is also possible to think of them as gatekeepers instead. If we cannot penetrate their operation, we will stay bound to samsara forever—bound to our problems, our negativity, and the fruits of our karma. Circling in the dualistic structures of 'from' and 'to', self and others, we will stay caught in concepts of our own creation. No matter how much effort we devote to practice and study, there will not be much benefit. Accordingly, in this book I explore the identity of 'I' and 'me', self and mind. I invite an inquiry into their structures and dynamics, and I ask what alternative forms of knowing may be available.

Another way to describe my goal here is to say that I want to deepen the understanding of mind. This is a theme I investigated in depth starting with *Revelations of Mind*, as well as in earlier books. When we make mind the target of inquiry, we begin to understand in a different way meanings, points, identities, and manifestations. We can open views of the mind, manifestations of the mind, projections of mind, and identity of mind. We can point out mind and transmit the faculties of mind. The dimensions of mind can become fully available.

In conducting an inquiry into mind, the question arises again and again how we can proceed when we seem trapped in the structures of samsara mind—when even our understanding of nirvana seems to be a projection of the understandings our present mind relies on and accepts. If we cannot open up, transform, and transcend samsara mind, going completely beyond a conceptual understanding, we will stay within the domain of language, concepts, ideas, and identity, of labels and meanings. We will never move beyond identifying with ever greater specificity the meaning of what 'I myself' have already pointed out.

Seen from within our ordinary perspective, this is a very real dilemma. We seem to be caught up in what is already established. We have no vehicle that could take us beyond our own projections, no door that opens into a whole new realm. The structures of 'I', 'me', and 'mind' are an example; the fundamental structure of 'from' and 'to' is another. Whatever knowing we apply will stay within the realm of mind, depending on it completely. We may run around looking for alternatives, hoping to sniff out something new, but nothing will change.

Still, these dispiriting conclusions also arise within the realm of mind. If we are willing to exercise our faculties in new ways, perhaps we can penetrate and transform our projections after all. To explore this possibility, we can draw on all the resources available to us: our intellect, our practical experience, our senses, our capacity for dialog, our openness to ideas. We start from a fixed conceptual point; for instance, that we are the meditator, the seeker on a journey, the subject trying to make sense. But this starting point can also be the starting point for inquiry. Instead of relying on our current search engine, perhaps we can find a different search engine, one that does not frame each inquiry in terms of intellect, feeling, thoughts, and sensations. Perhaps we can search within being itself, free from all restrictions.

This is not to say that the shift is easy. We believe firmly in 'I' and 'me', in mind and identity. We take it as established that I am the one who needs to learn, to do, to change, to know; that I am the one who understands and identifies and finds new ways to be 'within'. Even if I can loosen that sense of 'I', the fundamental sense of home, of identity, of place remains. I still belong 'to' and work 'for'.

Because the regime of mind operates whether I acknowledge it or not, the very possibility of searching or watching or questioning confirms that I am the agent—the actor, but also the one carrying out an assignment. It feels as though I am independent, that I am the one who sets the agenda, but in fact I have a boss who makes my duties clear. I have a purpose: I need to improve, or perform, or succeed; perhaps I need to transform. I have a problem, and I need to do something about it.

This is the message, whether we hear it in terms of feeling guilty or experiencing the fruit of karma. Whatever dialogs go on in the background reinforce the message: "Yes, you need to do it. No need to explain. Case closed."

Yet if we can ease the dialog, ease our sense of the way things are and the role we have to play, we can use the mind differently. We can find a way to prevent the four gatekeepers from blocking the path to understanding. We can manifest and communicate on our own terms. Like a doctor immune from the disease ravaging the patients he or she treats, we can apply the right medicine.

Once we know that the structures we have always taken for granted are not really substantial, we have new ways to understand and communicate. Like someone recovering from a poison that has racked our body with pain and disease, or someone waking up from a harrowing nightmare, we are free. We may look and act much as we did before, but now we can respond differently to whatever situations we encounter. No longer driven by the patterns of samsara, we act on the basis of upaya, or skillful means, sharing our knowledge, helping to uplift others and free them from ignorance and suffering, guiding them toward transformation. Having experienced incisively, we can show others a new pattern, a new way to be. For the sake of offering help, we may take on the role of having an identity, but that does not mean there is really someone there—someone subject to depression or anger or emotionality.

Our own experience in knowing the mind—the arising of knowingness wisdom—is inseparable from our ability to be of benefit. In Buddhism this is known as prajna upaya—the marriage of wisdom and skillful means. We have a method we can share, and our knowledge communicates itself through our actions. Recognizing that difficulties, problems, and conflicts are manifestations of the projection of mind, we can lead others to the same understanding.

To start this path, we need only to question. For instance, the usual patterns of mind depend on the structure of beginning, middle, and end, so it seems that time must be involved. This could be a good place to begin. How do we occupy time? How is time related to mind, or to the manifestation of appearance, or to cognition?

Then there is the question of place. Since we find ourselves located somewhere, we can say that we depend on space and identity. At once questions arise. Where do forms come from? If they arise without a 'from', how do they manifest? If appearance does not appear from point to point, how can it manifest at all, and how can we experience it? How do forms or objects occupy points in space, and how can there be changes and variations? How do thoughts and concepts, passions, and impressions take form? Who occupies? What occupies? How does 'what' take place? Can form arise without shape and character and energy?

Whatever appears in space and time happens with regard to me. I am the one who has a problem; it is my emotions, my conflict, my disruptions and distractions that I care about. The connection between 'I' and 'me' seems obvious, but is the 'me' mind different from the 'I' mind? How are 'me' and 'I' related to 'from' and 'to'? Who introduced 'I' to 'me', and who makes the bridge between them?

We can go further. Suppose at some point we say we understand; we say, "I got it." Who gave us this understanding? Who manifested it? Perhaps we say we understand through mind, or the senses, or feeling. But how are the bridges built, point by point? Can we be specific? Can we trace the transporting, from beginning to end; trace the transcending from here to there? Present here and now, can we make the link to past and future? What is the difference between now and then? What are the points of connection, the points where past and future meet? How are end and beginning transmitted? What is the role of the present in relation to past and future? Does it have its own being? If so, how does the door to the future open?

When knowledge comes, who owns it? Who knows? Who has the experience? Is there an identity? If so, it seems important to understand it, for otherwise how could knowledge or wisdom arise? But perhaps there is no identity.

Perhaps knowledge is free, not owned. Perhaps it is exactly the quality of freedom that lets the dynamics of knowledge manifest. Can we see? Can we say?

It seems that knowingness encompasses all directions. Infinitely seeing, it feeds back to itself. Once this realization comes, upaya grows. Whatever thoughts or emotions manifest in this world, we know how to deal. We can activate all our faculties. When we do, we look round at the landscape we somehow inhabit, letting understanding become bigger, like a student ready to pursue an advanced degree. This is the foundation for the embodiment of the real freedom of knowledge.

The Buddha's knowledge is free. Prajnaparamita, the perfection of wisdom, is free. Like space, no one owns it, and yet it manifests. To embody a totally open knowing—just that is what we could call freedom. If we could embody this, our lives would take on great meaning. We could offer the medicine that heals all ills and solves all problems. Mind itself, understood, can be that medicine, a treasure of knowledge. To manifest that vision can be our mission, our goal.

The treasure is already there, already within, but we have been asleep and do not acknowledge its presence. There is no journey of discovery to undertake, nothing to collect or acquire. We have lost the real jewel, but it is there when we learn how to look. Total freedom of knowledge— that is there.

We do not presently know how to touch the thereness, because we cannot find the right vehicle, the right language, the right concepts. But once the groundwork is in in place, the key is there. Then we may say that it is all not so difficult. We may find the right ways to connect to the entities we name, to mind and senses and fields. We can open whatever the intellect points out and labels; we can find the manifestations of mind. We can connect to our present mind, our thoughts, and our behaviors. We can discover the relevance.

This book took form over several months in a number of sessions with Jack Petranker. Our talks took the form of dialog and wide-ranging discussion. Jack took notes on these talks and later compiled and edited them into the materials that you find here. He also added in material from earlier discussions, dating back more than a year.

My sense is that the results offer points of entry for a variety of readers. I hope that you will find them enjoyable to read. You will benefit most if you approach the material in a direct, personal way, giving yourself permission to think about what is being said in ways that make sense to you. The book was designed to be clear and straightforward, without too many detours, but it also bears reading more than once, so that the ideas within it can unfold additional dimensions.

The themes discussed in *Dimensions of Mind* are important for anyone interested in deeper understanding. They link up to similar themes in other books I have published: the meaning of mind, the mind of self, our mission on this planet, the nature of reality, and more. In our discussions, I tried to communicate to Jack observations about the subjective orientation of mind and the objectivity of mind, as well as the mind of knowingness, knowledge, and self-understanding.

His responsibility was to try to capture my thoughts and express them in a way that fits with the structures of the English language and Western ways of thinking.

These are topics important to me, and I hope that the ways they are explored here have value to you. If you find yourself thinking seriously about what is said here, working with the ideas, exploring the exercises, I think you may find it beneficial. I have been on this planet now for over eighty years, and during that time I have done my best to study, read, know, and interact. Here I share some of my impressions. If you find them meaningful, I will rejoice.

Please look upon this book as your aid and guide into activating a self-search engine into the boundless dimensions of mind.

Tarthang Tulku
Offered on this Independence Day,
for all independent searchers
July 4, 2016

Prologue: Creation Stories

1

We can start with space. Science takes it as a given, and philosophy mostly accepts it as well. Space is said to be empty or mostly empty, but it also has the capacity to present. Within space, conditions emerge. Following traditional accounts, we can speak of the five elements emerging: earth, water, fire, air, and space itself. Each element has its own character or significant nature. Each has its own power and its own spirit or energy. Each element conditions every other element; each stands in relation to the others.

However, we have moved too quickly, assumed too much. Let us return to space. The character of space is to be open, to allow. Space allows appearance. In our usual understanding, what appears in space exists. Put differently, whenever the operation through which space accommodates is active, existents appear. It seems we can say that space is the mother of what exists, for it preserves a situation in which existence can manifest. Try to imagine that something exists without space to accommodate it, and you will see: space makes available.

Imagine that before existence there is a point with no dimensions. Due to space characteristics, the point manifests. In that original space manifestation, we may not need at first to speak of space, for at that point nothing exists: there is nothing that depends on space. But because space makes available, the point marks out. This is the first transition: from nothing at all to existence. Let us call what is marked out by the point a dot: the bare minimum existence.

This first existence is the starting point, prior even to the elements. Since we are now here, there must have been development. The dot that appears performs the conditions of existence. Through conducting that performance, the one dot becomes many. Existence becomes two characters, then more. Eventually a longer history unfolds through different stages. Character is assigned and duties taken up.

None of this would be possible without space, through which the ability to manifest gives form. Since that is so, existence, in taking up the duty of manifesting character, also manifests the character of space. The character that emerges from the form of the point is marked out. It appears; it becomes visible. Only the open ability, the flexibility, of space makes this possible.

The openness of space means that space has no dimensions at all. It is not flat: it does not have two dimensions. But it also does not have more dimensions, though that is how we sometimes speak: not three dimensions, not six, or eight, or ten, or sixteen. Yet space allows existence to appear, starting from points. Space allows points, in an allowing that has nothing to do with dimensions or shape. Perhaps we can speak of degrees of points. We might imagine there are thirty points: the number does not matter. Each point is a unity of all points, for each and every point embodies space.

As development proceeds, 'here' and 'there' manifest. These too are space. Not only does the object appear, but the subject as well. But how does the subject appear? It does not seem to appear in space; at least, we cannot point it out. We can say, however, that the subject appears as the pointer, pointing out what has been marked. Or we can say that the subject appears as the audience, pointing out dots. Here we arrive at a new capacity. The pointer, the subject, has the ability to 'point out' space. The pointer points out distance; through the pointer, pointing can make distinctions. The pointer becomes the receiver for recognition—recognition of the points, the marks, the dots.

The appearance of the subject gives another kind of audience: the audience of what is, the objects of appearance— reflections of an echo. The pointer points, and the objects of appearance point back. Reflected back to the pointer, they let the pointer point.

The point, it seems, is already established. But now there are dots to observe. The next step would be measurements of all kinds. When did it arise . . . how long did it take . . . what distances are there? Just a few sentences more, and the meaning would be there: "Once upon a time . . ."

But that is a different story.

2

What shall we call the observers, the pointers? Shall we say 'beings', or perhaps 'persons'? We may want to speak of the six senses: seeing, hearing, and smelling, taste and touch, and the mind. These are the faculties we have available. Responding back into space, they cognize. Now what has been marked is symbolized.

We are still at the very beginning. Points become dots, and dots become zero. Through the act of observation, zero gradually extends. What is it that is newly recognized? Perhaps it is distance. Perhaps it is the conditions placed on existence.

With conditions, things are not the same. Properly speaking, it is only now that we may call what appears the observer. The observer makes distinctions, recognizing that what appears is not the same. Now we may speak of beginning, middle, and end, and so of past, present, and future. In this way, we gradually establish appearances. There is an unfolding from 'A' to 'B' to 'C': time provides difference. The observer is established along with the act of observation. Both depend on conditions, on the object of space and the subject of the observer. Since conditions arise, we can say that both have the character of the conditional: time conditional, space conditional.

It may seem that I, the observer, have made all this up. That is one way to say it. In the beginning, there is a shape. The shape becomes highly visible to an observer. The observer has a point of view, and from that point of view, names have been given and changes have occurred. There have been transitions and a forward momentum.

Our observations come into play: seeing the transitions, we name the names. The past is different from the present. Trees are different from plants. Characters impose their character, and this becomes the basis for change. We recognize that the dot is not just a dot, the plane is not just a plane, appearance is not just appearance. There are not just three dimensions, or four, or six, or eight: we can apply many different dimensions.

We can speak now of 'from' and 'to', of a movement towards. This is a linear way to make sense of it all. The 'from' is the symbolic beginning, the 'to' the symbolic ending. An unfolding occurs in one dimension. In the unfolding, a narrow form takes shape, like a stick. Look closely at the stick-shape, and we can speak of a bottom and a top. It may seem there is growth, starting at the bottom and moving toward the top, pointing out space to the object. Look closely, and the 'I' is there.

Symbolically, 'I' is now the pointer. The letter that specifies 'I' has just this narrow shape, the shape of the from/to, the shape of a pointer, pointing out. First the point, then the dot. The dot gives rise to the 'I'—the dot of the 'i' makes 'I' the point. From the point comes the image of 'I'. That is what matters, first and foremost: to establish the 'I'. Now we have a home, a place that can be related to every other place.

Everybody starts from the 'I'. Whether we speak of samsara or nirvana, whether we use the language of psychology or religion, everyone has a 'from', a starting point. Everyone goes to the 'I' identity. That is the start of every operation. I propose; I make decisions; I make meanings and transitions.

Good and bad, happiness and sorrow all have to do with 'I'. 'I' is the carrier, and 'I' is the feedback. Sorting out is 'I', and eventual freedom from karmic obstacles also depends on 'I'. Without 'I', there can be no position. Without 'I', we have no home and also no duty.

3

The unfolding from point to 'I' is a kind of artistic creation. To start with, the structure of 'from' and 'to' gives the distinctions 'tall' and 'short'. But there is more. Since I can mark out measurements, I can make other shapes. I can stake out. There can be growth at many levels, appearance at many levels: beginning and end, trees, buildings, people. A process builds up. Steadily, we update it.

The whole process, the whole of what appears, is my image, my possession. It is made in the shape of 'I', the shape I represent and that represents me. It all becomes possible through the relation between space and sound. Space allows sound. 'I' allow the sound to be pronounced.

At the outset, sound is without form. Not shaped by anything external, it is the simplest of sounds: AH. But since there are rhythms, form unfolds. AH becomes AAAHHH. The rhythms put down their own shape; they move; they vary. They become thinner or more fluid, and more sounds emerge: EEEEE, and EYYY, and AAIII. Sounds emerge in the same way that the image of the dot becomes a pointer, narrowly connecting 'from' and 'to'.

Through this unfolding in sound, 'I' comes into its own. Now it can possess. Possessing, it can control, reducing the dots to fundamental particles, expanding them into elements, or setting them in motion so that they grow, perhaps even manifesting as DNA, giving form to life.

All these possibilities come together in the symbol of the image. What matters is to identify that image; it is this identification that makes the 'I'. First is the image of the existence of dots. Through sound, that image is established as the label 'I'. The image of 'I' is the pointer, and the pointer points out that very image, that unique position. This pointing out is the beginning of establishing ultimate points, of establishing home.

The meaning that belongs to the image belongs to the name. Before the name, there are shape and form and the character they bring, but only as the sound-symbol operates is meaning established. With the sound AH, the shape of character emerges. 'I', the possessor, possesses the character of meaning. Possessing the character of meaning, it possesses the symbol and the image.

Once this movement has been initiated, the next step is to recognize. First 'I' cognizes: "That is it." Based on the cognition, I identify. I establish the 'it-ness' of the it: its shape and form, character and meaning. When 'it' is complete, I can re-cognize: recognize and repeat. I have entered the realm of the predictable, so I can initiate and empower. Here is the origin of 'belonging to'.

The vehicle for all this is perception. When perceptions agree, we can build up and establish. We can say what is similar, and we can identify difference. Sound creates voice, and voice has many rhythms. Dots can manifest everywhere in space, making all forms and all characters. Starting with pointing we give meaning. From meaning, we can conclusively establish.

Look back again to the beginning. Space is the mother of all existence, and sound is the root of all language and all identifying. On that basis, someone is there, someone is trainable, someone can give identities and meanings. With the receiver there, conclusions can be drawn and knowledge can emerge. All points manifest, giving characters, nature, existence, and appearance. It all becomes detectable. Making names, we make the namable, the pointable, the recognizable, the identifiable. The point can take in and distinctions can establish. Each character, each situation can manifest.

There is more. As each subject and each object presents, we can agree: we can arrive at the meanings of knowledge. We can assign labels; we can describe the meanings of points and characterize them. Language, perception, and conception draw their conclusions. Instantly, they find their echo in the subject, which proclaims itself agreeable. Laws of existence are established completely, and the system becomes unitary. Each point is presentable to the subject. There are intellectual points, points to be known, points available for perception. Since space is infinite, pointing can go on infinitely. Space allows for transmitting continuity; it lets beginning, middle, and end occur.

Within the system, there is the pronounceable; there are perceptions that are recognizable. Holding fast to characters, to nature, to the perceptible, the rule of the system and positions of power come to be. As they feed back knowledge of meanings, character and identity gradually form. They are followed by 'pro' and 'con', virtue and vice, good and bad, and every other distinction or category. Any system that develops, any discipline at all, any situation that we come to know in this, our world, grows from these roots.

We sort through all these possibilities in countless ways. We investigate history or evolution; we rely on the experiential way or the way of observation. We make stories and legends. Different disciplines may speak of the world or samsara, of causal structures, or of truth. They may say, "This is the way it is." Each offers its own background; each lays out its own way—in each case, the byproducts of certain ways of knowing.

4

Once the object is, I am ready to start in on my assumptions. First come my perceptions. In perception, the agents of the mind point out, making the object possible. There is a correlation: the subject produces an echo, the reflection of an active engaging. Through the agents of perception, I point out the known, through constructions stimulated by the interaction of mind and matter, subject and object. Establishing recognition, I form my position.

Next comes the underlying order, established through labeling. This stage is easy. It unfolds in the same way a legislature makes laws once the constitution has been adopted. I, the legislator, present my position through the workings of mind. I identify and then go on to label, perhaps in a new way. The agent of mind, I stand also as the subject in relation to the object. The interaction, the echo, produces feedback that establishes recognition. That is the beginning of knowing—what we give the name 'knowledge'.

In the field of knowledge, there are rules and systems, together with a knowing authority that makes decisions and provides labels. As the flow of concepts interacts directly with perceptions, knowledge provides its 'yes' or 'no'. Knowledge-decisions may ripple through the knowledge field, like waves through a gravitational field. They flow outward, but they also provide feedback. Feedback produces clarity, sending the required message to perception.

Knowledge gives the foundation, but it needs an assistant, a tool. That is the role of language, always there to help present, to help make decisions, set policies, and produce labels. Once the label has been applied, it becomes possible to describe the meanings. Only through such feedback can knowledge generate ripples through the field.

Language provides the labels, and knowledge supports what language offers: perhaps through perceptions, perhaps through concepts that allow for entertaining various meanings. When perceptions are approved by knowledge, when the two combine, it becomes possible to pronounce verbally. The sound has its label, which can accurately describe. Knowledge either accepts what is described or offers another description. The ripples keep going, extending further.

In the course of these rippling rhythms that echo and feed back, the conceptual frame of mind is established. It is this that we often designate 'mind'. Having assigned that label, we reach one possible level of study, one possible form of education. But there is also a second level of education. We could say that what has been presented until now is a kind of theory or system, a philosophical presentation of what happens in subject-object communication. On the second level, however, these developments are just the pointers, the coordinators. We need to go deeper. It is like recognizing that the history of the United States does not begin with the first Europeans, even though we call them the founders—that the native Americans came first. We need to look at that level.

In fact, we need to look even deeper. In the universe, particles gather together to form elements; in history, a few people band together to establish a community that will found something new. But we can question appearance still more broadly. What is the fatherhood of appearance . . . the motherhood . . . the parenthood? What is the origin of space and time? How does knowledge first emerge? What is the source of creativity? What is the origin of the original? What makes transitions possible? If something just pops into being, like a bubble, how does the bubble bubble? We might answer that there is no answer to the question 'how', that bubbles just bubble. But then there can be no 'from' or 'to', and we will have a hard time establishing any ground at all: not for the place we find ourselves, not for the subject who names, not for the object that appears.

5

If we can discover a way to ask at this deeper level, we open the possibility for a therapeutic self-understanding. The first round of questions, though fundamental, maintains a certain distance. How have we come to establish the conclusions we rely on? What are the origins of the disciplines and fields of knowledge we use to make sense, to label: religion, philosophy, history, science? Going deeper, the question comes again: what is the origin of the origin?

Deeper still, we can ask about the origin of the searcher, the one who is asking. How is it possible to know? Perhaps we do not know. But if we do not know, what is reliable? If our knowledge is not grounded, our perceptions may be fantasies, no more solid than a rainbow: stories in a dream or stories born in echoes—magical displays. Perhaps we can see how a story is set up, but that does not show us that the story applies to what is going on now, or to where we are.

We may want to emphasize the importance of our present living experience, of this very moment in time. That way, we can dismiss questions about how that present moment comes to be. But when we try to pin present experience down in all its particulars, we quickly find that in each moment of present experience, subject and object are active. No matter how much we resist, there are conditions that condition the present. And the conditions we accept, whether we have learned to name them or not, have their own conditions.

When we look at conditions, we may find ourselves giving reasons. "This is why things are the way they are," we say, and perhaps we feel we have gotten to the root of the matter. But have we really made progress in our understanding? There are reasons enough to support whatever situation we find ourselves in, but how far can we trace the reasons? How do reasons arise? Do they just pop up, along with whatever situation they justify?

"Absurd!" we counter. But where can we go, what can we say or do, to know the source of the reasons we give? Must we step outside the present? If that seems beyond our capacities, can we be confident that our reasons give us reason? Can we truly be certain that situations do not occur simply by their own power?

When such questions begin to operate, we cannot readily communicate what is at stake. For us here, occupying our present position, questions like these seem to lead nowhere. They are simply confusing, or else irrelevant. Perhaps they seem like nothing more than words, running wild. The situations they suggest do not apply. We have a way of thinking, and according to that way of thinking the meanings we rely on are real. The way we think, the way we speak, the way we live all go along with that realness. There is no ready way to go further.

So we continue in the same way we always have. We are used to a story that starts at 'from' and moves toward 'to'. What does not go along with that story may seem to have nothing to do with us. Why should we care about what comes before our childhood, what leaves no trace in our DNA, what does not show up in the history of our becoming?

Still, we may not want to shut down our questioning too quickly. We know the shape of our lives, and much of what we know fails to give us comfort, fails to support the value of committing to the same. Whether we want them or not, we will encounter transitions in our lives that we cannot predict, cannot account for, and cannot easily react to in positive ways. On this point we are trapped in a no-choice world, subject to rhythms over which we have no control, changes beyond our ability to see or make sense of. So perhaps we do want to ask after all. There seem to be reasons to care.

If we could access what goes beyond what we see and beyond what we know how to make so, new opportunities might emerge—even if we do not know how to proceed or what to expect. Before we have found a new way to look or ask, all talk of such possibilities may sound like fantasy or fiction, but that is just because we do not know any better. There may be a different truth at work. What possibilities could we celebrate? What liberation could we enjoy?

We all know what it is like to experience the cycles of pain and pleasure, frustration and excitement, disappointment and hope. We know what it is like to think our knowledge closes off certain policies. We are used to accepting the tyranny of the past over the present. We know what is real, and we accept it. Now, imagine exercising a knowledge beyond our present knowledge. Would such new knowledge offer something different? Would we discover a new kind of creativity?

Perhaps we have not yet penetrated appearance actively. Have we really looked to our right and our left, instead of straight ahead? Have we looked up and down? Have we looked in all directions—360 degrees? We cannot say that knowledge is limited in advance. It comes equipped with its own search engine. We are free to look elsewhere, or differently, or more fully. We can become the agents of opportunity.

Our experience usually comes with its own witness. The witness proclaims what is so. It proclaims the consensus. Doing so, it claims an automatic power: the power to name and establish. What is established? Simply the power of what is so.

We stand in a certain relation to what is so. We are dominated and manipulated by what is so. We are subject to a regime we have no way to challenge. We are driven here and there, for that is how things are. The 'I' suffers, for that is how things are. Pleasure pulls us one way, pain another. There are things we cannot know. That is how things are.

All that is so. That is the truth. It is one level of truth. Still, since the search engine is available, we need to ask: is it possible to engage rhythms of flexibility? Consider the basics. We are driven here and there. One time we may want and enjoy, another time we may pull away or pull back. We can see in this the rhythm of sameness. This is the rhythm we know, the one we have pursued since earliest childhood, as far back as we can remember. But we may know other rhythms as well.

Look for yourself! We have found ourselves in so many situations, always responding, always reacting. Do we find in this the evidence of sameness, or can we equally chart in the records of the past a remarkable accommodation to change? Does conditioning point beyond conditioning?

6

Water flows, and air is always moving. Earth is solid, and fire burns. Each one of our perceptions, each of our engagements, is just like this. Each has its own specific capacity: the capacity of anger or lust; being greedy, or anxious, or confused; the specific capacity of not knowing. We know all these. We know the character of being puzzled, or lonely, or empty. We know what lostness is like.

Human experience is like this. We know different 'feels', each with its own character. But knowing them does not mean we have any way to change them. When we feel lost or confused, angry or impatient, we may find ourselves trapped in such feelings, helpless as the feel of the feeling goes on and on, bonded to the way things are, with no choice. A toxic current is flowing, and we are caught in the stream. The feeling grabs us and we identify with it, and our reality is frozen. Internally, an agent of the mind activates, and all our different faculties—our ability to think, to feel, to imagine—are put in the service of the feeling. Eventually comes a transition, and we find ourselves in another place, but the transition too is out of our control. The initial feeling is somehow imprinted as one possible variation. Later, it will be reactivated.

As these transitions and variations manifest, we play the role of victim, the one possessed, as if some other knowing force were in control, pointing out what is going on. The force grabs hold, and then that grabbing grabs hold, becoming a form of thought, becoming feelings and perceptions. The mind 'takes control', but all it can do is say, "Yes." It makes the case, irreversibly, and we call it true. A reality is established: perhaps animal experience, or hungry ghost experience, or hell realm experience. There is fear, there is darkness, there is misery. There may be unimaginable loneliness.

At this very deep level, there is no possibility for flexibility or questioning, no allowing for openness or change. Everything is solid. Originally I was the one who established, but now 'me' is possessed. I dwell in this territory, caught in its 'mineness'. I am the owner, the one responsible, the CEO. I am the one who is dominant. I say "Yes," and seal what is so. I confirm that this toxicity is the truth of what I say. Whatever I do feeds back into the truth of what has been witnessed, and I am caught. The power of mind, the role it takes on, sustains the circle of my reality, cycling through 'I' and 'me' and 'mine'.

Can we trace this development? Can we exercise our understanding to see these patterns, these cycles? Can we discover our situation? We already know the starting point. Parenthood mind makes the object, and the object creates the 'I'. Having been adopted, 'I' belongs to mind. Yet 'I' presents itself as the pointer, pointing out: creating the point, which becomes the existence-making dot. From this starting point, this pointing, come all kinds of creation. 'I' becomes me. Through sound comes language, through perception come images. Countless characters arise.

Part One

Getting Started

1

Using our Time

Imagine that your life is a big house with many rooms, built decades ago. You have lived there a long time, and you know it well: its good sides and its bad sides, what you like and what you wish were different. You know about the problems that keep coming up, the repairs that need to be made, the appliances that break down, the rusty pipes, the leaky roof, the cracking paint. You are aware of the many little flaws and defects, though you have probably stopped noticing most of them. As a responsible home owner, you guard your house against the threats brought by the changing seasons and the passing years as well. You know the landscaping and the view the house presents from the street. You know the property lines and you trust that your neighbors will respect them.

Looking at this analogy at a fairly simple level, you might think of the house as your body. You can enjoy and appreciate it, but you also have an obligation to take care of it, a responsibility that increases as you age.

Let's extend the analogy a bit. Imagine that the foundation of the house is under attack by termites. You could think of the termites as the thoughts and feelings that constantly cycle through your mind, pulling you away from your deeper concerns. You may not notice or even know that this is happening, but on some level you probably register this constant undermining activity as a force that interferes with your own intentions.

Now, to take it one step further, you know that you will not inhabit your body forever, so imagine that you are only renting the house you live in. Assume you are paying a fair rent: are you getting full value for what you are paying? The answer will depend mostly on your attitudes. Do you appreciate your home? Do you make full use of its qualities and enjoy its location? Do you enjoy its architectural details and take pleasure in how you have furnished it? Or are you too caught up in your own shifting concerns to notice much about the place you live?

Because we are alive on this planet, we have countless opportunities for enjoyment and appreciation. But if we are constantly turning our minds one way or another, worrying about satisfying this craving or that longing, fearful of some real or imagined threat, we will not be able to benefit from such opportunities. If our minds are taken up with an endless interior dialog, one thought or concept following another like the beads on a mala, can we really say we are at home at all? We may just be wasting the rent we pay.

Buildings or bodies, minds or complex social systems: in each case similar patterns apply. Appearance unfolds through points in space. Events manifest in accord with different rhythms, as in a grand and subtle dance. Our surroundings undergo change, sometimes dramatic, like the damage brought on by destructive storms, but sometimes hard to notice, like erosion or the slow seepage of toxic chemicals into the water supply. We may imagine that basics stay the same, but that is a narrow view. The bacteria in our bodies live out their lives in cycles vastly different from our own, and the biochemistry of our organs shifts unceasingly. Our sense faculties constantly register subtle changes: sounds and sights, smells and tastes and feels. Day in, day out, the heart is beating, and the breath does not pause.

Most of these dynamics go on 'beneath the radar'. If we look back at our lives, perhaps twenty or thirty years or more, we will acknowledge that there have been tremendous changes, but mostly they took place without our noticing them. Only looking back do we notice that our skin has new wrinkles, that our hair is thinning or that we are turning gray. Our sense faculties, limited in their capacities to begin with, deteriorate from year to year. As the days and months and years go by, we perceive differently and think differently. We make different judgments, not just from year to year but from day to day.

In many ways, change in our 'inner' world is much easier to detect. Our thoughts and feelings shift from moment to moment, often too quickly for us to be able to identify where they come from or where they go to. When our feelings do change, it is difficult to recall what we were feeling just a moment before. And even if we think we know what was going on earlier, we cannot project with any confidence what will be going on a moment from now. On the surface, this moment now is likely to resemble the one immediately preceding it, but at a more subtle level, we cannot predict even that much. As we find ourselves caught up in different concerns or chasing different goals, our feelings or mood may go off in a different direction entirely. Through it all, we try to guard against negativities, but if we are honest, we know that we can make no guarantees.

None of this is news. Time works changes that are largely beyond our power to control. A look at how most people's lives unfold, or a look back at our own, should convince us that events do not always turn out the way we hoped. How should we respond? Should we just give up and let go entirely, hoping that things will turn out? Should we trust in fate?

Exercise 1: Out of Control

Reflect back on times in your life when you drifted into an unhappy situation, or stayed for too long in a situation you knew was not good for you or those around you. Would greater awareness have led you to take decisive action, or did you see fairly accurately what was happening, but decide not to act on it? Imagine that you had acted on what you saw and on your own values. What do you think the consequences might have been? Resist the temptation to pass over such possibilities quickly. Let your questions deepen; take time to reflect on them and trace out the responses they evoke in you.

Whatever age you are right now, imagine that you have a hundred years left to live: time enough to do what you think has value. You know there will be changes and transitions during that time; you know that many of them are beyond your ability to control. Within that situation, what can you do to make the best use of your time? What knowledge can you rely on? What methods and techniques can you apply?

Let's look another way. How much time do you lose in a day? Let's work out a rough answer. Start with the 24-hour cycle. If you set aside 6-8 hours for sleep and practices such as meditation or body disciplines, 2 hours for meals and personal needs, and 6 hours for productive, focused work, you still have not accounted for roughly 8 hours.

What happens during these 8 hours? Perhaps you use them for entertainment or casual social interactions. Perhaps they go by in the form of daydreams, fantasies, and various kinds of distractions, or else they are taken up by worries, concerns, and idle thoughts. Let's assume that they are truly lost, that they have just melted away with no specific result. Those eight hours a day comes to about 250 hours a month, or 3,000 hours a year. If we really cannot account for that much time, we are losing 7 or 8 days out of each month and 4 months out of each year—in other words, a third of our lives.

Is that acceptable? Are you really willing to let a third of your life slip away? You, your parents, your teachers and mentors, and countless others have made an investment in your time on earth. Together, you and they have tried to create the conditions for living a meaningful and fulfilling life. Are you getting a good return on that investment?

You seem to be discounting a lot of activity that some people find rewarding. For instance, think about time spent playing with your children, or enjoying a hike, or visiting some part of the world we've never been before. Why can't those count as meaningful?

Absolutely! But I have in mind something different. It has more to do with pursuing our own highest ideals and values. For instance, it might have to do with helping others—our family, our friends, our community—or with making a contribution to the welfare of humanity. It might have to do with advancing knowledge or creating beauty. Your values may be very different from someone else's, and that's fine. But the question to ask is whether you are letting time go by in activities that have nothing to do with your own sense of what's important. That's what I mean by getting a good return on your investment.

Still, you seem to be encouraging us to feel guilty about every moment we don't use to maximum advantage. Suppose we do spend some time just relaxing and 'hanging out': is that so bad? True, not everything we do may have an immediate connection to our highest goals, but that doesn't automatically mean that it has no value. Some activities may just help us feel more balanced or healthier. For instance, I might meditate every morning, or do some kind of physical activity that makes me feel healthier or stronger. It doesn't seem fair to say that's wasting my time, just because I'm not working for the benefit of others.

That's not my point. If what you do brings you a sense of well-being and joy, you are building a foundation for positive action. Taking care of yourself, or of those you care about, is positive. You could certainly say that it contributes at some level to a meaningful life.

The kind of lost time I am talking about happens at a different, more subtle level. For instance, suppose you are doing work that you find important and satisfying, and in the middle of what you are doing, the mind wanders off and you lose yourself in some in some fantasy or regret. Or suppose you decide that it's a good time to check on your email, or get the weekend weather forecast. Even a minute or two to this kind of activity disrupts the flow of what we are doing and makes it more difficult to get back in focus. It may not seem like much, but you're undermining your own efforts.

That makes good sense to me. I've read that according to various studies, when you interrupt the flow of what you are doing, even briefly, it takes many minutes to refocus on what you were doing before. Sometimes it's easy to see how time is lost. I may look up some useful piece of information on the internet and then notice something else I find interesting. So then I go look at that, not really thinking much about it. Then I get drawn into some other little distraction, which of course is exactly what advertisers on the web are trying to make happen. This happens again, and then again. It may take twenty minutes or more before I decide to go back to whatever I was doing before I got pulled away.

Yes, that's the kind of thing I have in mind. It doesn't just happen on the internet. There are countless examples. We find ourselves worrying about some health issue or complaining to a friend about a situation in which we feel trapped. We worry about money, or about the state of the economy, or we get caught up in some political controversy where everyone has his or her own view. We fantasize about changing jobs or moving to a new location, or we remember the last vacation we took and wish we were still there. Moment by moment, feelings and thoughts like this take up our time and drain the energy we have left to give to other kinds of activities and intentions.

Exercise 2: Confronting Distraction

Notice your tendency to distract yourself from what you are doing, or your willingness to be distracted when the opportunity presents itself. Answering emails, surfing the internet, fixing a snack, engaging in a casual conversation—there are countless possibilities. When you see yourself headed in this direction, decide not to go along. What happens? Does the pull get stronger? Does it dissipate? If there is resistance to your decision, can you trace its arising? What form does it take: a feeling? A thought? Is there someone who wants to be distracted?

These are the kinds of activity that seem to undermine our commitment to leaving meaningful and satisfying lives. It's not that they're really very fulfilling in themselves, or even that they help us feel more positive or more relaxed. They're just habit patterns. It's as though we're programmed so that every now and then we feel an itch, and then we have no choice but to scratch it.

Exercise 3: In One Hour

Try keeping close track of your time for just one hour as you go about your day. How much time do you devote to your main task or activity, and how much gets sucked into other kinds of activity, concern, or patterns? You can ask this question at various levels. Do you get up and take a break? Do you go find someone and start up a conversation, or check the news? Do you imagine what else you would rather be doing? Do you let your mind wander aimlessly? You can try this exercise in various settings and at various times of the day: when you are working, relaxing, meditating, having a conversation. Even at times you set aside for relaxing activity, do other concerns come up?

9

2

Running at a Profit

Suppose your life was a business, and you found yourself struggling to make a profit. Probably you would try to analyze your situation to see what was going on. Are hidden costs eating away at your resources without providing anything of value in return? Are you confident that you are maximizing production? Do you have good ways to measure your results? Can you say for certain that your long-term business plan is on track? Are you headed for success or failure?

In a regular business, this kind of assessment shouldn't be too hard to do. At a simple level, you could just check your bank account to see if you're in good shape or not, or you could go a little further and analyze income and expenses. But in the business of running your own life, answers may not be as easy to come by.

Still, it's always possible to ask questions that help clarify what's really going on. Are you taking advantage of opportunities that present themselves? Are you applying methods or using tools that make it more likely you will get good results? Are you cultivating a global sensitivity to what is happening from moment to moment: global mind, global body, global feeling, global reality?

One clue is to look at your own attitude or outlook. Do you take a casual attitude toward what you do or what you plan, telling yourself it doesn't really matter whether you win or lose? Do you look back at the end of the day and ask yourself how well you've done? Does the question even make sense to you? It seems fair to say that many people never ask that kind of question, because it never occurs to them that they could do better than they are doing right now, or that they could make some kind of fundamental change.

When we consider our lives as an enterprise, we may notice some key indications that things are not going all that well. First, we seem to have very little ability to control the patterns to which we are subject. In business, that might mean that we were at the mercy of business cycles or external events that shape the economic environment. In our personal lives, the patterns are more internal. Sequences unfold in loops that repeat themselves—thoughts to feelings, thoughts to thoughts, feelings to thoughts, and so on.

Observing these patterns as they play themselves out, almost aimlessly, can make us feel powerless. If we have no sense of where to go or what to do next, we worry about our lack of direction or drive. If we notice problems, we may go to the other extreme, insisting that we are in charge, denying the evidence to the contrary, and insisting that we understand what gives meaning to our lives and how to achieve our goals. At that point, we risk settling for talking about

our values instead of acting on them. It may also be that
our sense of what has value is fundamentally hollow, that
we are just going along with a story someone told us a long
time ago.

Certain signs may alert us that these problematic patterns
are in control. We may experience feelings of dullness or
loneliness, of not knowing or ignoring. We may feel powerless, as though someone had hijacked our lives and is running all the operations. We may feel disconnected from a
sense of meaning, or feel we lack the motivation to seek out
a purpose for our life. Or we may simply shut down, not
feeling anything very strongly, whether positive or negative.

Living like this basically means that we have lost our way.
We go on living from one day to the next, but like someone
sinking into senility or trapped in a deep depression, we just
repeat the old patterns, not really aware of what we are doing. We go about our business, worn out by efforts that lead
to no clear result. The question of finding purpose in our
lives no longer makes sense.

An outside observer seeing us at such times might conclude
that we are very naïve. We act without knowing what aims
our actions support. We do not ask where we have come
from or where we are headed. We have no way to frame the
questions that are truly important, let alone seek answers.
Internally, we may see things in much the same way. Seeing
no lasting value in what we do, we may adopt a viewpoint
that is fundamentally cynical.

*Isn't that what the spiritual path is for—to offer us guidance in deal-
ing with these kinds of questions? I'm not just thinking of meditative*

traditions. Nowadays there's a lot of emphasis on positive psychology: learning to turn toward richer and more fulfilling ways of being and finding ways to take care of ourselves.

That's fine as far as it goes. But is it really all that helpful to try to turn our lives in a positive direction if the underlying questions about what is truly meaningful go unanswered? The authorities that people have learned to turn to in this culture—science and psychology, for instance—seem reluctant to offer real, practical guidance.

There seems to be a strong sense that it's up to each individual to decide how to live his or her life.

If that's your conclusion, you're acknowledging that science or psychology or even philosophy have little to offer when it comes to questions of value. For instance, science only takes positions on what it can measure, and its measurements when it comes to values and meaning are not very reliable. As for psychology, it's reasonable for the experts to say that decisions about values are up to the individual, but that means the psychologists themselves have no role to play.

But spiritual traditions are ready to offer guidance.

Yes, but many people decide that the price of admission—accepting various doctrines or beliefs unquestioningly—is too high to pay.

3

Getting Clear

For most people going about their lives, the bottom line seems to be that something is missing. It's as though we're cut off from the creative context of our own lives. We watch events unfold like someone who sees a mirage in the desert and wonders if it's real.

I don't know about that. My life seems very real to me.

We certainly do have the sense that we are here, that our bodies and minds are busy acting and interacting. But can we really be sure of what we see and how we react? Is there any basis for the mirage? Maybe we're making it up, at least at the level of meaning and value. Is our sense of personal identity—our conscious experience—just produced by the circumstances we encounter and the neurophysiology of our bodies? Do the decisions we make trace to an endlessly looping interplay of thoughts, concepts, and feelings?

For instance, as long as we are thinking, we seem to be able to say that there is a thinker. That seems reliable. But the idea 'there is a thinker' is itself a thought. We tell ourselves, "I know that I am thinking," but who is the one who knows that? If our knowing is the outcome of a thought or a series of thoughts, how does the thought know? We have plenty of ideas and opinions, but when we look more closely, our ideas and understandings seem to lack real cohesion or conviction. In the end, they just point toward each other. There's nothing more fundamental or basic that we can truly rely on.

When we look at the operations of mind, we see plenty of thoughts—they just keep coming! But assigning them to a thinker is another step, and then saying that 'I' am that thinker is a third step. We recognize the thought, and we automatically add the conclusion, "I have been thinking a thought." Can we be sure?

Exercise 4: Who's Thinking?

Experiment with challenging the automatic assumption, 'I am the one who is thinking'. As thoughts come and go, can you let go of your ownership claim? Can thoughts arise and pass away in somewhat the way that an itch arises and passes away, or a fly lands on the back of your hand? What obstacles to this way of seeing arise? Are you making commitments to your thoughts that make it difficult to approach them in a neutral way?

The closer we look, the more puzzling our experience turns out to be. For instance, sometimes I 'have' a thought, and sometimes a thought 'occurs to' me. Are those two events identical? Again, one thought comes and then another one follows it. Do they both operate in the same way? How do I know? What's the basis for comparison? Is there some neutral position where I can stand and compare the two?

Even if there were, by the time I make the comparison, both thoughts have passed on. Am I really remembering them accurately? And even while I was having the thought, was I really paying attention to what it was like to have the thought, or was I just focusing on the content of the thought?

A lot of people might say that it's a mistake to focus too strongly on thoughts anyway, because they cut us off from direct experience. It might make more sense to focus on sense experience.

Does that really help? We may rely on our senses and say that that's the real authority. "I saw it with my own eyes!" But we know that our senses can be fooled, and we also know that people may see or hear the same object or sequence of events very differently. Everyone knows about optical illusions where you are absolutely convinced that one line is longer than another, and even after you've measured them with a ruler and satisfied yourself that they are the same length, the visual impression that they're different lengths persists.

Consider what happens when we make a judgment about something or someone, or when we decide that we like or dislike something. I accept one thing as true and reject its opposite as false, or I decide I want this instead of that. It all seems very real in the moment, and I can be completely confident about my decision. There are real consequences too: I may form attachments or develop a craving as a result. But the next time, in the same situation, I may have just the opposite reaction. One time I really like a meal in a restaurant, but the next time I order the same meal and it's disappointing. How can a process this arbitrary give any guidance? How can I know what is truly so? Yes, a process of some kind is going on, but how well do we understand it?

We are full of assumptions about what's real or what's right or what we like, but when we look more closely we seem to be building on some very shaky foundations. Perhaps we are deeply confused, or we just don't know.

It seems to be that most of the time we go through our lives in a kind of routine way, not paying all that much attention. For instance, when we're walking down the street, we don't notice very clearly what's going on around us. If we were less distracted as we engage in mental activity, could we develop more clarity about how our mind operates?

Aren't these questions more for philosophers than for the rest of us? We may not be able to justify our choices in any rigorous way, but we can still choose what we want to do. We may be wrong sometimes, but usually things turn out all right.

I don't think you can make that assumption. In the first place, do things really turn out 'all right' most of the time? Are you being honest about how much suffering goes on in your own life, or in the lives of other people you know?

Beyond that, it doesn't seem smart to settle for things being 'mostly all right'. The question we have been looking at is whether we can live our lives in a truly meaningful way. To pursue that question, we need to bring our best resources to bear, even if we don't think of ourselves as philosophers or deep thinkers. When the basic structures that shape our experience are unknown, or the foundations of our knowledge are uncertain, how can we manifest a deeper intelligence? And without such intelligence, can we really take full advantage of our time on earth?

I may not always make the best choices, but mostly things take care

17

of themselves. I realize that at some point I may face a crisis or find myself confused, but why should I build my whole life around those kinds of possibilities?

You may assume that the course of your life just goes on by itself, without your having to pay any attention to it, and much of the time that's true. But when you just let the process unfold through its own momentum, it will proceed in a set way toward a predetermined goal, whether you want it to or not. You may not be all that happy with the results.

Is that really how we want to live? If we act without really knowing why, acting without a sense of purpose and priorities, we risk losing time and wasting our energy. In a way, this amounts to abusing our time, our lives, and our own intelligence. We give up on the possibility that we could know the very foundation for our own lives.

Of course, we may not notice that this is so. So much is going on from moment to moment that we can easily get lost. Feelings, memories, thoughts flow and proliferate; they are endless, like stars in the sky. Living in realms of yes and no, good and bad, we are occupied and preoccupied. One moment slips away, then another, and then another. Sixty years go by. Having gone by, they are gone, and with them, our lives. Is that really the outcome we are prepared to accept?

I do understand what you're saying. Sometimes when I tune in to what is happening in my life, I have the feeling that something fundamental is missing, that somehow I just don't get it. It's not that I'm unhappy, or uncomfortable, or depressed. It's just that there seems to be a great sameness. Things are always changing, but in another way, the basic patterns don't change at all. I have the same kinds of thoughts, I seek

18

out the same kinds of pleasures, I tell myself the same kinds of stories. I will keep going the way I've been going, and some things will go well and others won't, and gradually I will get older and lose my energy— at least if I'm lucky! And all the time I'll be wondering if I've really done everything I possibly can to live a meaningful life. And if I look at other people, I see the same basic pattern, whether people acknowledge it or not.

So what can we do? You're asking for something fundamental to shift. What's the first step?

If you're really serious about asking that question, that's a good place to begin. It doesn't have to be that difficult. In fact, the first step is obvious—one that almost no one could object to. Before we can do much of anything, we need to develop a sense of well-being and confidence—a positive foundation that can support us as we go forward.

Let's see how that would work.

4

Starting with Joy

The starting point for change is to cultivate a sense of well-being. We all have the capacity for joy, even if we sometimes seem to forget that's true. Whatever is happening on the surface of our lives, we can look within to discover positive, healing energies and experience.

You wrote about that in The Joy of Being. *You said that if we can develop confidence grounded in self-knowledge, we can develop a foundation of joy that can sustain us throughout our lives. Is that what you mean?*

Yes, that's what I mean. Life offers many beauties and riches if we just allow ourselves to experience them. So the exercises and readings in *Joy of Being* offer a good place to start. A powerful teaching in the Mahayana Buddhist tradition tells us that this very world, just as it is, is a perfect field of enlightenment. If we just learn to relax our usual ways of conducting our lives, the body, the senses, and the mind can all become gateways to deep inner peace. Even if we don't have much time to devote to specific practices, we can always work directly on our outlook—our view of life.

When the body is content and at peace, when joy is born in the heart, the mind turns toward the Dharma. It becomes natural to radiate the four immeasurables out toward all beings. So the starting point is to cultivate well-being.

Of course, that doesn't mean that you don't experience suffering. Suffering is a natural part of life, as the Buddha reminded his followers again and again. But when you live in joy, you can experience suffering without being caught up in it.

Exercise 5: Starting the Day

As soon as you get up in the morning, take three deep breaths, aware of the inhale and exhale. At first you will have to remind yourself to do this, but soon it will become a habit, one that can be deeply rewarding. Before the first thought or concern enters your mind, let this positive experience shape the coming day. Let yourself enjoy the way the whole body engages the breath, together with the way that breathing connects you to the world around you.

Later in the morning, but still before you begin your round of daily activities, take a few moments to reflect on your good fortune. Even if you are dealing with obstacles or with sad and painful circumstances, you can remind yourself how remarkable it is to be alive and in possession of your faculties. You have made contact with teachings that can help you get more out of life, and you can form positive intentions and act on your own values. Let this reflection inspire you.

With this feeling of inspiration active within you, take another step—a kind of visualization. Say to yourself, "Today I will be kind to myself. I will take care of my body, I will nurture my spirit, and I will cultivate positive feelings. I will create a positive atmosphere around me, and I will appreciate the riches that my senses make available to me." You don't actually have to repeat these words or even put your intention in words at all. If the intention is there, it will be like taking an inner shower that cleanses and refreshes you, opening all your faculties and encouraging your capacity for appreciation.

If we look carefully at the ongoing stream of experience, we find that the mind is always active, commenting on experience, conducting an ongoing dialog with itself, making judgments, and setting itself up for negative reactions. This may seem self-evident, but the more you track your own inner experience, the more you will discover that many of the mind's movements are so quick and so habitual that they tend to pass unnoticed. On the surface, we may have the sense that we are having a positive, productive day, that things are going our way. As we develop the ability to look more closely, however, we may realize that that is true only at one level. Like someone riding a bicycle, the mind makes constant adjustments, triggering a steady stream of reactions that include all sorts of negativities. That is one reason we may suddenly discover that we have fallen into an unhappy mood. The preconditions for that shift in attitude have already been established: the way has been marked out.

When you notice the mind starting down a negative path, you can deliberately cultivate reflections that will strengthen you intention to live in more positive ways. With practice, you may find that you can apply them at a very early stage, offering yourself encouragement at a point when it is most likely to be effective. Here are a few examples:

> Today I will not fall into dark and moody places. I do not need to get lost in feelings of darkness, emptiness, or loneliness. When I feel anger or resentment starting

to arise, I will remind myself that these kinds of feelings come and go—they have no substance. If I let them, they will soon pass. I do not need to act on them, nurture them, or go along with them.

For the sake of my body and my mind, which have been my supports for so long, I will not to give in to emotionality, negative judgments, or a sense of inner conflict. If memories of bad times or situations come up, I will confront them directly, saying, "I know now that I do not have to accept these feelings."

Whatever experiences I have during the day, I will not react in toxic ways. I will do my best to make this a good day. I will not bring feelings of conflict or negativity to my interactions. I will not poison my experience of the world, whether through my eyes or ears or the other senses or through negative judgments or comparisons. As much as possible, I will cleanse and purify my experience.

During the day, you can bring these positive intentions into every interaction: a casual conversation, a telephone call, a meeting, a simple encounter with a stranger. Make it your intention to benefit everyone you come into contact with. You can do a lot with a smile, a few kind words, a thoughtful gesture, or a helpful way of seeing some situation in a more positive light. The next day, you can make more efforts in the same direction, vowing to improve.

Joy of Being offers many practices that can help restore richness to your experience. It would be valuable to work with them over an extended period of time. But there are also simple things you can do that you can easily integrate into your life without thinking of them as special practices.

For instance, if you enjoy listening to music, give yourself opportunities to do that. It's probably a good idea to give some thought to what kind of music is best. Everyone is different, but in general it's better not to choose music with lyrics, because then the words may take over. It's also good not to choose music with a strong emotional content, especially emotions that encourage a driving, agitated energy. In the end, though, it's up to you.

In the same way, unless you are fasting, just about everyone eats every day. Usually we are in a rush when we eat, too distracted to notice as we taste, chew, and swallow. We may also use meal times as social occasions or times to connect with our friends or family, or as quiet times when we take out a book and catch up on reading. All that has value, but it is also valuable to take the time to enjoy your meals deeply. A good place to start is to chew well, enjoying each bite. Imagine that you are distributing the inner essence of the food you are eating through the whole body, giving each cell the nourishment it needs.

You can apply the same kind of simple attention and appreciation to all of your daily activities. When you walk, even if it's in a busy, crowded setting, you can enjoy the sensations associated with the way your body moves. You can also appreciate the input you receive through the senses: bright colors, a wide range of sounds both pleasant and unpleasant, aromas, and so on. When you interact with others, you can be open and attentive, keeping a basic balance.

Exercise 6: Panoramic Seeing

This exercise condenses a series of three exercises in *Joy of Being*, all related to developing a relaxed way of seeing:

Gaze softly at something you enjoy looking at, focusing on color and form. As the body relaxes, the eyes can look more gently, without making any particular effort to focus or take in specific details. To encourage this relaxed seeing, you could also just let the eyes take in what appears before them, not focusing on anything in particular. Cultivate a sense that the objects you see are inseparable from the space that allows them to appear. Gradually let go of the sense that you are the one doing the seeing. Let yourself take pleasure in the light that enters your eyes, and let go of the strong distinction between the subject that sees and the object that is seen. Eventually, you may sense the field of awareness expanding to encompass all objects panoramically. In this meditative way of seeing, all objects take on a luminous light, and the act of seeing transforms your being toward openness, compassion, beauty, and deeper purpose.

When you structure your life in this way, it's easy to develop a positive attitude toward your own experience. It also comes to seem natural to be kind and gentle in your interactions with others. You don't need to make special efforts.

That sounds like a wonderful way to live—much more refreshing than how I usually go about my business. But . . . I don't want to sound disrespectful . . . there are many self-help books on the market that seem to say something similar.

In one way, living in a positive, appreciative way is nothing special. That's what everyone wants. But it's not how most people live, and that is really unfortunate. So it's nat-

PART ONE: GETTING STARTED

ural for people who feel that they have learned something
about how to live in a more positive way to be eager to
share their understanding, and it's also natural for people
to seek help wherever they can find it. The real issue is
whether the methods people adopt go beneath superficial
reactivity to get at the root causes of unhappiness and dissatisfaction.

*How can you tell? You can't try out one method after another—that
would take many lifetimes.*

It's better just to focus on this moment, right now. Here
we are, in this particular situation, having these particular
experiences. So just cherish the present opportunity. Don't
worry about making comparisons or second-guessing yourself. If you are appreciating your experience, that's enough.
You don't need to wonder whether you could (or should) be
doing even more.

We are on a journey, and we want to enjoy every moment of
the journey. That means staying right with what is going on
now. What we are experiencing at this moment will never
be repeated. Even if we remember it later, those impressions
from the past, no matter how sweet they are, will not capture every nuance of what is available now.

The world of our experience, the expressions that manifest as the unfolding story of our lives, is a kind of dream
world, impermanent and transitory. One day, it will simply
be gone. Knowing that, you realize how important it is
to recognize each moment for what it is, and not to lose
the chance that this immediate situation presents. If you
embody your own experience, you can cherish life as it

26

unfolds. Then, very naturally, you can share what you have discovered with others.

You might say that we owe that much to the impressions we receive and the actions we express. This life offers a rich abundance of sights, sounds, colors, textures, and tonalities. The past has given us the present opportunity. If we don't treasure it, we have no chance to pass on meaningful knowledge and benefits to others. First we can develop a positive orientation toward all that is going on in the field of being, and then we can share it. Many could benefit from what we might have to offer: people alive today, who are in so much need; the next generation; even animals and insects.

The world is offering us its riches in a spontaneous act of kindness Although we do not usually notice, there is a precious knowledge within the ordinary. Everyday experience contains marvelous seeds. If we cultivate them with gratitude and appreciation, beautiful fruits may come forth. If learn to see with grateful eyes, we can truly discover a sacred quality everywhere we look.

When we understand this, the ordinary can become monumental. You could say that this dimension has been hidden, a secret that no one knows. But when you share your own joy and appreciation with others, the secret reveals itself and becomes sacred.. Make this secret available in the life of each individual, and you will discover unending abundance.

I sense that you're talking about something precious, but it seems very remote from my own experience. How can we activate that beauty and that abundance?

Why do you insist on its being remote? It won't stay remote if you just let yourself experience it. Our problem is that we set up rules for ourselves that determine what's allowed. We say, "You're only entitled to a certain amount of pleasure . . . the world will only allow you a certain degree of happiness. You shouldn't expect to be happy all the time." But those rules are not binding. We can just set them aside.

We have a way of setting limits on our own possibilities. A certain amount of positive experience is fine, but at some point we have used up our quota, and it's time to go back to being ordinary again. It doesn't have to be that way. If we let ourselves, we can learn to accept positive thoughts and good feelings as natural. The strong tendency is to reject the very possibility that this could happen, but that's just based on what we've learned to accept. We don't have to go along with it. Just decide to embody what is positive, as fully as you can. You can see the results for yourself.

Of course you may encounter challenges. You may feel lonely or insecure, or have to deal with pain or loss. But none of that has to stop you. You are not the first to have such feelings—many people know that kind of suffering. So now you have to ask yourself how you are going to react. If you just go along with the negativity, nothing will change for the better. About the best you can do is wait for the painful parts of your experience to pass. When you make that choice, though, you are undermining your own possibilities.

How much you contribute to the world is up to you. If you choose not to accept the fundamentally positive parts of experience, you make it highly unlikely that you will be able to engage in meritorious action or add to the store of knowledge. How can you generate positive karma if ripples of negativity are constantly spinning out from the center of your experience? But when you turn toward the positive, all that can change. You can create a healthy environment for yourself and for others—at the physical level, the social level, and the emotional level.

Exercise 7: Building Positive Energy

Sit quietly and relax tension in the body. Do a few gentle head rotations and relax some more. Then focus lightly on the breath, letting the sense of breathing as an ongoing activity expand into the whole of your sense of being embodied, and also into whatever sense fields may be active, such as seeing or hearing.

After a few minutes of breathing in this relaxed way, take a deep breath and be aware of how the diaphragm expands to allow air to enter the body. You should have the sense of the abdomen rising and falling. Take a few breaths like this. If you are not sure you are breathing into the belly, you can put one hand on the belly and experience how it rises and falls with each breath.

When you are comfortable with this way of breathing, take a deep breath, let it expand into the abdomen as fully as possible, and then hold the breath. Draw the abdomen in a little toward your spine. Let the belly be warm and energetic and lightly focus there. Hold the breath for a little while, just past the point of comfort, still very relaxed. Then slowly release the breath. Sit quietly for a few minutes, letting the feeling of warmth in the belly flow through the body and especially into the heart. Let this inner massage bring a sense of joy and well-being.

Continue to sit quietly with these feelings for a few minutes, then repeat two more times. When the cycle of three breaths is complete, sit for a few minutes longer. Allow any arising thoughts or images to dissolve into the warmth and stillness that the breathing brings with it. Repeat this exercise twice a day for at least 20 minutes, for two weeks or longer. Note: this exercise is adapted from Exercise N in *Mastering Successful Work* (Dharma Publishing 1994).

Exercise 8: Choosing the Positive

Over the course of several weeks, keep track of how you are feeling during the day. How often and for how long do you feel positive? Negative? Are there times when you are overwhelmed with a sense of difficulty or sadness? Times when you spontaneously appreciate what experience offers you? When you notice that you are feeling negative, ask yourself if it has to be that way. What happens if you try to switch to the opposite—swiftly, strongly, without thinking about it? When you notice that you are feeling positive, let the feelings accumulate and expand. You may find it helpful to do a Kum Nye exercise that encourages positive feelings to expand.

A good time to bring this practice to mind is just before you connect with other people, whether it's a social occasion, a business meeting, or a casual encounter. What energy do you bring to the interaction? Can you turn it toward the positive? Can you trace the impact of your own feelings or attitudes on what happens?

5

Bringing Joy to Others

So many people we meet as we go about our lives are lonely and restless, lacking support for what is beneficial in their lives. Because they don't know how to take care of themselves, they go through their days hoping for a few simple pleasures that will balance out their unhappiness. If you have developed a positive attitude toward yourself, you have the resources to help them. When your own life, day by day, becomes a celebration of the opportunities you have been given, you can share your blessings with others. In fact, sharing your own positive feelings with others happens without your having to make any extra effort. It happens naturally.

As you develop appreciation, your sense of well-being can ripple outward. Eventually, each routine thought or action can become a carrier for joy that radiates out in waves of well-being to all sentient beings. You can start with your friends and relatives. Later, you can bring others to mind: those you know and those you do not know, those alive today and those who have gone or who have yet to come. All beings yearn for positive feelings and thoughts and for encouragement. Through your own positive feelings, you can offer them what they wish for.

In some ways, each of us lives in a private world. The people you meet do not know what you are thinking, nor can they sense in a direct or obvious way the good wishes you are sending their way. That does not matter. Just resolve to share your own sense of enjoyment and well-being with all beings, known and unknown alike. Wish for them everything positive, whatever form it may take: radiant light, soothing breezes, positive thoughts, delightful tastes, infectious laughter, inspiring music, or beautiful sights. As you think of them, let waves of energy expand in all directions, each one carrying your intention to be of benefit.

Exercise 9: Mood Ripples

This exercise is related to the previous exercise, but it takes a more challenging approach toward your own experience. Start by simply being aware during the day of your moods and attitudes. When your attitude is positive, you can expand it, as in the previous exercise. When your feelings tend in the other direction, approach them lightly and carefully, with an attitude of acceptance. For instance, you may feel heavy or blocked. You may have negative thoughts racing through your mind: a sense of inadequacy perhaps, or regret for something you have done wrong or some way in which you have caused another person pain. Stay with such feelings, without trying to change them, but also without accepting them as the truth of the way things are. Where do such feelings lead you? Take a survey of your present situation and how your mood is shaping it. Where is this attitude headed? What do you expect will happen next? As you trace out your feelings, how do they change?

In doing this exercise, be sure to stay very attentive to what you are feeling without getting lost in it. This is really a practice in staying present and awake. Notice the stories you are telling yourself, without necessarily going along with them. You might think of this as cultivating mindfulness of mind. If you sense that you are losing your ability to observe with equanimity, take a break. You could also alternate this practice with the previous practice, 'Choosing the Positive'.

Even though samsara is marked by suffering of countless kinds, there are many positive elements in our daily experience. If we make the choice to turn those elements toward the well-being of all that lives, we can make a real difference in the world.

Think back: what has happened to you today or in the last few days that brought you pleasure? Did you have sense experiences that you enjoyed? Perhaps it was the sun shining off a body of water, or the leafy green of a potted plant. Perhaps you heard a sound that gave you joy, or you lost yourself for a time in a piece of music. Perhaps you had a conversation with a friend that left you feeling a sense of connection, of being supported and understood. Perhaps you had the opportunity to engage in creative work that brought you the pleasure of accomplishment and expanded opportunities for positive actions and healthy outcomes. Or perhaps there was a moment of insight, confirming that wisdom is indeed freely available in the world.

Whenever you have such a feeling or experience, you can send it out to others, serene in the intention to share the blessings. While you may not be able to trace or recognize the results, you can be confident that sharing such feelings, even if you only do it inwardly, will bring healing energy to the hearts of others. Feelings of deep joy and satisfaction go beyond your own limited concerns and patterns—that is what makes them so rich. By channeling such waves of energy through your conscious wishes for the well-being of others, you can multiply their impact.

Traditional Dharma practices also offer powerful opportunities for sharing what is positive. When you chant mantra, you can chant for all beings. When you pray, your prayers are not for yourself; they are prayers for the welfare of all, for an end to suffering and the growth of bodhichitta, the mind and heart of enlightenment. Similarly, when you visualize the Buddha or Guru Padmasambhava, you are inviting their energy to transform the whole of samsara. You are not asking for some kind of abstract blessing: you can actually feel the energy you are invoking being activated throughout space and time.

There are no limits to how such positive energy can spread. Imagine that you set out to share your positive thoughts and feelings with people who do not like you and have no interest in spiritual matters. Whether they know you or not, whether their negativity is based on grievances that they cling to tightly or on stereotypes that they have simply accepted unquestioningly, energy that manifests through positive intentions will soften the hardness in the hearts and allow positive and noble thoughts to enter the stream of mental events that course through their minds. If conditions allow, they may turn naturally toward joy and light and move closer to the healing powers of samadhi.

Practicing in this way is deeply worthwhile. Choosing it, we embark on an extraordinary journey, one that enriches our lives with beauty and meaning. This is the path of the Bodhisattva, the path of wisdom and the path of compassion. Put simply, it is also a path of thoughtfulness. It is a path we share simply in walking it, even if we do not pronounce to others what we are doing. Meditating and practicing for the sake of others, secretly, silently, invisibly, we send good thoughts and intentions into the universe. Through the medium of space and the energy of time, waves of wellness spread in all dimensions.

There is no great difficulty in expressing and activating such intentions. Whenever we have feelings of faith and devotion, we simply allow them to expand outward. As our awareness deepens, awareness becomes available everywhere. Whatever sweet or pleasant or positive feelings we have can be shared. Even if we simply witness an act of kindness or recall a generous action we performed at some earlier time in our lives, we can develop that recollection and pass it on. Multiplying and extending whatever has benefit, we can let our attitudes and impressions radiate outward, benefiting those close to us, strengthening our community, and creating a beautiful environment for all. Our actions and our thoughts affirm that it is worthwhile to be alive.

Much of our daily experience as human beings can be deeply toxic and negative, but it can also embrace the creative, joyful, and healing aspects of being alive. Caught up in the patterns that feed negativity, we may not be aware of the positive dimensions that life unfolds, yet the positive remains available, like a secret paradise, like the beauty of art, like the stars on a moonless night when the lights of the city have been left far behind.

As we move through life, we can choose to focus on such positive dimensions. We can think deeply, think toward a mind that engages the world without falling into negativity and depression. Why not do so? Haven't we had enough of 'business as usual'? Aren't we tired of seeing what is wrong in the world and having no way to address it? There is no profit in fighting, killing, and putting others down: that is not the way to happiness and well-being. We need to learn to respond to our circumstances with wisdom and with all the knowledge we can muster. We need to make this human mind great again.

Once we decide to undertake a journey toward goodness, we have countless treasures we can draw on. The power of love and generosity, of thoughtfulness and openness, can guide us toward freedom. The examples of the great teachers and sages of the past, the deities, the Buddhas, and the Bodhisattvas can inspire us. Even for those who dismiss such figures as nothing more than legends, the possibilities they introduce into our ways of thinking can encourage us to improve ourselves in ways both small and vast. There is no real cost to aiming to guide our lives in accord with such models. If we can live in a way that is selfless, our capacity for joy will not be diminished. Instead, we may find the greater joy of being truly alive.

Every day, every hour, positive ripples of time radiate outward. Engaging such ripples, we can discover a joy beyond direct expression and share it with everyone caught up in the endless problems that beset a life lived in samsara. There may not be much we can do directly, but that should not stop us. Even kind words may help. When we encounter someone in pain or in need, we should not be afraid to ask how we can help. We have our limits, known and unknown, yet we are free to think and speak and act in ways that encourage and uplift others. We can offer small gestures intended to bring benefit, and we can manifest to our fullest capacity whatever understanding we have.

6

Easing Negativity

We are all familiar with thoughts and emotions that veer toward negativity, depression, or anger. That is just a part of what it means to live in samsara. People who begin meditating often become more aware of such negativities, and they may find it confusing. If meditation stirs up unhealthy patterns, is it really a good idea to continue meditating?

The truth, however, seems to be that the greater awareness that comes with meditation lets us notice such patterns for the first time. Until we learn how to focus on the quick bursts of disappointment, criticism, anger, pride and the like, they may rumble through our minds too quickly and silently to acknowledge, especially when they challenge our self-image. "I am not someone who feels superior to others," we tell ourselves. "I am a fair, accepting person." When we start to notice thoughts and feelings that go against the stories we tell ourselves about who we really are, we may feel uneasy and even demoralized. It's good to be honest with ourselves, but it may be easier and more comfortable to look away.

Meditation intensifies awareness. It brightens the mind, letting us see more clearly. What we see may not square with our cherished assumptions, but that doesn't mean that meditation is creating problems where none existed before.

That makes good sense. But my question is this: if meditation does make us more aware of our negative patterns, why isn't that awareness enough to put a stop to them? Nobody likes being trapped in negativity. So why is it that we have such a hard time letting go of the negative patterns we discover?

There's a paradox at work here. A mind at ease will not generate such feelings or thoughts, but being at ease is not easy. That is simply not the direction mind has learned to go. So we need to train ourselves to ease the mind. Specific exercises can be helpful.

Isn't that what most forms of meditation aim at?

Not exactly. If we try to relax the mind, we are fixating the mind on the idea of relaxation. If we try to contemplate, using a particular practice we have been taught, we are fixating on doing the practice. If we give up on the idea of practice and just try to be kind to everyone, we are still fixated on the concept that we want to be kind.

The patterns of samsaric mind go deeper than that, and it may be that our usual approach to meditation does not reach that deeper level. For instance, we say we want to *be* this way or that way, or that we don't want to *be* some other way, and we hope that meditation can help us reach that goal. That approach can be beneficial, but what matters more is to ease the identity that underlies 'to be'.

OK, I'm ready to try. What do I do?

There are exercises that can help, but it's better to start with a very gentle approach. For instance, think back to a time when you were very young, say four or five years old, or a little older. Perhaps you have memories from that time when you felt very calm. It might have been when you were playing alone, and there was a feeling of vast space, or a sense that time had stopped. Does a memory like that come to mind?

Yes, I think so. Of course, I wasn't describing it to myself that way. But when I look back now, that's a good description.

Looking back, what is the feeling associated with that calmness?

Warmth . . . support . . . . More fundamentally, though, I would say appreciation.

OK. That's a good start.

But let me make a jump. You seem to be asking why I can't just go back to that feeling. Have I lost some ability I had when I was little?

You don't need to think in terms of getting or losing. We can start at a more basic level. We all have certain habits of mind that are connected with labels and identities. For instance, we have the name 'mind'. Because the name is there, we give mind an identity, and then we go on to assign it certain characteristics and judge its operations. We say, "My mind is relaxed; things are going well." Or we say, "My mind is feeling agitated. That's not good."

That whole way of going about things is not very helpful. It doesn't lead to a sense of ease. It's habitual for mind to operate in those ways, so our descriptions and judgments are not necessarily wrong. But the habitual patterns we identify and judge may not be a solid as we are pretending. It may be that those patterns themselves can become space.

So developing space is a kind of meditative approach that can help us develop ease?

You don't need to call it meditation. In fact, if you do, it just plays into old habit patterns and old distinctions. It's better to just practice secretly. I don't mean to keep it a secret from others. Keep it a secret from yourself. Practice without calling it meditation. You don't want to have a conversation with the mind, telling it what to do. If you treat the mind that way, you block it from opening up. You have to treat the mind gently. Don't even tell it, "I'm going to practice secretly."

Is that because this kind of ease is beyond language?

That's already saying too much. When the speaker says, "I'm looking for a state beyond words—I can't talk about my experience," that's again a case of shutting down the possibility for openness. Now there's something the mind is not allowed do to do. Try opening that 'not allowed'; just let it be.

Can you say something more about "just letting things be."

The nature of 'to be' is inherently good. But usually we turn 'being' into a question of identity. We say, "I am this way; that's how I am." Now 'to be' has become a problem. "Am I this way? Am I not this way?" 'To be' has nothing to do with identity. When you've lost identity, when you don't know the meaning, then you can be. That's a big difference.

I don't understand. The two kinds of 'to be' sound the same to me.

It's better not to worry too much about distinctions. Too many words! Just organize experience in a positive way. Be caring, kind, friendly, and thoughtful. That's the way to be. It doesn't have to be very complicated. When you follow out ripples and rhythms in your interactions with people in ways that create a positive environment, you will see the benefits. Then you can deal with negative situations easily.

Could you say more about how to deal with negative situations?

First you need to recognize that reacting to a difficult situation with negativity will not lead to positive results. Most people know that; they just don't know what else to do or how else to react.

Right. I'd put myself in that category.

Don't agree too quickly! It's helpful to take time to see how you react when difficulties come up, or even when you just find yourself in a bad mood. Do you feed that negativity? What happens when you try to change your mental state? Does a forceful response bring about change? There's not necessarily a right answer here. You have to see for yourself.

Suppose that you agree after looking into it carefully that you don't have very constructive ways to deal with difficulties and negativity. Once this is clear, you realize that negative situations are potentially very useful, because they may help you discover a better way. You can take advantage of a negative situation to see what other possibilities there are for dealing with it.

This is different from our usual way of responding. When you are feeling negative, don't look around for something that will change your mood or distract you. There's no need to take any particular action at all. Just contemplate how you are feeling and your response to how you feel. Take some time to do this: at least a few minutes.

But in the situation you're describing, I already know how I'm feeling. I'm feeling some sort of negative feeling. Maybe I feel depressed, or confused. What else is there to know?

That's just the very surface level. If you give your feeling a label and then move on, nothing valuable is likely to happen. The question is this: how do you feel when you feel negative? There may be many layers to explore, many subtle dimensions that shift from moment to moment. How you feel is the target, so explore it, get familiar with it. That's what you need to open up, and the time to do it is now, not later.

Simply contemplating your feelings in this way, without trying to change them, may lead to strongly positive outcomes. Rationally, that may sound like a paradox, but if you stay with the experience, you don't need to worry about paradox.

What kinds of positive outcomes?

You'll have to discover that for yourself. But to give just one example, there may be a sense of light radiating out, accompanied by a feeling of peace that exhibits in new ways. It may be something you have never experienced in quite this way: feelings and sensations that are out of the ordinary. It's a sign that you are making contact with the treasures that lie buried under our usual responses.

Is this a question of developing inner calm?

Not exactly. It's more like discovering some new sense faculty. You don't have to develop it; you just have to realize it's there. You may never have looked that way before, but now you can, and when you do, you realize that you are no longer stuck. Transformation is a real possibility. It's like discovering you can fly when you never even knew that you had wings.

I've had dreams like that. I just realized that if I walked a certain way, I could walk up into the sky. It was very realistic. Often after I had those dreams, it seemed like it must really be true that I could do that.

Then you have a sense of what I mean. But this is not a dream.

This society generates all sorts of toxic patterns, which are reflected in the operations of the mind and senses, in words and thoughts, and in individual character. So it's safe to predict that when you trace out your feelings, you will discover various negativities. Most people recognize that this culture stimulates more and more cravings—it operates on that basis and couldn't really function otherwise. You can see it most easily with drugs and other forms of addiction, but in fact the same dynamic operates in countless other ways. Growing up in this society, we learn to want more goods and services, better vacations, more exciting news, more approval from others. It never stops. The craving itself becomes toxic—even if what we crave seems harmless enough, the craving causes us harm at the deepest level.

What kind of harm?

44

I think you know. We become slaves to our own desires. Our opportunities for beauty and meaning are lost. Our best impulses are doomed. Our dreams become small and uninspired, our attitudes are twisted by the constant grasping after something new and different. We lose the ability to feel love and affection. Our throat, our heart, and our senses close down, and we seldom experience real joy or depth of feeling. Something positive within us dies, and life itself comes to seem worthless.

That's certainly not how most people would describe their lives! They would point to the things they value: family and good friends, feelings of accomplishment that let them feel good about themselves, new sensations or experiences.

It's not a very long list, is it? But in fact, we often fool ourselves about what is really going on in our lives. We imagine that we are having rich experiences, but that may just be on the conceptual level. Can we really say that we feel nourished within? Wonderful treasures are available—love, joy, happiness—but we have thrown away the key that would give us access to them. On the one hand, we are so committed to controlling our situation that we refuse to allow feelings to enter in at all. On the other hand, we try to control each new situation we encounter, and the result is that we shut down our feelings of joy and the other treasures that life offers us. It's a strange trade we make. We give up our positive feelings, but we hold on tightly to our anger, our confusion, and cravings. And what do we get in return? Fantasy, imagination, temporary pleasures, and an endless stream of thoughts. Or suppose we do have positive experiences. Most of us do not have companions to help us make

positive choices, so there is no way to share whatever sweet-
ness we may experience.

You make it sound very grim.

It *is* grim. We are losing our humanity. You could say we are
almost bankrupt.

*Is that why you're presenting these other alternatives? Are you trying
to restore us to a more sane way of being?*

We need to connect to our own experience through the
heart. It doesn't matter whether what you are feeling is positive or negative—just bring it close to the heart. Once the
heart-feeling is there, it naturally opens up in positive ways.
It begins to expand, and the sense that you are separate
from others becomes very questionable, so that you can easily imagine sharing your positive feelings with others. You
don't have to work out in advance what you want to do or
how you can be of benefit. All that comes naturally. You
can find ways to communicate that don't depend on external conditions or circumstances or on holding to the same
values and ideas.

That is really the starting point for compassion. The body,
mind, and senses can all become sources for healing. That
is what we would like to show others. Everyone is born into
a life full of rich and nurturing potential. If they contact it,
their lives become meaningful.

We know from our own experience what it is like to be cut
off from inner healing, so it is easy to develop sympathy for
others in the same situation. In the beginning, we can focus
on our friends and those close to us, but eventually we can

have the wish to help anyone, even people who have not been kind to us. We understand the way their minds operate, and we can recognize in them the same kinds of emotionality and ignorance that we have experienced ourselves.

The more deeply we connect with our own inner knowing, the more we find it natural to devote ourselves to acting in worthy ways. Each thought, each perception, each feeling, each gesture is an opportunity for uplifting the lives of others. Whatever understanding we develop is a gift to be shared with others. We recognize how important it is to see with more clarity, and we want to contribute whatever knowledge we embody. The culture itself may promote bankrupt policies and conduct, but we don't need to go along. The Bible has a saying, "An eye for an eye and a tooth for a tooth," but even Western religions would agree that we don't need to accept that way of thinking. We can choose generosity and healing gestures, because we know that acting in this way is the gateway to the riches that life offers.

Our teachers and friends have given us great gifts. Now we can pass on what we have received to others. In fact, if we relax into our experience, this will happen naturally. We will find ourselves thinking of others, looking for ways to be helpful, making an extra effort even when it comes at a cost. If each of us could imprint that understanding on our soul, so that it shaped our intentions, the world would be immeasurably richer. The Bodhisattvas call this intention Bodhichitta, the loving compassion identical to wisdom.

How much is Bodhichitta a question of intention and good wishes and how much does it mean that you really do act for the sake of all beings?

47

There's a gradual development. Even forming the intention to be of help to others is already an advanced stage. First we have to acknowledge our present situation. For many of us, the heart has become a desert, dry and barren, with little sign of life. It may take some time to realize that. In fact, you may resist that description; you may say that it doesn't apply to you, and you may be right. Still, you need to look closely, because this is a dimension of our experience where it is easy to lose sight of what is truly happening. Once you get used to being cut off from deeper positive feelings like compassion or love or enjoyment, it starts to seem natural, as though there were no alternative. If that's your situation, Bodhichitta can seem like just a nice idea, a conceptual model for how to be a good person. The concept is important, because it at least shows us that another way of being is possible. But if we just stay on that level, the concept will gradually fade away. Whatever inspired us to imagine being of benefit to others will lose its intensity, and we will lose our connection. The words are not enough.

If you recognize that your ideas and your intentions do not fully match up, the next step is to dig deeper, as though you were digging a well in the desert, looking for a source of water. One way is to cultivate Bodhichitta through your imagination. What would it be like for your heart to be filled with love? Perhaps you have experiences of feeling that way, and if so you can draw on those memories. Little by little, imagination can cross over into feeling. You can bring your own positive feelings back to life, nourishing your own heart. Once the feelings are there, they flow out toward others without any special effort. There is nothing to restrain them. From there, it is natural to express what you are feeling through words and gestures or through simple acts of kindness.

The riches we can discover in our own hearts are a precious resource for all humanity. They don't just belong to us— they come alive when we share them. That is why it matters so much to cultivate love, joy, and compassion. We do it not just for ourselves, but for everyone. We are the carriers of realization for all beings, so the more we understand, the more important it is to devote ourselves to sharing what we know. Discovering this knowledge, tracing and expressing our own creativity: that is a project to which we can dedicate our lives.

Perhaps you have heard about such possibilities before, but at some level they have seemed like a myth, like the Garden of Eden. But when the desert within us begins to bloom, we recognize that this is no myth. Genuine caring and spontaneous kindness are very real.

That is not the view that this society teaches. Few people today trust the truths passed on in the ancient knowledge traditions. We have learned to be suspicious, even paranoid. We suspect that people who look for what is positive are fooling themselves, telling each other stories to feel better instead of facing up to the harsh truth. If we think that we are especially clever, we try to trace out the ways that stories like this support the power and privilege of the few who are in charge, and we congratulate ourselves on our ability to strip away the layers of deception. Perhaps it was views like that—insisting on the most negative interpretation as the most honest and real—that made the desert spread to begin with. But the reason may not matter. The truth is that many people today are cynical or nihilistic.

It's good to acknowledge such negativity, because it does sometimes seem to be pervasive. I'm not completely convinced, because the picture we get from the media may be misleading. It's always easier—and more 'interesting'—to point out what is negative and wrong than to communicate examples of what's positive.

Even if the negativity we find reflected in the media is accurate, though, that doesn't mean we have to accept a negative view of experience or of our situation as true. We have other possibilities available to us. We can try to learn for ourselves how to bring the head and heart and senses together, how to feed and nurture what is most positive in our lives. When the senses and the thoughts that run through our minds become more 'expressionable', our lives from day to day can become richer and more healthy.

This is the way to benefit from our lives, to use our time and energy well. We do not want to end up bankrupt and defeated, wasting our lives in idle, meaningless pursuits, secretly convinced that there is nothing of value to live for. We do not want to pass that message on to others through our actions, our sidelong looks, our sighs and complaints. There is already enough negativity in the world.

So what can we do?

Be ready to nurture your body, your senses, your mind, and your heart. Do not think that you are being selfish when you take care of yourself in these ways. It is urgent that you do this, for that is the only way you can reach out to others in gestures of love and healing. Others may not notice what you are doing. If they do notice, even just a little, they may

50

not understand your motivation. But that need not concern you. Act from your own deepest knowledge, the knowledge you discover when you are most at peace, most clear. Let the truth you rely on guide you, and you will find that you can guide others as well.

7

Cultivating the Immeasurables

Can you say more about practice that leads toward Bodhichitta?

One powerful method in the Buddhist tradition for transforming the negative patterns of samsara is practice of the four immeasurables: love (or loving kindness), compassion, joy, and equanimity. If we train ourselves gradually in developing these four, we will come to know the special flavor of each of them, and we will be able to bring more aliveness, more 'juice' into our experience.

We all experience various kinds of negative emotions and attitudes and orientations: what Buddhism calls the kleshas and upakleshas. Many of them could be thought of in psychological terms as different forms of neurosis. When they begin to spill their toxicity into our lives, everything in our experience 'indensifies'. That is the point when we can apply the immeasurables.

Most religious traditions, or even most religious thinkers, would probably agree that it's a positive thing to cultivate feelings of love and com-

passion toward others, and joy and equanimity are also really positive. But you're saying that the four immeasurables can help us overcome our own negativity. Can you explain how that works?

The immeasurables have an inherent, magnificent power that can transform experience toward joy and serenity. It's not just a question of doing what is morally right, though of course that is valuable too. When love and joy and compassion fill our hearts and minds, we change at a deep level, and negativity has no room to take root. So cultivating the immeasurables is a distinct practice that we can activate in the face of our own negative patterns. We can choose to turn our thoughts in this direction: in the beginning, when we notice the direction the mind is headed, in the middle, when we begin to activate one of the immeasurables, and in the end, when we actually taste the result.

You can start to cultivate the immeasurables by reflecting on the pain and suffering that everyone you know—and everyone you don't know—has gone through in the past. Sometimes it may be physical pain: illness, exhaustion, disease, or injury. Sometimes it is some form of inner mental torture: lostness, regret, longing, embarrassment, or grief in all its forms. You may not like to think about those situations, but you know it is true.

The first step is simply to acknowledge this. Then you need to develop sympathy. For instance, think of your parents before you were born, or even as you were growing up: they were no different from anyone else. They had problems and difficulties, the same way that you and your friends do. Before you were born, they were just trying to live their lives and to find happiness. Sometimes they succeeded, at least for a while; other times, they ran into obstacles and frustrations or found themselves in painful situations. Everyone goes through difficulties and has problems: rich people and poor people, the powerful as well as the weak, the famous as well as the unknown. Of this there can be no doubt. The patterns of negativity repeat themselves from our earliest moments to the time of death, and then beyond death, from one life to the next.

Think of all the instances of suffering you hear about every day or see for yourself: people you have known in the past, friends, relatives, victims of catastrophes that you learn about in the media. Sometimes it can be almost too painful to see the reports of suffering, unhappiness and loss that make up the daily news: the ongoing reports of war, sudden tragedy, or grinding poverty. Yet what we learn about is not even the tiniest fraction of what people experience every day. If we add in the suffering in the animal realm, it is literally too much for our ordinary mind to comprehend.

If the sheer mass of suffering that goes on each day and each hour seems overwhelming, take steps to keep you heart and mind open to what is happening. Think of what you have experienced in your own life. Remind yourself what it truly feels like to suffer. Even events that seem trivial now—a small disappointment, a minor pain or irritation—may have caused you great unhappiness at the time. Let those memories be very real. You could also take time to engage whatever limited form of suffering you may be experiencing right now, in this very moment. The point is not to make yourself feel bad, but to look at suffering in an honest and heartfelt way. Whatever unhappiness may befall you now or in times to come, there are countless other beings going through something similar, or perhaps far worse.

There is a story in the Buddhist tradition about a woman who lost her son and went to the Buddha to beg that he restore her dead son to life. The Buddha told her he would do so, provided that she bring him a mustard seed from a household where no one had ever experienced death. As she went from house to house asking for this small gift, she heard and again, from each person she spoke to, of their dear ones who had passed away, dying in old age after great suffering, or cut down unexpectedly in their youth or before they had even matured into childhood. Gradually she realized that her loss, real as it was, was common to beings everywhere, and her bottomless pain began to ease. We too can understand that suffering is universal. In moments when the time is right, we can share that knowledge with others.

There are also people who suffer because they have lost all hope for meaningful change. Trapped in the conviction that all action is futile, they have given up on their lives. Here is a place where the active expression of compassion can be helpful to them and also to you. Perhaps you can find the right moment to encourage them. Be sensitive to what they are feeling, and also to the possibility that they have their own psychological reasons for wanting to hold on to their negativity. You may be able to show them the possibility for breaking through the patterns that make up their own special form of suffering. If they are carrying the burden of guilt for some past action or failure to act, perhaps you can help them see that they have the power to forgive themselves for whatever harm they have done to themselves or to others. Although all beings suffer, no one has to repeat the patterns that produce suffering. Compassion gives us the clarity and stability to see that for ourselves, and it helps us see as well how to share that understanding.

Someone without much experience in the world might think that people would not willingly cause themselves harm, but that seems not to be the case. We have all had the experience of choosing some course of action we know will make us unhappy, going ahead even though in the very moment we act, we have already begun to feel regret. We have all heard the voices in our heads spinning endless stories or giving endless reasons to justify doing what we know is wrong.

Even when we try to act in positive ways, our surging emotions can often get the better of us. We feel ourselves falling into resentment or dullness or irritation, and even though we cannot really say why, we are powerless to check the momentum. Although we do our best not to fall into loneliness or despair, when such emotions arise, they exercise a kind of hypnotic attraction. We find ourselves reliving memories that feed into such feelings, we fall into the energy they sustain, and we shape our experience so that it confirms the negativity we are feeling.

Most of us are deeply familiar with certain characteristic negative feelings that cycle through the stream of our mental activity. We may remind ourselves that such feelings come and go, and that today's unhappiness will seem ghostly in tomorrow morning's light. Yet it does us little good to tell ourselves such things. Instead, we pronounce the negativity we are feeling to be the truth of what is so. What starts out as a tendency toward a particular form of unhappiness—bit-

56

terness, envy, fear—becomes in the course of time a familiar companion. Our personal psychology gradually reshapes itself to conform to this understanding, until we can see no other possibilities. We may waste precious time—even years of our lives—convinced of the truth what we experience, when it would be more accurate to say that we are simply living out a story that we have chosen to accept as true. Many people have fallen into such patterns, choosing a past that confirms the present, and then shaping a future that matches what has come before. We ourselves may follow the same course.

How sad to realize that we are not taking full advantage of all we have received! Our parents gave us the opportunity to grow into adulthood, our country and culture created the conditions that make a deeply fulfilling life possible, our friends and teachers helped open our minds to endless possibilities, and the earth itself—indeed, the whole cosmos—created the conditions for being alive. Can we really let these fortunate conditions go by to no good purpose?

I do realize that we have fortunate opportunities, including the opportunity to hear teachings that can really have a transforming effect. But I have to admit that hearing this, or reflecting on it, is a two-edged sword. If I am already feeling basically positive, it can be inspiring to cultivate a sense of gratitude. But sometimes, when I am already feeling negative for some reason, it just makes me feel bad to think of how I let precious time slip away.

It doesn't do you or anybody else any good to feel guilty for squandering your opportunities. It also makes no sense. You may think you are special in some way, but sometimes it helps to remember that at a basic level, you are no different from anyone else. Tell me, is water wet?

Yes.

OK. Water is wet, and human beings manifest negativity and toxicity. That's just how it is. It's like having a disease for which there is no cure. There is no agent to purify it, no medicine to heal it. The thoughts that cycle through our heads will reflect it, the feelings that fill our hearts will manifest it. It is like living in the middle of stinky garbage dump, so wide and so deep that you can never find your way out.

Is that supposed to make me feel better?

How you feel is not really the point. What matters is to be honest about our situation. And our usual situation is not very promising, even though we have so much potential. Left to ourselves, we will never be able to set out on a path of virtue. We will never be able to develop faith in what is truly positive or discover a more profound vision of reality. We will have nothing of value to share with others, no way to bring inspiration to those we care for. We will not know what it means to feel joyful in body or spirit, and we will have no way to take care of ourselves at a deep level.

Is that the basis for the negativity and anger that seem to manifest all over the world in political movements?

It's related. When we live lives that are shaped by destructive tendencies, we cultivate our own negativities. And because we never taste the juice of experience or know perfect enjoyment, we are prone to let others take over our lives, telling us how to feel and think.

Would you like to hear more about the negative situation we have gotten ourselves into, or have you had enough?

I don't exactly see the point of wallowing in misery, but I realize that the Buddha taught the truth of suffering as the foundation of his path. So maybe I need to hear more, even if the idea doesn't thrill me.

You're on the right track. If we are willing to look honestly at our situation and what outcomes it is likely to produce, we are on the way to understanding the four noble truths taught by the Buddha: suffering, the cause of suffering, the end of suffering, and the path that leads to the end of suffering. We are ready to ask how to develop the qualities of love and joy, of happiness and inner health, of all that is positive. We are ready to discover how to embody, empower, and teach. That is the mission we can decide to take on.

So yes, let's go a little further—let's try to look with a fearless heart and open eyes.

8

Our Samsaric Condition

The Abhidharma teachings developed in the Mahayana recognize six root emotionalities (Sanskrit
'klesha'; Tibetan 'nyon-mong'): greed, anger, arrogance,
ignorance, doubt, and distorting views. Out of these arise
20 forms of negativity (nye-nyon, upaklesha): disturbing
emotions or neurotic patterns that agitate the mind and
produce waves of toxicity in the mental stream. The suffering of samsara manifests through these negative patterns. Here is the list, with several standard translations,
as given in a text by the great master Asanga. (For the
Sanskrit and Tibetan, along with some alternate translations, see the Appendix at the end of the book. For a detailed discussion, see *Mind in Buddhist Psychology* (Dharma
Publishing [1975]).

1. rage/fury; indignation
2. resentment
3. concealment, slyness
4. spite

5. envy, jealousy
6. avarice, stinginess
7. pretense, deceit
8. dishonesty, hypocrisy
9. self-infatuation, mental inflation, self-satisfaction
10. malice, hostility, cruelty, intention to harm
11. shamelessness, lack of conscience
12. lack of propriety, disregard
13. lethargy, gloominess
14. ebullience, excitement
15. lack of faith, lack of trust
16. laziness
17. heedlessness, carelessness, unconcern
18. forgetfulness
19. inattentiveness, non-alertness
20. distraction, desultoriness

Exercise 10: Reflecting on Neurotic Patterns

Instead of just running down the list of neurotic patterns given in the text to make sure you understand what is being said and how it applies to you, take some time to reflect on them. Which ones do you recognize from your own experienc? Which ones seem puzzling, as though they don't belong on the list? The twenty upakleshas do not form a natural grouping in terms of our ordinary understanding. We would classify some as emotions, others as states of mind or moods, and still others as character traits. Try classifying them in these ways, and then notice whether your classifications shift over time.

After you have reflected in this way for a while, perhaps over several sessions, choose a few patterns to work with in more depth, over a period of several weeks. (You can do this while you continue reading through *Dimensions of Mind*, or you can set the book aside for a time while you go more deeply into the investigation.) In deciding which patterns to focus on, you might choose patterns that you can readily identify in your own experience; alternatively, you could focus instead on one or two that seem foreign or unfamiliar.

In working with a particular pattern, look at your experience in a fine-grained way, ready to trace the arising, manifestation, and consequences of the pattern you are working with. How do patterns manifest? Do they always have the same basic feel, or are there significant variations? Are there certain situations or interactions that are most likely to trigger them? Do they come up more often at certain times of day? Are there characteristic thoughts that accompany them? Do they come in clusters? Are they associated with feelings or blockages in the body? Are there thoughts that typically accompany a particular pattern? If so, do the thoughts arise before, after, or during the manifestation?

You may wish to trace out connections between different patterns. For instance, when you are distracted, you are likely to be forgetful. Does forgetfulness happen as a result of distraction, or are the two operating at the same level? How is envy related to self-infatuation? Notice that some of these patterns are presented as the absence of a positive; for instance, lack of faith or trust. Does this make sense to you? Can you identify the absence of a positive state (in this case, faith or trust) as having its own characteristic feel?

As an example of this kind of inquiry, here are a few reflections on laziness, or what might be considered procrastination. Suppose you have something you need to do, but time passes, and you simply do not do it. What is going on? What happens when you tell yourself that it is time to get started? What do you feel? What voices do you hear in your head, pro and con? What kinds of emotions do you notice? What stories do you tell to justify your laziness? Do you really feel unable to act, or is it more that you don't want to? Can you imagine what it would feel like to get started? Where would that lead? Are you afraid of what might happen? What do you imagine?

If you experience your laziness as a 'not wanting', what do you want instead? If you seek out some sort of distraction to keep from getting started, do you enjoy it? What happens if you choose not to follow the impulse toward distraction? What feelings arise? Does the pull toward distraction come back, stronger than ever? If you continue to resist it, what happens? Do new patterns arise? Is the drive for distraction a kind of need, almost like an addiction? What about addiction? Is it included in the list of neurotic patterns? Should it be? Can you track its operation in your life?

As a variation on this exercise that you could also do over a number of sessions, develop your own list of negative patterns. For instance, the traditional list does not include anxiety or guilt, both of which seem quite common in this culture. More surprisingly, it does not include fear. What does this suggest to you? As you conduct these inquiries, keep in mind that you are not proceeding on the basis of some theory or model, but are investigating actual feelings or patterns, and the events associated with them, as they arise in your own experience.

Most of us are fairly familiar with neurotic and negative patterns, whatever our particular flavors happen to be. We may not have noticed, however, the ways that they produce obstacles to clarity that are difficult to penetrate. When we find our experience shaped by feelings of resentment or jealousy or depression, or when we fall into patterns such as pretense and hypocrisy, our lives 'indensify'. Without really choosing to do so, we call forth residues of previous experiences that support our negativity. The result is that we cause pain to ourselves and disturb the well-being of others. We stumble along through the events of our lives, moody, dull, or depressed, or perhaps agitated and restless. Clumsy and ill at ease, we are annoyed by everything. The mind is unwilling to cooperate, either internally or externally, and we find it difficult to turn toward anything positive, even when we are clear on what needs to be done and no real obstacles stand in our way. Our experience is tense; we could even say that it carries within it the seeds of violence.

Exercise 11: Tracking Negativity

Notice in your daily routines times when you experience dense, negative feelings. Usually we focus on the specifics of our negativity: we realize that we feel irritable, indignant, or resentful, or we see that we are being dishonest with ourselves or someone else. Here, however, the inquiry is at a different level: you are looking at the feel of the mind caught in one or more of these negativities. As you explore a variety of negative feelings over time, can you recognize qualities or feelings that are shared among them?

Many people have trained themselves not to notice their own negativity, so it may take repeated sessions to discover how much negativity the mind actually generates. One clue is when you find yourself seeking distraction or feel restless. Are you looking for something that will take your mind off the negativity you are feeling (or not letting yourself feel)?

If you can identify a characteristic feeling that operates in all or many negative states, see if you can also notice it operating in the background in situations that feel more neutral. For example, is there a characteristic feeling that manifests when the mind is wandering from one thought to the next, one image or memory to the next?

Finally, when the 'normal' feeling of negativity is operating, notice your relationship to the flow of time. Do you have the sense that one moment is simply following another, with no particular rhythm or dynamic? How does this compare to other situations where you have a strong sense that what you are doing is meaningful, pleasurable, or valuable? Look from the other side too: when your relationship to time feels negative—pressured, bored, etc.—is the same feeling present?

When experience feels dense, we grow discouraged. The environment itself feels dark and thick, with no way forward and no way to activate change. The density spreads out, which means that we encounter it everywhere. In this way, it feeds back to itself.

These feeling tones are active for most of us much of the time. Though we may do our best not to notice, much in our experience is inherently unpleasant and unsatisfying. We are easily angered, quick to judge, and easily emotional. We may sense dimly that there are things going on that we do not want to think about. Why look too closely, when there is no way out?

These attitudes and experiences are self-fulfilling. When we are alienated from ourselves and from our own best impulses, we begin to feel that we cannot really accomplish anything of value. We rehearse in our minds all the reasons why we cannot succeed, or why the results we get will not have any real benefit. Even when we are convinced that we are working toward a positive goal, we find ourselves spending many minutes or hours in aimless activity, unwilling to face up to our own negative judgments or our fear that we will prove incapable or incompetent. At such times, all possibilities for what is positive—inspiring thoughts, virtuous conduct, beauty—disappear from our lives, as though they were lost forever, leaving us with nothing in our experience to enjoy or appreciate. Nothing seems interesting enough to engage us. Not knowing goodness, happiness, and positive qualities, we waste our lives.

It all sounds deeply discouraging.

It's certainly sad, and if that were the whole truth of our lives—the fabric we weave from day to day—you would be right to be discouraged. But before you get too caught up in your emotional reaction, you should take time to acknowledge what we're really talking about. Living in this way is not something that happens to someone else. It's not the theme of a novel you read once, or a film that people are talking about. It's happening now, and will happen time and time again. If it doesn't seem to be an accurate description of your own life, it applies to someone you care about. If it doesn't seem true today, it may well be true tomorrow.

We can know this for certain, because it happens to everyone. From what we know of history and our observation of the world around us, it has always been this way—for all human beings, and perhaps even for animals. And unless we can introduce some possibility for change, things will just go on in this same discouraging way.

Why do things unfold in this negative way? After all, it's not as though people want to be unhappy.

When we are trapped in negative patterns, we have no control over our thoughts. They just keep going, round and round, whether we want them to or not. The senses are dull and flat, so we have no way to enjoy expericnce; at the same time, anger, desire, and aggression are never far away. It is too difficult to think of making any real change: we tell ourselves that it would take too much effort and produce no result. The same toxic pollution keeps being generated, and we move from one moment to the next almost mechanically: from yesterday to today to tomorrow, from past to present to future. Each situation generates the next: each new moment repeats the one before. Your patterns will be different from everyone else's, but history and our own observations teach us that similar conditions have always operated.

In fact, the patterns may in some sense be larger than our own individual psychologies. For instance, there may be cycles in time that exert their influence. Western astrology takes that view—it holds that the exact time someone is born into the world influences the way their lives unfold. Even if you don't accept that idea, you would probably agree that circumstances we encounter in early childhood can have an impact on us, and then there is the influence of culture. But all these are variations on the same theme. We can see in ourselves and others that an underlying negativity is universal.

That's why you said it's as though we had been born in a giant garbage dump.

Right. If that image seems too negative, you could imagine that we are seabirds living in a bay polluted by a toxic oil spill. Everything is tainted, and there is no way out. We cannot live as we are intended to live; cannot accomplish what has value. Though we may survive, we cannot prosper.

So what's the right response? What can we do? Can we clean up the pollution? Can we transform our situation into something positive, wholesome, and truly good? I accept your point that we have to be honest about what's going on. But let's say we are willing to open our eyes and take a long hard look. Now what? What approach can we take? What is truly trustworthy?

Let's look at one of the traditional answers to that question. The great Mahayana master Shantideva wrote that all unhappiness and negativity in the world come from clinging to the self. Countless other teachers in every Buddhist tradition have said very similar things. Cultivating the Four Immeasurables—love, joy, compassion and equanimity—offers a way to undermine the commitment to the concerns of the self, which fuel the neurotic patterns of the mind. They turn our mind instead to the welfare and happiness of others. Because they are not bound by the patterns of samsara, they can serve as the antidote to suffering, negativity, and emotionality.

The four immeasurables are the healers we need, and we need to invite them into our lives. Teachers through the centuries have emphasized to their students the importance of practicing them. In our own publications, you can find a detailed discussion by the All-Knowing Longchenpa in *Now that I Come to Die* (2007). The translation there, following the earlier work of the scholar Herbert Guenther, refers to them as the Four Immeasurably Great Catalysts of Being. Longchenpa suggests starting with equanimity, but he also says that they can be practiced in any order. His discussion of how each of the immeasurables interacts with the others is highly illuminating.

With sustained practice, the four immeasurables can become our home. When that happens, everything changes. Inspired by the four immeasurables, we can do something meaningful with our lives. Our actions and qualities can pervade the atmosphere in which we and others live with a subtle, healing fragrance. We can do this for ourselves, our friends, and families, and our community. We can do it for the past, the present, and the future. We can do it for the sake of preserving all that is positive. Our journey through this world can bear rich fruit, and we can become a model for our friends and for future generations.

I can certainly see the value of approaching others with compassion, wishing them well and taking joy in their attainments. And I can see that approaching each situation in a kind of balanced, unbiased way, is likely to yield good results. But can you say more about why this practice is considered so powerful? Why are they "immeasurable" in their impact? To use the term you mentioned, how can they serve as catalysts of being?

It would take quite some time to really lay out the basis for this way of understanding. But we can also look at it in fairly simple terms. If we truly appreciate what goes on in the lives of others and learn to notice the patterns that loop endlessly through their minds and ours as well, we may find that we are naturally more kind, and that we feel joy when they are able to turn their lives in more positive directions. When we see how they set themselves up for unhappiness and understand the basic structures at work, we may naturally react with sympathy and empathy. The reverse also holds. When we cultivate the immeasurables, it becomes much easier to see with clarity.

For instance, our parents gave us so much when we were small and depended on them completely. It is natural to feel deep appreciation and gratitude for what they did. Now, thinking of the suffering they have experienced in their lives, both known and unknown, we may find it natural to ask how we can help. There is a tendency to turn away when we encounter the suffering of others, but if we let ourselves experience it fully instead—if we simply pay attention—it is natural to care.

Exercise 12: Forming Intention

Sit in a relaxed way and let the mind settle down. Don't make any effort to think or notice or perceive anything special or to focus on a particular object. In this relaxed state, ask yourself: what is your intention right now? What are you aiming at; what do you have in mind?

Notice that the answer to these questions might relate to one or more of several different time frames: your intention in sitting here, following the directions in the exercise; your intention in working with these materials; your intention for the coming stages of your life, and so on. This may be true at a very simple level; for instance, you may intend to wash the dishes because you intend to watch a movie later. Feel free to move back and forth among these different levels. What matters is that you really let yourself feel as fully as possible whatever intentions you are aware of right now.

Once you have spent some time in working with your sense of intention, perhaps over several sessions, experiment with deliberately putting a different intention into effect. It might be an extension of a previous intention, but it could also involve some other intention, linked to a different part of your life or to a wish or concern that you have left undeveloped or have not previously paid much attention to.

Finally, choose to develop an intention based on the four immeasurables. For instance, you could cultivate the intention to work for the benefit and happiness of others. You might also focus more specifically: you might decide to get a specific training because you wish to help others. In that case, you would be operating with two related intentions.

In doing this practice, a number of questions may arise. What is the difference between intention and desire? Intention and the kleshas? Can you hold multiple intentions in your mind simultaneously—either intentions at different levels, as described above, or intentions that conflict with one another? For instance, you may have the intention to do a good job on the project you are involved with right now, but also the intention to finish the project as quickly as possible. Can you merge two intentions into one? Some intentions just seem to be built in to a situation: for instance, you form the intention to walk to the store, and leave your house to do so. A block later, is the intention still there, guiding your steps? When you are walking through city traffic, do you have the intention not to be hit by a car?

How can we develop such caring?

The starting point is to educate ourselves internally, to become aware of our own situation and the patterns that play themselves out in our lives. That way we can form the intention to take care of ourselves. Eventually it becomes natural to extend that intention outward toward the wish to benefit others.

As soon as begin to know ourselves more accurately, we have taken the first step toward allowing positivity back into our lives. Eventually, we can learn to let gladness and appreciation fill our own hearts. On that basis, we can resolve to benefit others.

All beings are trapped. All beings are caught in not knowing. Seeing this, we can form the wish to work on their behalf, in the past, the present, and the future. It is especially valuable to focus on your parents, whether they are living or not. By practicing in that way, you can gradually gain confidence that this world, just as it is, with all its unhappiness, can be transformed into a Buddha realm. We can dedicate ourselves to that aim, and we can rejoice.

Part Two

Making our Way on the Path

9

Progress

Think what it is like to born as a baby into this world. We cannot refer back to our own experience to know what it must be like. But we could perhaps compare it to travelers who arrive in a completely foreign land, with no sense of what to expect. They are ignorant of the language, ignorant of the customs. They find themselves in a new world, and they know nothing of its history or its resources. They can only guess at the concerns, the wishes, and the fears that motivate the people they see around them.

Of course, it's actually much more dramatic than that. As newborn babies, our senses may be functioning, but we do not know how to use them, and we have no access to language. Only gradually do we learn how to connect with the world to which our eyes and ears and body introduce us. It takes many years for us to learn how to reason and develop a sense of self, how to use language effectively to communicate with others, how to express our feelings in acceptable ways. We may know from the outset what we like and dislike, since that seems almost instinctual or biological in its foundations. But that basic reactivity will only take us so far. It takes a long time to discriminate good from bad at the level of ethics or aesthetic judgment and to develop more refined tastes.

We could not learn any of this without our parents, our friends, our teachers, and other guides. Patiently they correct our mistakes, introduce us to new sensations, new places, and new kinds of experience. They teach us what we need to know to survive and to carve out our sense of who we are and what has value. It is a long and challenging process. There are times when we are filled with wonder and joy, but those feelings often trade places with feelings of confusion, uncertainty, pain, and disappointment.

By the age of twelve or so, the basics of this process are in place. We have learned how to navigate through the events of our lives, and we accept as inevitable the pain, frustration, and emotionality that go with the journey. As part of this process, we have learned a fundamental skill that is not always acknowledged: we know how to follow by heart an internal map that guides us as each new encounter comes into view. The map tells us what reactions are acceptable, what judgments will harmonize smoothly with what we already believe, and how to respond in ways that others will go along with. It doesn't always work smoothly, but for the most part we have learned how to read the map and follow the roads and pathways it identifies.

This fundamental situation forms the basis of our development as we go through life. Of course, we may change

75

our outlook and our opinions in fundamental ways. We may have experiences or meet people who upend some of the assumptions we start off with. As we grow older, we will continue to learn, and our understanding will shift, perhaps radically. Still, by the time we enter adolescence, we have a rough understanding of the way things are. We know enough to continue the journey on our own, without the need for almost continuous guidance from others.

Unless traumatic experiences have made us deeply distrustful, we enter these years of growing independence with a strong sense of curiosity and an eagerness to learn more. Now that we have developed our capacities, the world becomes a bigger place, with much that is unknown. We explore and experiment with new possibilities and sample new experiences. We learn new vocabulary, discover new kinds of social relationships, and awaken to new sensations as our bodies mature. If we are fortunate enough to be exposed to a variety of influences, we may realize that the reality we take for granted has not always been here, that change is a constant. We learn new ideas and explore new ways of thinking or feeling. Perhaps we investigate more deeply philosophies or belief systems that seem attractive or match up with our own expanding sense of what is true and good.

Although we gradually form our own opinions and understanding, we cannot simply go off on our own. The world is too complicated for that, and our own emerging personality too fragile. We continue to look to others for guidance, unsure that we are doing things the right way or thinking the right thoughts. We crave acceptance from those whose approval has become important to us. Perhaps we give our allegiance to a new set of friends, guides, and teachers, or perhaps we continue to follow the lead of those who helped make us who we are. Either way, we learn to make our way through a web of social interactions that now become increasingly significant in our lives.

In these transitional years, we still need to rely on others for all sorts of support, some practical, some emotional or spiritual. There is still much we do not understand about the complicated world unfolding around us and within us, and in some ways the challenges we face are more difficult than those we confronted when we were young. We are reaching the point at which important, life-changing decisions will have to be made. Still, we are heading toward independence.

In the Western world, the age of eighteen typically marks a kind of formal transition, when we are said to be ready to go forward on our own. Even then, however, our education—formal and informal—continues. If we do not deliberately choose to shut down the possibility for fundamental change, we will continue to face new challenges—and new opportunities—for the rest of our lives.

A similar process unfolds for anyone who begins to explore a spiritual path. As beginners, we have only vague ideas about how to proceed. We look for guidance to teachers and friends who have more experience; perhaps we try to gain instruction from books or videos. With their instruction and example, we begin to form ideas about how to act. We learn the meaning of key terms and develop a better understanding of how to conduct ourselves. Our sense of what is right and wrong, valuable and harmful, may shift. If our connection to one particular tradition or approach deepens, we may gradually take on a new set of values, turning away from things we previously cared about and shaping our lives in ways that might have surprised the person we were at an earlier point in time.

As we continue on the spiritual path, gradually making the journey our own, new concerns may arise. The path points toward a final goal and promises specific attainments along the way, but it may be difficult to say whether we are making real progress. If we do not have the kinds of experiences or insights we were hoping for, we may grow anxious. Are we doing things the right way? Are we following the right teacher? We may have imagined arriving at some wonderful state as the result of our journey, but like the end of the rainbow, the goal may remain out of reach. We know we are seeking something, but we may not be able to say exactly what it is. We are on a path, and we may feel that we are experiencing real benefits, but the question remains: will we ever graduate?

Questions about how to proceed may come up again and again. Shall we take a path that emphasizes prayer? Shall we cultivate devotion or a relationship to a teacher? Shall we study philosophical texts or turn instead to meditation? Shall we go on retreat or devote ourselves to actions that benefit others?

In the background, another set of concerns may rumble along: here we are, following the path we have somehow been led to, whether through choice or through various circumstances over which we have limited control. Yet people in other parts of the world or from different backgrounds follow completely different paths. What does this tell us about the value of the path we have chosen? Is every path equally acceptable? That seems difficult to believe. Still, how can we be certain that we are on the path that is best for us? Shall we just trust in the seemingly accidental circumstances that have led us to be in this setting, following these teachings? Shall we call it our karma?

We may also find ourselves questioning what our commitment to a spiritual path has actually accomplished—what have our efforts achieved? We may know the right words and concepts, and we may be confident in our judgments about what has value, what is right and what is wrong. When it comes to what is actually happening in our lives, however, where has our path led us? Do we know how to shape our experience in satisfying and fulfilling ways? Is our attitude always positive and joyful? Are our actions consistently meaningful? Are we bringing benefit to ourselves and to others?

Despite our best efforts, the path we are on may not unfold smoothly. The road we take may prove bumpy, with many obstacles along the way. There may be times when we feel stuck or our practice grows stale. We may find ourselves looking longingly at other options, whether these are spiritual or worldly. What does this tell us? Should we be concerned? Should warning signals be going off in our minds?

Traditional teachings say that the obstacles that arise as we follow a spiritual discipline or way of life can themselves be part of the path. When we find ourselves in the middle of some difficulty, however, it takes a certain degree of trust to be confident that our problems are part of the path instead of a sign that something has gone wrong.

Times of disillusionment or disappointment are challenging enough in themselves. The real problem, however, seems to be that such negative states of mind imprint themselves on our consciousness. Even after they have passed, they leave residues that are not easily washed away. A mind shaped by negative attitudes—even those that go underground or seem to have disappeared entirely—may not easily turn back toward higher wisdom and deep appreciation. The patterns that accumulate in the mind or soul linger on. They may color our experience more than we realize.

10

Tracing the Patterns of Mind

Once we recognize the patterns of mind, we can also see what needs to be done. We need to ask where such patterns—parts of ourselves or our way of dealing with the world that we do not like, do not understand, and may not even acknowledge—come from. We need to sort them out with care. Only then will we know how to work with them in an effective way.

You make it sound like that would be an almost impossible task. You just said that negative patterns can be deeply ingrained. They may even be difficult to see, because they are part of our makeup. In fact, it seems that the more fundamental they are, the more invisible they become.

That's true. The kleshas—which is how Buddhism names these patterns—are deeply rooted. We have to be ready to do a kind of self-therapy. It's self-therapy, because even though others may help us see more clearly, we are the ones who have to recognize and accept what's going on. So yes, it's difficult to know where to begin. Still, it's not as though we've identified a separate problem: a difficulty that we have to resolve at the outset, before we even get started with exploring our minds. It's the same problem. It's hard to explore the mind because we don't know the mind.

Most people don't think much about how their own minds work. They may not know how to get started, or they may not realize it's possible to ask this kind of question. Still, some individuals seem to be naturally curious about the way the mind works, and that can be a good starting point. Others may just get tired of feeling that their lives are out of control. For others, it may be some sort of profound shock or loss or sudden realization that leads them to ask this kind of question.

The motivation is not that important. What matters is that everything you need to look into the patterns of mind is already available. It's not like a scientific experiment where before you begin you need years of training, a fully supplied laboratory, and special equipment. As soon as you look, mind is right here. At one level, we are all already experts in the operations of our own mind. We just need to know how to look, how to ask unexpected questions.

Whatever is going on right now, the mind is active. You can engage that activity. You can trace out the patterns that are unfolding right in the moment. You may even be able to trace the patterns that the mind has enacted in the past and look to see whether you can discover general themes.

So that's one way to begin, and you may find it very fruitful. Still, that's only one level, and you may want to probe more deeply. If you ask about the roots of your own mental patterns, that's a completely different story, and it can take you in a very different direction.

What direction? Where would you start to look?

It's one thing to track our own thoughts and concepts and see how we respond to different circumstances. But that is just at the level of appearance. Whatever patterns we identify, we don't know in any very useful way where those responses come from or how they arose. We don't understand the fundamental structures in play.

The most basic patterns shaping the operations of mind were laid down a long time ago. They may even be built into our human way of functioning. You could say that they're imprinted on the fabric of the mind. Those are the ones we want to understand, because whatever we do, however we act, however we react to events reflects those pre-established patterns.

Day and night, twenty-four hours a day, we base our actions, our thoughts, and our emotions on the pre-existing structures of the mind. Mind sets up an image of the way things are, and we live within that image. Mind directs our responses; it shapes our thoughts and feelings and conditions our decisions. All of that happens whether we choose it or not. The way the mind operates may not match up very well with our ideas about how we want to act or should act. But that's exactly why it's important to conduct the inquiry. We often act in ways we might reject if we had a chance to reflect on them more deeply. We may even act in ways that we know at the time go against our own values and beliefs. Don't you think it's important to make the effort to understand what's going on there?

I'd like to ask a more practical question. If I do want to develop a deeper understanding of the patterns of mind, does it help to practice Kum Nye or some other body-focused discipline? People might say that the mind is not the body, or that there's a difference between cultivating certain kinds of physical feelings and promoting deeper understanding. But it seems that the kind of deep inquiry you're describing becomes much easier if I have learned to relax tensions in the body or have stimulated energies that promote clarity and settle the mind.

Yes, that kind of practice can be helpful. The patterns of the mind are imprinted in our bodies, our way of being embodied, so we can learn a lot by loosening physical blockages and just more generally finding ways to be at home in the body. But don't expect that this will be easy either. The patterns of mind are laid down at a very deep level, and it may require a lot of discipline to unearth them. And even if we learn to recognize patterns that we didn't know about before, that doesn't mean that we can change them.

What kinds of patterns are you talking about?

The list is probably endless. The Buddhist tradition says that the Buddha taught 84,000 different teachings because beings are caught up in 84,000 different errors or wrong ways of being. You could think of the mind that way. But there are some basic themes it's good to recognize. One is the pattern of resistance. We just don't want to know, or don't want to make some particular change. Then there is the pattern of misunderstanding. We may be clear about what's going on at one level, but at another level, we may not understand at all. Not understanding is not a problem in itself; it may even be fruitful. If we look more closely, however, we may recognize that our not understanding is based on mis-understanding.

Some misunderstanding seems to be deliberate. It's a kind of defense mechanism against seeing or understanding something we would rather not acknowledge.

We also have a basic problem with communication. It's not just how you communicate with other people; it also involves communicating with yourself. You may know at some level that you're responding to what's going on in ways that will have significant negative consequences. You may even see clearly where you're headed, where the choices you're making in this moment are leading you. But because of resistance, misunderstanding, and poor communication, the knowledge doesn't get through. The pattern goes unchallenged.

One sign of such a failure to communicate is when you assign blame for some emerging difficulty or recently discovered mistake, or for something that has clearly gone wrong. Of course, it's easy to blame someone else. But you may also blame yourself, or blame some established pattern that feels out of your control. You say, "I shouldn't have done that . . . I always do that . . . I let myself down . . . I fell into the same old pattern." It may seem that you are being honest, clearsighted, and direct, but in fact your willingness to accept the blame may just be a way of covering up what is really going on. If you agree that whatever happened is your fault, you can put an end to any deeper questioning. Of course, it's difficult to pin this particular pattern down, because we mostly believe in the messages the mind communicates.

Exercise 13: What's Happening

What is actually going on in the stream of mental activity that cycles through the mind from moment to moment? Ask yourself this question over a series of sessions, keeping track of what you notice so that you can look for recurring patterns or for differences that arise at different times. There is no need to manipulate what you find; just describe to yourself what you discover. When something interesting or unexpected comes up, you may want to make a note of it in a journal, which you could consider a kind of lab manual.

What is likely to come up when you do this kind of inquiry? At the first level, you will probably discover events familiar to everyone from daily experience: thoughts, memories, feelings, emotions, desires, moods, judgments, fantasies, and so on. At a second level, there are the interactions among these different events. For instance, one event may support the arising of another, or lead to it automatically, or block it from appearing, or make it more likely to appear. Events may arise in clusters. For instance, in the course of what seems like a single moment you may have a negative thought, then get upset with yourself for having that thought, then tell yourself not to get upset, then feel like a failure when you're still upset, and so on.

Again, an event that seems positive one time may seem negative the next (assuming we can call it 'the same' event.) You may also want to explore how the kinds of events that arise in the stream of experience are influenced by other aspects of what is going on: the time of day, the general tone of mental activity, and so forth.

If you have a meditation practice that emphasizes developing inner calm, explore how this kind of inquiry relates to your meditation. Does greater calm shift the nature of mental activity? Does an inquiry into what's happening in the mind promote or hinder the arising of calm?

Another pattern—one of the most basic of all—is that the mind understands everything in terms of 'I' and 'me' and 'mine'. We are always seeing the world in terms of 'my mind', 'my behavior', 'my soul', 'my path', 'my ideas', 'my me'. Mind sets up the I-me-mine framework, establishes a realm of reality within that framework, and then clings to what it has established, holding on tightly to the more specific patterns that grow out of this fundamental structure.

Can you give an example?

This pattern is so basic that almost every experience counts as an example. For instance, we establish 'I' as the coordinator of experience, the one who fires up the experience-engine and starts it running. It may seem natural, even indisputable, that this is how things are, but putting 'I' at the center may actually reflect a very limited understanding.

Exercise 14: Not Mine

Think of the claim 'that is mine' as the way we grasp an experience. This holds for almost any experience: a thought, a feeling, a perception, a desire, a memory, a judgment, or anything else. Whenever you recognize something as 'mine', you are giving it a certain status that you don't usually question. However, that status can be challenged. When an experience comes along that you ordinarily view as 'mine', challenge that assumption. Say to yourself, "That's not mine!" For instance, a thought may come into your mind, and you simply know that it's 'my' thought. Try telling yourself the opposite. Yes, the thought is there, but allow it to be there without making it yours. What happens? Thoughts may be about events. Does releasing the 'mine' also release the event's hold on you?

As you grow more familiar with this exercise, ask yourself about the difference between releasing a negative feeling (for example, anxiety) and releasing a positive feeling (for example joy, or gratitude). Are you more reluctant to release one kind of 'mine' than another? What happens to the status or operation of the feeling when it is no longer 'mine'? Try this with other kinds of mental events as well.

It does seem that 'I', 'me', and 'mine' are about as fundamental to experience as anything I can imagine. But isn't that exactly the role of a spiritual path—to call that commitment to the 'I' and its supporters into question?

From the point of view of understanding 'I' and 'me' and 'mine' and 'mind', the spiritual way offers a deeply interesting journey. It allows a different set of questions to arise. For instance, 'I' and 'mine' play a role on the path, but can we say for certain that they are real? In ordinary experience, this might be a strange question to ask, because we can hardly conceive of a world where 'I' and 'me' and 'mine' are not central. On the spiritual path, however, the commitment to these structures loosens, and asking questions about their status starts to seem natural. And then there's another, related question: what is the relationship between 'I' and 'mind'?

Would you say that we have to give up our commitment to 'I' and 'mine' if we want to make progress on the path?

In ordinary experience, we are completely familiar with the roles that 'I' and 'mine' and 'mind' play, which is one reason we never question them. But as we inquire more deeply, we enter unfamiliar territory. We don't know if the identity we usually function with still occupies the same position.

Sometimes our experiences on the path can be very vivid, very alive. They almost seem tangible: we can touch them directly. Are such experiences 'mine'? Do they happen to 'me'? Do they fall within the ordinary operations of mind, or do they somehow go beyond them? These questions seem reasonable, but it is not clear how to investigate them. If we try to question our 'special' experiences analytically, we run into problems. The closer we get, the more carefully we contemplate them, the more they shy away, like a wild animal.

The result is that we end up with only a series of questions. How do such experiences relate to our usual mental structures? In the middle of such experiences, does the 'I' fall away? What about the 'me'? Which one—'I' or 'me'—is responsible for the experience? Which one continues to operate? Who is manifesting this way of behaving? Who is sponsoring the experience, or directing it? In a sense, it seems that 'I' and 'me' and 'my' and 'mind' are coordinating with each other. Can we describe their cooperation, or does it go beyond our ability to express? Who is offering the I-me-mind description? Who is asking such questions?

'I', 'me', 'mine', and 'mind' seem to depend on each other, like actors who come together put on a play. But that does not tell us how they cooperate when it comes to following the spiritual path. Do they support such efforts? For instance, am I the one who makes progress on the path? If not, who does?

11

Four Gateways

The knowledge that guides us in our lives is constructed by concepts and built out of words. Meaning is
married to the labels we assign. Nouns give us identity,
verbs specify the range of possible actions, and prepositions—'from' and 'to', 'beyond' and 'within', 'before' and
'after'—mark out limiting structures. What can we make
of all this? In one sense, we are just describing the surface
of our lives. Yet that is where we mostly look. We have
been taught to focus on the external world, so that we
ignore the workings of our own minds. Eager to know
what will come next, we journey on and on through the
world, shaping the space of our experience and carving
our own personal stories out of the dynamic of time.

If we can begin to look more deeply, we soon discover the
operation of the four gateways through which all our experience passes: 'I' and 'me' and 'mine' and 'mind'. 'I' is the one
who knows and acts, the one who names, turning naming
into a script for being. "Me' attaches to 'I' in order to establish a role and place. By grounding the relation between 'I'
and whatever appears in the world, it lets 'I' represent itself;
by basing itself on longing and belonging, it serves as the

witness for 'I', confirming its identity. 'Mine' sustains the relation of 'me' to 'I', satisfying the claims of longing and belonging. Through 'mine', the world makes itself available for ownership, offering boundless possibilities for subject-object interactions. As for mind, its function is to know or recognize what 'I', 'me', and 'mine' establish. Mind frames 'I' and its world, and then keeps watch to guarantee that all unfolds in appropriate ways. Its regime embraces and encloses us.

The operations of 'I', 'me', 'mine', and mind affirm a reality beyond questioning. 'I' takes a strong position, and 'me' has territory to defend: I need to protect what is 'mine', what belongs to me. Mind tells us this is so, and what mind asserts becomes our reality, a realm shaped by cause and effect and 'from' and 'to'.

Are you saying that 'I' and 'me' and 'mine' literally create the world that we know?

It's more complicated than that. The creative power of sound gives rise to naming and language. 'I' emerges. Whatever is named holds its character and proclaims its truth. 'I-ness' is the starting point: from that, the whole world of meaning opens, from 'tree' to 'freedom', from 'history' to 'space', from 'cause and effect' to 'from' and 'to'.

'I' alone is baseless and homeless, but 'me' makes it possible to represent 'I'. For its own needs, 'me' accepts 'I' as owner, and now 'I' has found its witness; now it can 'come into' being. At the same time, in order to function, 'me' must be part of the world of objects and things. 'Me' and 'mine' work together to establish a relationship with whatever

91

appears in the world. That relationship is based on belonging and attachment. More fundamentally, it expresses longing: an insatiable wish to gain substance—a kind of protection—through connecting with 'this' and 'that'. Whatever appears is 'to me' or 'for me', even though we take this so much for granted that we seldom name this relationship in words. In effect, 'me' establishes itself as the opposite of 'thingness'. It serves as an absence that is also a proclaiming.

'Mine' sustains the relation of 'me' to 'I'. It ensures that 'me' will have a role to play. At the same time, 'mine' confirms and satisfies the belonging and longing claims of 'me' with respect to the world of objects. 'Mine' is like the constitution that gives order to the realm of appearance. Based on that constitutional order, a world is constituted, just as a legal constitution makes it possible to enact and execute countless laws. Through 'mine', a world of boundless possibilities can emerge.

In the end, the constitution of the world is made possible by 'mind'. The function of mind is to know, to recognize, to understand. Suppose that mind emerged from deep sleep: in the first instant, there would be a not-knowing, a kind of fuzzy blankness. But once 'I' is established, recognition comes, and with it all the responsibilities of maintaining the mind regime.

Then is the mind the one that is really in charge?

That's one possible description. But you could also say that mind functions automatically, doing what needs to be done. We could say that mind produces thoughts, but at another level, mind is not separate from thoughts and not separate from feelings. These are simply the expressions of mind, with no possibility to separate out or quantify or locate what manifests 'in' mind. For instance, where does happiness arise in mind? Where do thoughts emerge, and where do they go? We cannot ask such questions; we have no way to think the question through.

These are complex issues. I have my own way of speaking about them, but there is a long history in Buddhism of investigating the relation between 'I' and 'is', between mind and reality. What is the nature of 'I-ness' and 'me-ness', of 'mine-ness' and 'self-ness'? There are no simple answers. Just think, if you wanted to understand the human body but did not know anything about biology or chemistry, you couldn't make much progress. If you wanted to analyze someone's identity but didn't know anything about how they had acted in the past, what could you say?

At least we know where to focus the inquiry, because in the end, it does come down to mind. So we can ask: who created mind? Who appointed it to its central role? How did it become the decision-maker? I am not sure that the Western tradition has analyzed these questions very carefully.

For myself, I have been trying to understand the relation of body and language and mind for many years. Just in the last few years I have published Revelations of Mind and OK Mantra, which introduce some of these themes. Soon there will be a new title that I hope can offer some guidance for people who would like to take this exploration further. So I am doing what I can.

I am not asking these questions out of some kind of intellectual curiosity, or because I have my own theories and I want to brainwash people into believing them. I am asking because we have all been living in toxic ways for far too long. You might blame Western culture, or you might say it's because we have let our conceptual approach to knowledge lead us astray, or you might just say these are the patterns of samsara. Whatever your understanding, the point is to find ways to undermine the forces that are in control, so that we can be free of the basic causes of unhappiness and suffering.

For most people, it seems completely natural or even inevitable that we operate on the basis of 'I' and 'me' and 'mine' and 'mind', but I think it is important to ask whether we could develop an understanding that did not rely on those structures. My own sense is that if that happened, we would be on the road to complete freedom. We would not need to adopt any belief systems; we would not even need to maintain a particular moral code. We would not need to pay the crushing 'samsara tax'.

Do you think that your efforts in this direction are bearing fruit?

So far, I would say that readers and students of what I have written have not been able to take these ideas as far as I would hope. They seem to approach them too much on the intellectual level. You need more depth; you need to be honest with yourself. The point is not to have conceptual insights, but to have insight into your own nature.

How can we go deeper?

If you want to question the basic fourfold 'gateway structure', observation seems the right place to start. Look at it this way: structures unfold, objects appear, and I engage

94

what arises. How does this happen? Asking that question is not so difficult. You are not being told you have to train in new skills, or that you somehow have to start over. You do not need to put yourself in the wrong. You do not even have to puzzle out the solution to a difficult problem, because in a way it is very simple. You only need to be curious and willing to learn. Can we let that motivation guide us?

Observation leads to understanding, and understanding gives us a choice. It offers a knowing that does not depend on language or thoughts and the structures they uphold. When we understand, no one is telling a story to anyone. We simply know how we know. Because we are not bound to the four gateways, we can discover space, experience time, and recognize a different knowledge. Such understanding can be shared with others in ways that invite transformation. If we act according to these approaches, we can make a different world.

I understand why observation is important. But how do we observe? Usually when we observe, we are just applying labels to what we see. That doesn't get us very far. We see the same problems, the same opportunities, the same limits that we have always seen. For instance, we may say: "I feel unhappy . . . I feel lonely . . . I'm afraid of growing old." Even if try to let go of emotional responses, we still say, "I see a tree," or "I am watching the breath." So I'm still caught in the structures of subject and object, or self and world. You clearly have in mind going deeper than that.

Yes, that's so. But it's good to start from our present circumstances. If a specific problem is occupying us right now, we would like to know how it is produced. Is it the 'I' with its claim of ownership that produces the problem? Is it the relationship between 'me' and the object or situation? Can I trace the polarities?

Asking these kinds of questions leads to the central role of duality. As long as it is structured through 'I', 'me', and 'mine', the mind's way of knowing cannot be anything other than dualistic. The egg has been laid, and now it must hatch. 'Wrong' emerges together with 'right'; 'this' emerges along with 'that'. The subject points toward the object—no other way of thinking is available. 'I' think; 'I' know; 'I' see; 'I' have been such and such a way. A world comes into being, with its past tense, its present tense, and its future tense; with its shaping prepositions that mark out the connections of belonging and longing; with its automatic 'mine'. The structures of possession and territory present themselves to be accepted. It's the conceptual frame of mind. When we talk about being caught in samsara, it's these kinds of entanglements we're pointing to.

But you're saying we wouldn't need to stay tangled in these structures if we could understand the operation of 'I' and 'me' and 'my' and mind.

That's right. Once we understand how the four gateways work, how they lead us into samsara, we can gradually exercise their power in a new way. We can look without pronouncing. We can see how they make us what we are.

Buddhism refers to the world we experience as the play of maya, the magic of illusion. Knowing the operation of maya, the magic show of mind, is deeply useful. Right now we are caught in a dream, a nightmare that shapes our destiny. It will keep doing that until we wake up. Dismissing the nightmare—pointing out that it is an illusion, is valuable, but it's not enough. It's when we embody this understanding that the obstacles we face in samsara themselves become illusion.

If you're saying that mind creates our reality—or is it the 'I' that's doing the creating?—then is the point to use that creativity for something more positive?

Creativity and inquiry are closely related. It's true that there is a samsaric creativity at work in ordinary appearance. Sounds lead to names and names lead to meanings. We recognize and capture what is meant, and we are captured in turn. Time manifests appearance, and we awaken into the dualistic subject-object order, which manifests through the four gateways.

In the world as we know it, these structures have taken on characteristic qualities. The mind is forever busy, and we constantly cope with distraction. We cannot calm down, cannot understand ourselves. Fundamental toxicities poison our ways of acting. We are like prisoners who cannot leave their cells: our lives are ordered by a regime from which escape is impossible. The same patterns play out, and once again we enter samsara through the four gateways. There is no possibility for new consciousness, new awareness, or new knowledge. Even if we pursue the possibility of freedom, whatever we do or think or see takes form within the same system.

All that is true, but it is not the only truth. If we can exercise a kind of inquiry that is playful and friendly, more about questions and dialog than answers and pronouncements, we can show ourselves and others the possibility of engaging directly with everything that arises. It's that possibility of engaging directly that matters. If that's there, nothing else needs to change. Without any special effort, we can live our lives with increasing confidence and inner joy.

What is the relation between this kind of observation and the way most people nowadays seem to practice meditation?

There are many ways to meditate, but if your goal in meditation is to develop inner calm or release stress, it won't help with this kind of observation. Experiencing short periods of peace will not heal the patterns that dominate the rest of our lives: the mind patterns, the 'I' patterns, or the 'me' patterns.

But what's wrong with just dropping all the patterns and resting in peace?

The gateway patterns generate all sorts of thoughts, distractions, and inner conflicts. They guarantee that we will stay committed to our ego duties and our self-image. We all have experience with living that way, so we may well want to do something about, and that can be a motivation for taking up meditation. And in fact, meditation can be helpful. It can put those patterns on hold, which can be a great relief. But sooner or later, they will start to operate again.

Practicing meditation to develop inner calm may have significant beneficial effects for the way our experience unfolds, but we're not talking on that level. If we could find a way instead to free ourselves from the underlying patterns that shape samsara, our whole lives would be different. You could put it this way: our ways of behaving and of exercising our senses imposes certain obligations, but if we understand the underlying patterns, we can drop those obligations. We can access space and time differently. We can enjoy a new kind of knowledge.

You have written extensively about a new vision of time, space, and knowledge. Can you say more about what the practical impact of adopting such a vision would be?

We live in time and inhabit space. It's a fundamental truth about reality. If we gain access to a different kind of time and space, we may find ourselves living in a different world. Even though on the surface the world of appearances continues as it is, we can deal more flexibly with the challenges life presents. We can discover real freedom.

Does living within a new version of time and space depend on letting go of our commitment to 'I' and 'me' and 'mine'?

We don't need to do anything special or let go of anything or adopt any particular view. We can just start by asking some basic questions. Who made the structure that shapes our lives? How did it come into being? If we fully understand the answers to these questions, we arrive at a knowledge that is true and real. We reunite with the meaning of life and with our own nature. The whole of life become a spiritual practice. By developing this understanding, we can become a model for a new way of living.

This is a practice to embody in every moment, not only in short periods that we set aside and call 'meditation'. The difference is fundamental. For example, we are often instructed in meditation to be aware 'of' something. Or we may say that some kind of experience happened 'to' me, or that we 'had' a certain insight. But this way of practicing and judging the results of our practice reinforces structures based on distance and dichotomy. Once we experience in this way, the world has been cast into a particular form. Now we have no choice:

we must rely on identity and on the relationship between subject and object. Our mind energy, our body energy, and our sense faculties work in specific and limited ways. We lose the possibility for being genuine, natural, and open.

These old patterns are in some ways childish and immature. They contribute to samsara, and they produce karma and all the suffering and unhappiness we know so well. What we need is a way of understanding that cuts through those patterns. We could call it a new way of meditation or a new way of thinking, but it is one that can operate in every moment of our lives.

If we look closely at experience, we see that it is changing from moment to moment. Usually we assume that we live in a world where things have solid identities, but this cannot really be true, because then change would be impossible. The Buddhist tradition explores this point extensively. In terms of inquiry, the Abhidharma teachings offer ways to investigate a different view. For instance, it identifies 51 mental events, each with its own unique character or way of manifesting. These events operate in our lives in different ways. We may have very strong experiences: happiness, intense sensations, being awakened, or powerful energies. We may discover stages where experience loosens up or manifests in a more casual way. There are all different kinds of experience, and each of them seems to have its own unique reality at that point in time. But at the same time, they are momentary events. They do not have their own enduring identity.

It is just at that point that we trick ourselves. Based on recognition, we embody our experiences with great intensity. Each mental experience seems to have its own gravity, operating within its own field. The four gateways come into play, and those momentary experiences are automatically structured into the samsaric mode of cause and effect.

Once we enter the four gateways into samsara—and we are doing it all the time—they slam shut behind us, and we are prisoners, bonded to samsara. Concepts set up the way things are and tell us what we have to do. The language of 'I' and 'me' and 'mine' announce how to behave, and prepositions and projections establish what is happening. We have our duties and responsibilities, and we make commitments accordingly. We manifest fear, worry, caution, doubt, skepticism, and all the rest. The fundamental structure is one of dualism: 'this' or 'that', with no other alternatives.

These rules are so strongly and firmly established, so much in control of everything, that we do not even recognize them as rules. Once I have entered through the gateways, I do not feel that I have to obey or follow; it's just my own, automatic way of being. "Of course this is how things are," I say, "How else could they be?" That is how the structures we know so well are confirmed. Yes, confusion is mine; yes, suffering is mine; yes, conflict is mine. All the emotional manifestations I adopt are mine—could there be any doubt? Pain, suffering, and not knowing are just what mind presents. There is very little choice to act in any other way.

In this skillful, indirect way, the regime of mind takes away our freedom and replaces them with various toxic forms. We have been taken advantage of so completely that we do not even realize what has happened. Knowingness has run away, but we cannot acknowledge what has been lost. All we know is that things do not work well: not now, and not at any time in all of human history. Fear, worry, and conflict between peoples, natural disasters, damage to the environment, famine, disease, and insecurity are the only reality we know. Having money will not help, having a place to call home is not enough. Meditation only provides temporary relief and a little measure of peace. Any chance for real security seems to be lost.

You could say that it is natural to accept the truth of our unique experiences. Yet these experiences, each shaped by the force of its own inner gravity, may not be real in the way we believe. They may be more like a bubble. If we apply the right method—if we contemplate or visualize—we may be able to pop the bubble.

And then?

And then it is just gone.

12

How to Look

The samsaric way is always creating edges or boundaries between specific points or identified entities. This is this and that is that; this causes that and that is the result of this. It all seems very reasonable from our usual perspective. In fact, it may be hard to see that there could be any alternative. But that way of understanding, whatever benefits it brings, is responsible for all the problems we experience. Why? Because it establishes the regime of mind.

So is there an alternative?

In one way it's simple. Right now we understand appearance in terms of interacting things. If instead we understand appearance as an expression of dimensionless inner space, we have a master key for opening each mental state. When we go beyond dimensions, we enter the field of the mandala. One we have the master key of knowledge, we do not need to carry on with a world of separate points. There is no need for methods that will let us get somewhere or produce something, because we transcend time.

103

But don't you need methods?

Whatever methods we may use are temporary. They don't establish anything as true, or as the way things are.

Of course, we need to borrow conceptual structures such as 'time' and 'space'. We need to speak of finding the key, or being the observer. We need to describe what is going on in terms of 'identity' or 'points'. If we did not do this, we would have no way to navigate, for there would be no directions marked on the compass. But speaking in this way is a trick. We have to use it because all we're familiar with is the frame of mind that gives identity and subject and object. We can use all such points and meanings, but we do so in a way that goes beyond all points and meanings.

At the conventional level, we say, "I know; I understand; I identify." So someone might reply: how do you know? We answer, "I contemplate; I meditate. These are the processes I use to reach the non-conditional, to arrive at the fundamental, real nature." But again, we have to distinguish. The real or true nature is not 'nature' as given to us by the regime of mind. It is uncreated nature. It is not the nature of the sun shining, or fire burning, or the mind knowing. It is not part of the causal frame. We might speak of genuine or primordial nature, but of course when we do, we are again relying on making points. We do not want to get stuck in the point, even the point we call 'absolute'.

It seems we can't help getting caught in language. We always say more than we want to—or maybe less.

Language has its limits, and our mind says those limits are absolute, because we have no other vehicle but language, no way to go further. Still, we need that tool. We need language, just as we need sense experience, mental activities, and projection. But in a way these tools are really primitive. They are like stone-age tools used for breaking open nuts, or putting a sharp point on a spear, or building a fire for cooking. We need to develop other tools.

Once we have entered the four gateways, the ideas we accept set limits, the vision that guides us sets limits. What other choice do we have? The four gateways have a function, but for what we have in mind, their way no longer applies. They do not give us the master key.

Then how do we proceed?

In the beginning, we can look at how the mind projects. Later we need look back at the projector. When you have thoughts, what is behind them? What is in front of them? What is in the middle? The same questions apply to the senses. When we can open such structures, we may find ourselves in a very peaceful environment, where we can conduct our way of life, our way of embodiment, very differently.

It's like starting out on a journey, a journey that is all about asking questions we have not asked before. We need to proceed on our own, and we need to be ready to follow our own inquiry wherever it takes us. We start from the perspective that the patterns laid down by the mind exercise control over us, but that is only a preliminary assessment, a kind of fundamental orientation. How do those patterns manifest? Can we spell that out in detail? We play certain roles, but how do we learn those roles? How are the four gateways involved in that process? If we come to understand the gateways more fully, can we make use of them? Can they become our friends?

Exercise 15: Thoughts without Ownership

All day long, as we go about our business, thoughts pop up. Some thoughts seem to suck us in, so that we lose ourselves in the contents of the thought. Other thoughts, however, just seem to pass by, like cars on the freeway. If we observe with some care, we may notice how they are triggered; for instance, some thoughts may show up whenever I pass a particular place or see a specific object.

As you grow more familiar with this whole process, notice the ingrained tendency to accept that the thought belongs to you, as in the previous exercise. It is 'my' thought; it occurs to 'me'; 'I' am the one that has thought it. When does this ownership claim arise? Is it only there when you recall what you were thinking? Is it 'built in' to the thought from the outset?

We also automatically assume that thoughts arise 'in the mind'. What does this mean? Are we referring to a specific location, perhaps associated with the head? Does there have to be a mind for thoughts to arise in? What if we assumed to the contrary? What would change?

These are just a few ways to explore the relationship of thoughts to the four gateways. Over time, you can develop your own questions and your own style of inquiry.

Isn't there a fundamental contradiction here? When we set out to investigate the mind, we have to use the mind to do so. It's like trying to see beyond the self by looking in a mirror: all you see is the self, reflected in the mirror. In a way, it seems you are condemned to stay on the surface, while the more fundamental patterns that might be helpful to investigate stay invisible. I'm reminded of the old example of the finger that cannot touch itself or the knife that cannot cut itself.

It's a good question. But the mind has a way of asking questions that sets limits on what we can find out, even if that's not our intention. For instance, the mind relies on the structures of 'from' and 'to'. One of the first questions we ask when we notice something new is "Where did it come from?" And then we ask, "Where is it going to . . . What's going to happen to it?" We are interested in causes and conditions, in histories and in plans for the future. Your question about the mind investigating itself has similar assumptions built into it.

Suppose you asked instead: how does the 'from/to' structure itself arise? How does the mind organize experience in such a way that questions that call for answers in terms of 'from' and 'to' become the most important questions to ask? Are such questions even legitimate? Now we are going into areas that the mind would rather keep secret, but that is how to get beneath the surface. It's not easy, because the investigator, the analytic thinker who wants to understand how all this works, tends to shy away from that kind of question.

I'll have to work with that, but what you're saying makes sense to me. Somehow we have to extend our inquiry into the fundamental mental structures we use to make sense of the world.

Right! For instance, do we really know how 'yes' and 'no' work? Do we know what it means to say that you've contradicted yourself? Why can't the whole be greater than the sum of its parts—and when is that not true?

I'm sure there are philosophers who think about these things a lot. But at some point don't you inevitably reach the foundation, a point where you just can't go any further? I know that some Western thinkers say it's a mistake to believe that the human mind is able to understand the most fundamental structures of the world, like time and space. Why should we just assume that we have that capacity?

It's interesting: Westerners have great faith in reason and in the evidence given by the senses, but they get uncomfortable if you ask why that faith is justified. It seems as though they are only willing to accept certain kinds of answers. If it would take a different kind of answer—an answer that in a sense isn't tangible—they are likely to say it's a mystery; something we just can't understand. Maybe they are giving up too easily.

How would you answer the same question? What is the basis for believing in sensory evidence and reason? What would "a different kind of answer" look like?

First we need to be clear on why we are asking, so that we don't use our energy and intelligence in fruitless ways. I'm sure you know the story about the Buddha refusing to answer certain questions that we might call metaphysical: does the world have a beginning or an end; is the universe infinite, and so on. He said that this kind of theoretical question was not fruitful. So, keeping that in mind, the first question is the value of asking questions about the limits of inquiry. Not necessarily questions about logic and the law of contradiction—we may need to go deeper than that.

OK, I can go along with that. So let me ask: what is the value of challenging our ordinary ways of knowing?

You can probably anticipate what I'm going to say. We have accepted certain ways of knowing and understanding, and they rule our lives. We depend on them completely—now, in the past, and in the future. So if we are interested in the possibility of self-liberation, we need to look at those foundations. If we start from that basis and let it shape our inquiry, the answers we get may not look like our usual answers at all.

It's a level of question we don't usually ask. For instance, when we use a search engine on the internet, we are really only interested in the results of the search. We don't ask how the search engine operates. We don't think we need to understand the computer code behind it. Why not? Because we think the results are trustworthy—and to some extent we can actually prove that to ourselves. When it comes to the operations of the mind, though, it's a different story. If we look from a different perspective, the results of mind operations may not be trustworthy at all. What would count as evidence one way or another?

I understand your point. Relying on reason and the senses is very effective in some ways, but not so much when it comes to how we live our lives. Still that doesn't say anything about how we could do it differently.

The first step is just to realize that this is a very interesting and important line of questioning. If we are deeply interested, we will look more closely. We will trace the interaction of our mental operations, and we will discover we can open areas for inquiry, areas for experience, that we usually think of as closed. We can open space, open time, open knowledge; we can open thoughts and senses and feelings. We may not know what we are looking for, or understand the meaning of what we find, but that doesn't really matter: we can just keep looking, opening more and more dimensions.

When we open experience enough, our inquiry may lead us to the four gateways, the agents of our experience. We can look at the positions they take, the roles they play. In a way, the four gateways are also gatekeepers. They hold the keys to what we can experience and know. There may be some areas that they keep locked, but if we are committed to openness, we may find that that gives us our own key.

Does that mean opening the structures that the mind puts in place—the rules, the policies, the systems—what you call the regime of mind?

That's right. As long as the usual rules are in place, there is no possibility for engaging in any kind of penetrating dialog. But when you open the structures that set everything up, you eventually start looking at the one who has is responsible for setting it up in the first place. The starting point for that kind of question is to look at the one who is looking, and also to look at the operation of the search engine. Look at the projection of awareness.

That approach can be very useful. Once you look at the agent of action, the conditions that shape where we are right now come into question. You can look back at the history of how we got to this place, and that can trigger a totally different way of operating.

Is this kind of inquiry something you would do in meditation?

A meditative way of engaging what is going on can let us see more clearly, and at that point what we see becomes inherently interesting. But if we keep the focus on questioning the foundations of our ordinary ways of knowing, we may end up going further than what usually happens in meditation.

Why is that?

When we sit down to meditate, we have not really looked into the aspects of the meditation experience that we take for granted. For instance, we are committed to the idea of the self that is meditating, or the object of meditation, or the situation in which the practice of meditation takes place. That is taking too much for granted. It's important to recognize that we don't need to make any of the usual commitments: no 'thingness', no forms, no shape, no 'I', 'me', 'my' and mind.

There is another level of commitment we make as well. Suppose I ask you about your meditation, and you tell me how it's going: what kinds of experiences you have had, what kinds of feelings arose, what new insights you've had, and so on. But that whole response is going to the wrong level. You're reporting on your experience, which automatically creates distance.

Well, yes, I'm reporting, but that's because you asked me for a report!

No, that's not the main point. The same structure applies even if no one asks you for a description. When you meditate, you are steadily sending messages to yourself, giving an update on your opinions, your feelings, your insights, and so on. It's like a politician who tells voters that he has traveled all across the country talking with all sorts of different people, and now he understands what it is that's on people's minds. You don't need to take that role. You don't need to be a politician. You've already been elected for life, so you can relax.

The real problem is that you are constantly labeling your experience, based on language. Your concepts are like representatives who report what is happening, but those reports become your only reality. Everything is at a distance: the messenger delivers a message, and the message reflects the concept of the image of what is going on.

But how can we understand what is going on without labels and language? Aren't we going round in circles?

No, the problem goes deeper than that. Look at what you're asking: "How can we understand . . . How can we do it differently?" You always want to know 'how'. That's how Westerners operate: they ask 'How did this happen? . . . How did that happen? Always howling 'how'! If you cannot get an answer to the 'how' question, you are not satisfied. You send out 'how' as your agent, and you expect your agent to return with something you can make sense of.

Knowing without labels and images is actually very simple. It's only hard because we are not familiar with it.

That doesn't seem accurate. We do know without labels. We can experience directly. We can feel directly. That has nothing to do with labeling.

It's not that easy. We expect that when we let go of labels, we arrive at direct experience, but 'direct experience' is another label. It's part of a system of knowledge.

If you call feelings and experience into question on the one hand and concepts and language on the other, what's left?

You're the one who's saying, "Something must be left!" That's your problem. You are not satisfied with the situation the way it is. You project some alternative; you head off in some direction. You start by saying, "Here I am," and then automatically you look around for what is going on, sure that there must be something to make sense of. You project it; you look for it. The subject is there, and the subject looks around everywhere for something. You always want to find the right direction. You start off being dissatisfied and you remain dissatisfied.

It all makes good sense, once you are part of the system. But tell me, does the sky have directions? We are the ones who make directions. We point things out and we set things up. Who points? It's my mind, my projection, my idea. I insist on an 'according to', so that I can form the right opinion. The subject is 'here', and it has to relate to the object 'there'. Someone somehow has to relate to something somewhere. Without the label, it means nothing; it's meaningless. That's what samsara mind does. The West thinks that's the only option. That's just the way things are. Don't you think so?

13

What Comes Next

I'll ask again: if you get rid of everything—no labels, no identities—what's left?

Just manifestation! How does it usually happen? We detect something that unfolds in a causal, linear way. The sense faculties come into operation. Then we try to make sense of it—through common sense, or through psychology or philosophy or biology. We see actions and consequences, and we offer logical explanations.

Wait! You just named most of the fields of human knowledge. Don't we need to move a little more slowly?

Why? Whether we can work out all the details intellectually is not the point. When we get to the heart of the matter, what we're really looking at is the searcher and the search engine. If we really look right there, the searcher itself opens up. That means activating a different way of perception. It becomes easier to encompass change and open new realms or new fields. We think we know who we are and where we are, but when we open this new space, we learn something new about identity and realness. We see how identity comes from language and concepts. We see how things are established.

And that gives us freedom?

Well, we could say it makes us more flexible. For instance, if someone insults us or hurts our feelings, we don't just react in the predictable emotional way, because the usual patterns don't automatically operate. We may have better ways of handling what we encounter.

It still sounds like you're offering the possibility of freedom.

Now you're the one who wants to move too quickly! The bottom line is that if we don't accept the defining reality of what manifests, we discover that the ways we have learned to respond and the truths we have learned to accept—about ourselves, about the world—are open for questioning. We don't need to respond on the basis of received truths.

For instance, we may go from one day to the next reacting to whatever happens based on some simple models. We are unhappy, or we are confused. We get distracted, or we get angry. We like, or we don't like. We feel attachment or isolation or a sense of loss. Based on which of these labels we accept as the truth of the situation, strong waves and energies manifest, and specific situations in time and space unfold. We follow that manifestation because we accept it as real. At that point it is not easy to bring about any fundamental change.

It doesn't have to be that way. Imagine that the realness of what manifests opens: that is the key we have been looking for. Once you see that you are on a journey through life, and you see how that journey has unfolded since before you can remember, and you see all that without being committed to the truth of what has unfolded, then yes, that does seem to give the possibility of freedom.

It seems we would also gain a kind of power: the ability to turn things in a different direction.

That's right. We have a new way of engaging our experience. We see how we have been conducting our lives, and we understand the rules in operation. Whatever happens, internally or externally, we know how to deal with it. We know how to change things in a positive direction. We see and experience differently, and that means we have a choice. New opportunities open up, and problems cannot get in our way.

So often we find our way blocked. It feels like we've come to the end; we've used up our chances or run out of options. Now that whole way of seeing is transformed. We don't have to be the victims of our destiny. We don't have to play out the limited range of possibilities available to us. Whatever manifests is an extension of a journey of transformation. We have a new way of searching and experiencing and seeing, and that makes all the difference.

I spoke earlier about what it's like to grow up and reach the age of independence, which this culture defines as being about 18 years old. Now we could say we are going further. We are getting a higher education, like someone who goes on to college and then continues on to advanced studies. At that point, you see endless possibilities opening before you. You're not limited by the way things are. You're not so interested in the usual structures of 'from' and 'to'. Appearance is just appearance. It's bottomless and seedless. Whatever appears is a projection, or a reflection of a projection.

You mean because reality as we usually understand it is just a projection?

It's not quite that simple. The projection itself is a projection. Something begins, and something moves 'to' somewhere else, but that 'to' is not necessarily 'there', not necessarily anywhere at all. The subject becomes the object and the object becomes the subject.

Whoa! That caught me by surprise. I didn't think that's where you were going. But if I accept what you're saying, what would it be like for subject and object to become the same? Would they still interact? Do they just melt together? If that's so, how can we ever be clear on what's happening? Are you saying that everything is a matter of subjective experience? Or do concepts like 'subjective' and 'objective' still apply?

When subject and object interact at this level, it's like a shining ball of light. Think about the dreams you have at night. Somehow a whole world is created. We don't know how it happens, but there it is. Is it subjective? Yes, in a sense, because no one else can be in my dream. But the world that's created in the dream does not seem subjective. As long as I'm dreaming, it has a reality that is very much like waking reality, even if it does follow different rules.

Again, consider the example of a colorful rainbow. You can't take hold of the rainbow; you can't touch it or hold on to it, but it still shows up. Questioning the reality claims of the world of subject and object is like that. Manifestations appear, and events may continue to unfold in ways that seem familiar, but something basic has shifted.

If things continue to manifest in the same way, what is it that's shifted? If I came to see appearance as a projection, or a reflection, how would that affect my experience? What kinds of new possibilities would open up?

One way the shift might manifest is that you would no longer experience obstacles in the same way. The subject/object interaction and the grasping tendency that supports it depend on the claim of identity, and now that claim has become hollow. The language we use to assign labels, the cultural presuppositions that tell us what things mean and how to relate to them: all that is transformed. At that point, there is no ruler in charge of experience, no regime, no one forcefully insisting on this or that. There are no positions, no roles, no system to catch us up and set us in place. Slavery is abolished. The die is not cast.

When you get a sense of this, you can see more clearly how everybody is ordinarily caught up in a pre-established structure. It doesn't matter whether we occupy a position of power or feel completely powerless. No matter what role we play—ruler or rebel—we are all part of the establishment.

At the same time, because you see what is happening, you do not necessarily have to participate. You don't have to take a position within the structure. You reach a new level of self-understanding, a very fundamental freedom. Experientially, the world becomes very rich, very full. There are no hidden corners, just total openness in all dimensions. You can respond flexibly to each new situation.

With this kind of understanding, we can operate at two levels at once. We see how experience manifests and how the structures that shape it—the forms, the identities, the history of this present situation—have developed. But at the same time, it all seems rootless or baseless. Think of light, and how it can manifest any form. It's like that.

This kind of knowledgeability can inspire us to act and to respond differently. We understand how we have been caught up in patterns over which we have no control, patterns based on our own psychology, or our environment, our culture, the belief systems we accept, or our self-image. We can acknowledge the parenthood of our present circumstance and the journey that has brought us to this place in time.

So it goes back to the power of the labels we apply and the language we use to shape the roles we take on.

That seems right. We are shaped by concepts, and concepts are constructed by systems of words. For instance, Buddhism analyzes experience in terms of the interactions of the five skandhas: form, feeling, identification, conditioned patterns, and consciousness. That can be a very useful way of understanding our situation, because it challenges our usual roles and rules, our self-image and self-concern. But even that kind of analysis puts limits in place. Linguistic structures are like a two-edged sword: they offer clarity, but they also condition us.

Is that why Mahayana Buddhism challenges all constructs?

It's important to see both aspects of the conceptual structures we adopt. For instance, in the Mahayana, it's fundamental to develop a sense of compassion—to engage others with empathy. That is very much at the heart of the Bodhisattva path. To do that, you have to recognize how people get trapped in circumstances they do not control, how they feel isolated, how they suffer. I relate to the suffering of others because it makes sense in terms of my own experience. Now, all of that is based at least partly on a certain conceptual understanding. It is very positive, but in the end we need to open up that understanding as well. We need to see how our own sense of compassion is a manifestation; we need to recognize its source.

Will arriving at that understanding make us more effective in being of benefit to others?

Yes, it will. If we can see clearly how suffering arises and how the response to suffering arises, we can move beyond sympathy and tears. We can avoid the trap of hopelessness in the face of so much unhappiness and misery. We may be able to discover effective ways to cure the pain of others, like a doctor who traces the root causes of an epidemic.

All of that depends on going beyond conceptual mind. It involves a different kind of mastery, where we embody the highest knowledge. It's like finding the right combination to open the lock that will free us from samsara. That knowledge is available—others have discovered it. We need to do so also.

If we can learn to see clearly the nature of all manifestations, we will eventually make contact with a sacred power of transformation. In one way, we already embody that power, but we have put it in the service of self-image and identity, like putting a black shade over a brilliant light. Can we just let the inner light shine, for ourselves and also for others? When that happens, there are no more obstacles, no hidden dark corners where misunderstanding and sorrow remain.

So in the end, what matters is transcending all our ordinary perceptions and seeing in a new way.

That's fundamental. But even then, our work is not complete. We also need the power to activate that understanding. We might call that power 'blessings'; we might speak of the power of merit. Think of light again: it's luminous, but it also carries power, like sunlight. If we can transmit light into darkness, it will naturally illuminate what it encounters. That is the mission we need to take on. First we do it for ourselves, and then we share it with others.

In speaking this way, we are not just coming up with new concepts and labels. The light of realization transmits with complete immediacy. There is no longer 'before' and 'after', because time, space, and knowledge have been completely unified. There is no more separation and no positions or locations to carry forward. The unity of power takes over the samsaric way of manifesting. You might speak of this way of being as mystical, but also blissful.

Can you say more about how to share that with others?

Sharing does not depend on talking or showing. It has to do with natural blessings, natural positivity. It has to do with the power of truth. I truly believe what others have said: the truth does not fail. It can be embodied in any situation, and it manifests as empowerment. Its light does not just go here and there. It is universal, available to all beings in all realms. In religious terms, we could speak of gaining entrance to heaven, or the Sukhavati realm, or we could speak of bliss, or nirvana, or absolute freedom. Of course, these are all just concepts, but that does not make them false. They are actually produced by the power of the manifestation of truth.

How can we possibly express this, when language and even experience set limits and depend on limits? Perhaps we could say that truth's power generates a kind of gravity that exerts its force on all beings in all directions, throughout time and space, active in all forms of knowledge. It goes beyond concepts, beyond our thinking, our ideas, our images. At the same, as we make contact with what is true, we do not discard the realm of appearance and ideas. Once the journey is completed, truth can manifest in countless forms. All appearance can manifest the power of wisdom and embody the truth of understanding.

When we know for ourselves that the power of truth is available everywhere, our actions and our intentions grant universal access, grounded in a universal unity. We become capable of bringing benefit and value everywhere, sharing the blessings of liberation.

This sharing is the path, and it is also the journey. It is a path without language, without teaching—a path of internal realization and comprehension, not shaped by the products of mind, not conditioned by consciousness, concepts, thoughts, labels, or images.

For now, we may be stuck at the level of concepts and fantasies, where we inevitably encounter limits. We know we need to go beyond that level, to the limitless. Do we know what that means? No, we do not! We don't know how to think, or what to think about; we don't know what the next step should be. We don't know how to bring about transformation. So do we give up? What do you think?

14

How It Happens

As long as you rely on language and labeling, you are going to have problems. Once you have a problem, you feel the need to get to the root of what is going on, so you can come up with a solution. But that's a very self-referential approach. You want to know what to do, how to respond, so you go ahead and tell yourself—you send yourself a message. It's all about your own opinions, your own feelings. That's why asking 'How?' doesn't really lead anywhere.

In Revelations of Mind, *you write about "tracking back the how."*

Yes, but it's easy for that kind of inquiry to stay on the intellectual level. You need to ask in a very simple way. Can you ask without language, without images? It's more simple than you imagine! It only seems complicated or hard because you are not familiar with that way of doing it.

So go more into feelings and direct experience?

No . . . that's what you expect to find when you set aside language, but that's not it.

Then what is 'it'? If there are no concepts and no language, but also no feelings or experience, what is there?

You're still tied too closely to your usual ways of using the mind. You say, "There must be something . . . tell me what it is!" But as long as you are looking for something, you'll never be satisfied. You are projecting something that you have to find; you are looking for it. You start from the position of the subject, and then from that position, you look out in every direction. You are 'here', so there must be a 'there'. Whatever you do, you are always headed in some direction. But we talked about this already. We are the ones who make directions, through pointing.

The same structures operate when we talk about 'my mind', or about 'mine'. It's always my project, my idea. There has to be an 'according to', because otherwise we would have no way to form an opinion. There has to be a 'someone' and a 'somehow'. That's what it means to take the position of the subject. Right away we are in the business of labeling, because without labels, we don't know how to relate. If we can't label it, it doesn't mean anything to us. It doesn't fit within the framework of our normal way of thinking. That's how samsara mind operates. It's what Western mind does. That's why it's so important to understand the operations of mind.

People today are looking for methods for dealing with stress, and they may find ways to do that that are temporarily effective. But they don't understand the operations of mind that are at the root of stress. For instance, even the idea of understanding on the one hand or not understanding on the other is based on our normal way of using language. We think that these kinds of contrasts are necessary if we want to communicate—even to communicate with ourselves. But if we rely on making those kinds of distinctions, there is a strange, unexpected consequence. We find ourselves depending on the meaning of each word. That sets up limits. It cripples our ability to understand at a different level. We need to develop a different way.

Western language involves relying on all sorts of established patterns, which we analyze at the level of psychology or philosophy or social structures. There's no problem with that. After all, we need to communicate, and the only ways of communication we have available are the ones we have learned in school or in growing up. The difficulty is that we think that when we use that kind of language, we are really communicating something about the mind. We think we are establishing the meaning of mind.

It seems that if you go to sense experience, you don't have to rely on language. But you already rejected that possibility.

Right, because it stays at the same level. It doesn't matter whether we try to understand what we experience based on 'my senses' or 'my thoughts' or 'my feelings'. The structure is the same. It doesn't help break through limitations. It's like putting a band aid on a wound or giving someone a placebo. There may be some temporary benefit, but it doesn't mean much. We are still holding on to the name 'mind', and saying 'mind' makes us think we know what we are talking about. If we don't understand that fundamental pattern, we can't penetrate very deeply. The same is true for the senses.

What's the alternative?

We need a special way to communicate. In Buddhism, if someone wants to develop deeper understanding, first they study Abhidharma, perhaps for eleven years. Then they study Madhyamaka for three years, and then Prajnaparamita for three years. So that's about 17 years in all. At the end of all that study, they may be ready to say: this is how the mind operates; this is what consciousness means. Each school has its own level of understanding, and each approach has its own value.

The West doesn't have those approaches, which are very sophisticated. But that's not the real point. In the Buddhist tradition, we go through all these stages, all these different approaches, but we don't claim that they are the final word. They are not wrong, they are not lies or deceptions—they help develop understanding. Transformation, however, goes deeper than that. If you don't reach the level of transformation, then even the insights that come from this kind of study are only a temporary fix. The West never reaches that level.

The West does have very sophisticated philosophies, and its knowledge of psychology is growing all the time. Are you saying that all that misses the point?

Western thinkers do have some understanding, but they are always trying to establish the base—the place 'I' come from. Once the base is there, they may identify a detailed approach for increasing knowledge and work it out through very subtle reasoning. Suppose someone says that there are 35 steps you have to complete, and then maybe there is another level beyond that, with more steps. Just naming all those steps and levels already seems like progress. Now there's a structure in place, and they insist on following it, because they are confident that that's the way to reach the goal. It lets them say, "Right now I'm at step 29, and I have to get clear on what's going on at this level before I can go any further."

All that can be very satisfying. You feel that you're getting somewhere, and that going step by step in that way is really worth it. This is not just true for Western thinkers; it's how our intellect works. It's a product of our current mental capacity. Psychology, philosophy, science: they're all based on language and logic and on being rational; on proceeding step by step. They all insist that there have to be reasons and explanations for each step. If we can't know something on that basis, we just ignore it. If we can't talk about, we label it as a mystery, or we say it isn't relevant. It's like saying, "I live on the second floor. I'm not interested in what happens on the third floor."

Tell me, what does the West say is the difference between wisdom and knowledge?

It seems similar to the distinction you're making. Knowledge is what operates within a particular structure that we already understand. Wisdom goes beyond that.

In that case, perhaps we could say that knowledge is related to the mind. We rely on our experience and the framework we use to assign meanings. As we develop more knowledge, we recognize more aspects, or we see in a broader context. The aim is to know every aspect, both inner and outer: to recognize each element. We cognize, and then we get feed-

127

back based on recognition. It's a steady process, and gradually we become more knowledgeable.

There's a debate in Western philosophy about whether there is a kind of knowledge that goes beyond whatever rational or scientific framework we adopt, although they don't call it wisdom. Are you making a similar point?

I'll leave that to you to decide. What I'm saying is that the framework seems to establish what counts as knowledge. It provides the definitions or conditions for knowledge. For instance, if I am operating within a scientific framework, that shapes the possibilities for knowledge. It only counts as knowledge if it comes about through applying the scientific method. Those are the associations I make and that's the purpose of my inquiry. If someone using a different framework says, "But you've left out a whole different way of knowing," it doesn't matter too much whether I agree or disagree. In one case I modify the framework; in the other case I keep it intact.

For instance, someone may say, "Did you ever meet Einstein?" And you answer, "No, but I have read every biography of Einstein; I know all the facts about his life. I know where he went to school, and who his friends were, and what he wrote about, and where he went for vacation, and all his favorite foods." Is your knowledge complete? You could answer either way.

Does it depend on the kinds of observations you make?

Observations are relative too. For instance, nowadays astronomers are discovering many new planets orbiting around distant stars. But from what people have told me, the astronomers don't actually observe the planet: they only observe the effect of the planet on the light we measure from the star. Within that framework, that counts as knowledge.

In the end, knowledge requires language. You need gestures and symbols too, but language seems essential. There's no way around that. But one day you may realize that any description based on language cannot fully capture what is known. That is knowledge worth knowing, because it operates at a different level. It lets you recognize that the knowledge you usually rely on is based on projection, on reports that you receive from your agent. You can see that your standard knowledge operates within a regime specific to you—your frame of mind. You begin to realize that you have a specific way of presenting information to yourself. First you establish similarities through feedback. Based on that, the whole range of responses arises—feelings, ideas, models, theories, intuitions—all of it.

Are you just talking about information now, or does the same structure apply to practical knowledge?

There's a wide range of applications. For example, people say that they experience lots of stress, or they feel trapped by their own neurotic patterns or addictions, or they find it difficult to focus on what they think is valuable. Or they just feel unhappy or afraid or anxious. Within the realm that our society recognizes, all this is real; it's undeniable. Stress, conflict, emotionality: that really is their experience. That's how they respond to what life presents.

In the face of that reality, what can we do? If you have cancer, you need to treat it with whatever therapies are available.

The same is true for stress and the other kinds of negativities we experience. So if you are operating within the standard knowledge framework, you set out to solve the problem. If you're feeling stress, you look for ways to relax, such as meditation. Can that be helpful? Of course. You can pause the cycle of negativity and taste real inner calm. At that point, you may say, "My mind is at peace." If you go deeper, you may experience pleasant or joyful or even blissful sensations. It may seem like you've made an exciting, fantastic discovery, whether you call it samadhi or satori or enlightened mind.

It sounds great. But if understand you, you are saying that there's something wrong with that.

There nothing wrong with it. The experience can be very positive. But it's limited. It all comes as a response to the sickness, the distraction, the anxiety, and the conflicts of ordinary mind. If those dimensions of mind were not relevant to our experience, or if they were exaggerations, or if in the end they were just not true, then there might not be any problem to solve or any method to apply. Even the most positive states might be the answer to a question that never needed to be asked.

15

How to Respond

It seems completely natural, even indisputable, that there's a difference between positive, wonderful states from ordinary states. But you're saying we need to question that basic distinction.

Right. We don't ask those kinds of questions, because we accept the basic framework. If someone sets up or understands a situation in a certain way and then discovers a problem within that situation, they naturally try to come up with a solution to that problem. But it's all based on projecting the initial conditions forward.

Actually, we start with a projection—that's how the fundamental situation gets set up. First there is a projection. Then the shape and form of what we project becomes more and more real, For instance, it might be 'my emotional conflict'. We've established that there's a problem, so the solution to the problem becomes important. It might be meditation, or relaxation, or in-depth study, or a special relationship, or really anything else. But right now we're focused on meditation.

I wonder: do the Bodhisattvas meditate to solve a problem? Does the Buddha meditate like that?

As far as I know, the Buddha never says that the reason to meditate is to feel better.

Imagine that you met God. Maybe you don't believe in God, but we're just imagining. So because you are interested in how to work with the mind, you ask God, "Do you meditate?" Is that a valid question to ask? Who would be the meditator? Usually we say that mind is the meditator, but what if there is no label 'mind'? Does meditation require a mind that meditates? Does the mind that meditates have a fixed nature? Mind seems to be more like space.

What do you mean?

Space is not an object. You can't program space; you can't give it characteristics.

In the TSK Vision, you say that appearance depends on space.

It may well be that for the images and points and marks and letters and numbers we identify to be real or appear, they have to enter into a partnership with space. But that's not my point right now, because saying that doesn't tell us anything about space.

In the West, people say that God is the creator. We might say, theoretically, that space is the creator, the sponsor for all appearance, because space makes appearance possible. But what aspect of space is the creator? Suppose I am space. Is it my *power* that creates? Is it my *energy*? Can I create through my knowledge, or through my link to time? Does creation happen through my inventiveness?

Creation is actually very puzzling. If there is an act of creation, it seems there has to be a 'before creation'. What can we say about that? There must be some condition, some set of circumstances that makes creation possible. If the act of creation—the whole manifestation of the universe—is like firing a bullet, where did the bullet come from? Before the moment of creation, you did 'this'; after, you did 'that'. What is the difference?

Now you've brought in the question of time.

Yes, now time has a job to do. But the question is still the same. What was the product that produced creation? Is the answer 'time'? If so, is there a 'before time'?

Somehow we've jumped into questions about time and space. I thought we were talking about the mind that wants to relax or find peace and joy.

Exactly! We are looking for what to do with mind. So it seems we need some instructions. We have to know how to meditate, how to follow a spiritual path. Do you see where that approach takes us? Whether we like it or not, we are caught up in concepts. We have the label 'mind', the label 'senses', the label 'feelings'. Something needs to be done to arrive at some goal: we have to do some particular practice; for instance, a visualization, or some special kind of breathing.

What does that have to do with time and space?

All those concepts relate to the subject, and the subject has a particular relationship with space. As the subject, I am located 'here' and I have to get 'there': that's just what it means to have a purpose or mission. To do that, I have to go in a particular direction, or I won't reach the goal. So even though we start off with concepts, the content of our concepts—words, labels, ideas—doesn't make any sense without space and time. The content needs a context, and the context has its own content. Without that, there would be nothing to do, nothing to relate to, so there would be no point in even getting started. But that option doesn't make sense to us. We accept that we are obligated. There is something we have to do. We have responsibilities.

Suppose instead that there was nothing at all that we had to do. There would be no conflicts, no agitation, no frustration or anxiety. At that point, even the concept of release from suffering would not apply. If the conditions are never set up, then you have no job, no business.

Let's say that this is our approach—the 'doing nothing' approach. In the usual approach, benefits come as the reward from your efforts. In the doing-nothing approach, the benefit is that there are no problems that need to be solved. The conditions for having problems have never been set up.

It seems we could just take one approach or the other, but we may not actually have that choice, because we are committed to our problems and to needing to get rid of our problems. We accept the truth of that commitment as more basic than any choice we might make. We sort things out into 'good and bad' and 'pro and con', and that means we always have problems. And nothing is more important than finding solutions to those problems.

And when we look for solutions, we're really committing ourselves to the problem. We get involved, even if we say we don't want to. We interact with the situation we have identified.

That's right. Searching for a solution, we set up one condition against another. We're creating conflict.

So no conditions means no problems! But how do we arrive at 'no conditions'?

'Arriving' is part of the difficulty. You could say, "I am on the path." But your being committed to a path distracts you. It means you have duties and obligations. For instance, you may sit down to meditate, and you tell yourself, "concentrate . . . be aware . . . do what's right . . . avoid what's wrong . . . practice morality." All those polarities, all those distinctions! It all comes from being on the path.

Then do I just give up? Maybe I say, "Being on the path sounded like a lot of work anyway. No path for me! I like this 'do nothing' approach."

That's too easy. It's not really a serious response. It sounds like you are making a decision, and in a way you are, but the choice arises within a framework, a language system that defines your possibilities based on a set of pre-established concerns. The choice you imply does not apply; the meaning you choose does not describe what's going on. You claim to be leaving the old logic behind, but that's not what's going on at all. You may tell yourself you're heading off in some new direction, but more likely you are still operating within the realm of the familiar.

It's like someone who likes to eat at McDonalds, and every day they go there and they always have the same lunch. One day they say, "I think I'll try something else on the menu." But they're still eating at McDonalds. If someone said to them, I have some tasty caviar for you to try, they would say, "No, I like what I can get at McDonalds. That's what I'm familiar with." We're all like that. We all have our habits.

Can you really say that the opposite of having a habit is still part of the habit? Suppose I recognize that I am trapped in a set of habitual responses: doesn't that give me a new possibility? If I'm inclined to be adventurous, why can't I give up my McDonald's habit? Or is that just because I have a habit of being adventurous when it comes to food?

Your possibilities are shaped by the operations of mind. When you dream, the image in the dream is not real, but because you are inside the dream, you don't know that. The mind is the one that 'manufactures' the dream. Or think of a movie projector: mind is like the light that projects the image on a screen, but is also the one that creates the images. Look at the screen, and you see all sorts of things—feelings, attitudes, imaginations—but they are all projections, and mind is the projector.

Now, suppose that you ordinarily project a set of habitual responses, but under the right conditions, you project cutting off those responses. That may lead to a very different understanding, but it will still be an understanding projected by mind. That's more fundamental than whether you stay with the familiar or strike off in a new direction.

That doesn't make sense to me. If I have an experience that's completely new, that I never imagined could be possible, why would you call that a projection of what I already accept as true? I know that I have insights or experiences that come as a complete surprise. Are those all projections too? How can letting go of all habitual ways of thinking also be a product of habitual ways of thinking?

136

It's not so hard to understand. You don't recognize the projection as your own mind, and you don't recognize the forms the projection can take. That's the place to start. Whatever the specific shape and form of your experience, none of it would appear without mind. There's a loop: the subject presents and projects, and then what is presented feeds back to the subject, and then come interpretations. If there's no projection and no feedback, there's no experience.

One reason we don't see this is that it all happens very quickly, so quickly it almost seems magical. But whatever your experience is, it doesn't show up all it once. It has to have a head and a tail and a 'between'. It may be strongly creative—it may be 'never before imagined'—but it still depends on the same feedback loop, the same projection mechanism. You could put it this way: whether what appears is good or bad, new or old, whether you accept it or reject it, whether it's familiar or unexpected, the cause of the experience is 'me'.

You could also think about it in terms of fields. Eye consciousness has its visual field, ear consciousness has its auditory field, and so on. The body has its field too. With thoughts, it's more difficult to understand, but they also have a field or territory. Each field is separate, but we organize our experience based on the fields merging together and interacting. The conditions for experience—subject orientation, object orientation—come about through that interplay. Mind pronounces all of it. If you want to investigate further, the Abhidharma teachings and the analysis of the Chittamatra school work all this out in great detail.

We organize experience according to different categories: the subject who experiences, the object that appears, and so on. Do those categories name something real, or are we making it up? We lay it all out and we proclaim that it's true. Is that the final word? Perhaps it's more like a computer program that we wrote the code for and set in operation. Now it's running, and for us, that's the way it is.

16

How to Question

I don't have any good way to think about these issues. It all seems frustrating, like always skating on the edge of saying it's hopeless; that there's nothing we can do. Maybe it's just my problem, but I wonder whether it may have to do with the way the Western mind has been trained to think.

If I compare the West with the culture I grew up in, there's a real difference. There's a problem here, and it may affect the possibility for transmitting Buddhism to the West. It's a language problem. English is missing the right vocabulary.

Maybe we just haven't found the right words yet. English has a very rich philosophical vocabulary. And then there's the language of psychology and the language of science. So what's missing? There are so many possibilities for communication!

The problem is not about developing a sophisticated vocabulary. It happens at a more basic level. In this culture, people focus on how to be healthy and happy and free from inner conflicts. That is fine, but then they stop there. They don't go any further.

If we do go a step beyond that, we may recognize that we experience the world in terms of the projections we make and the labels we assign. We see that the mind sets up particular ways of experiencing. We realize also that we don't know the nature of the mind, so we try to go to that level.

It's at that point that our language systems let us down. We recognize the pattern of projection and feedback, but can we go any further? Can we investigate who is receiving feedback? Do we know who is supposed to understand what is being communicated? Which is more accurate: that mind has knowledge, or that knowledge knows mind? We understand in a general way the relationship between the operations of mind and what we know, but we don't know how to make sense of it. If someone asks how the world we inhabit manifests, how it is established, what can we really say?

Exercise 16: Don't Know Mind

Imagine that you have arrived in this world as a visitor from another planet or realm. Thanks to your preparation before you arrived, you speak the language and know the customs, but you soon realize that the inhabitants of this world make use of countless concepts that you simply don't understand. As you investigate further, you begin to appreciate that they structure their experience in ways that you cannot really grasp. For instance, you do not know what they mean when they use the labels 'mind' or 'mine'. You do not understand categories such as 'here' and 'there', or 'from', 'to' 'on' or 'at'. You do not know what they are referring to when they speak of being agitated or feeling inner conflict, states that they seem to refer to an 'I' or 'me'. There are many other similar expressions they use for which you can find no equivalent in your own experience; for example, 'like' and 'dislike', 'taking responsibility', 'dealing with negativity', and so on.

Practice operating in this 'don't know' state, both with respect to yourself and in your dealing with others. Since this represents a fundamental break with our ordinary way of experience, it is not enough to consider this possibility casually and then move on, reverting to your usual mode of experiencing. Instead, give yourself at least 20 minutes to conduct this inquiry, at least once or twice a day for two weeks. Do not try to describe to yourself the outcome of the practice or your 'success' in doing it, either while you are practicing or afterward. Do the practice and then move on.

It's easy not to take these kinds of questions seriously, because the very idea that our usualunderstanding could be called into question make no sense. Imagine the following dialog:

You know perfectly well what I'm talking about.

Who are you talking to?

I'm talking to you! Don't pretend you don't understand. You're listening, aren't you?

Who is listening?

This is ridiculous! You are denying something that is obviously true.

What does it mean to deny? What is the basis for denying? Does denying come from thoughts? Does denying happen before thoughts? Does it arise at the beginning of a thought? The middle of a thought?

Your questions are just nonsense. I know what I'm thinking and I know when I'm thinking.

Who is the knower? Do you know the knower? Does the knower know you?

I am the knower!

Is that so? Perhaps you are using the knower. Or perhaps one part of you knows another part. Is the self the one that knows? If it is, how does it get the knowledge that lets it know?

I can play that game too. Tell me, who is questioning? Who is denying that you know?

I don't know.

If you say you don't know, you don't know what you're denying.

At this point we seem trapped by a logic of 'including' and 'excluding'. If we say we know, we are including. If we say we don't know, we are excluding. Once we exclude, we no longer know what we're excluding, so perhaps we need to stay with including. When we do, we open up a realm of possible reactions and structures: identity, perception, sensing, knowing, and so on. As we explore each of these, we may have the sense that we are at the cutting edge of experience, but inevitably there will be a lot that is excluded. We do not know what happens before we know; we do not know what happens after we know. Do we know knowing itself?

For me to know, do I need a place from which to know? Do I need to be at the edge of what I already know? If I occupy some particular place, that means I have a location in space.

142

Do I also have a location in time? What limits does that set on the potential range of my knowledge? Is my knowing activity limited to what is available to me right now? If so, how can I know at all?

In our everyday interactions, there is a great deal that we take for granted. I say 'this'; I believe 'that'; I distinguish one set of conditions from another. But what is the basis for any of it? We may feel we can trust the knowing of the eyes and ears and nose and body, but what is the basis for that trust? The closer we look, the more the meaning is lost. Is the content of experience really there? Is the object real? If I cannot question the knower, how can I be sure of what I know?

Don't we have to make certain assumptions or start from certain premises? I can see that it's possible to call anything into question, but if I'm going to function in the world, I have to accept that 'I' is real, that the world is real, and so on.

Yes and no. Whatever we do, we are always confirming 'I' and 'me' and 'mind'. It is always 'my' experience that matters to me. Whenever we point out some object or react to some situation, we are also pointing back toward 'I' and 'me' and 'mine' and mind. That's why we can call them the four gateways: they are the opening through which we emerge into experience. We are just pointing, but the pointing becomes very real. Still, we can't really rely on that kind of evidence. It's like a rainbow: when you see it in the distance, it looks very real, but when you go there, you can't find it.

It's not easy to point this out in a way that makes sense in terms of our ordinary experience. Right now, we rely on a certain set of circumstances and conditions, but if we look backward in history, or maybe just a few moments back into the past, the things we call real now may not have existed.

There is a story in the Buddhist tradition about a village woman who lived by herself in a small hut who chose as her meditation object a tiger. She meditated intensively for many years, and the power of her concentration was so great that she herself turned into a tiger. She kept to herself, but at night, she would go out to relieve herself, and eventually the other villagers saw her. Terrified they ran away. We are not great meditators, but even ordinary mind has similar powers. We concentrate on our projections and ideas and concepts, and we impose them so strongly that they become real.

Is that true of the idea of 'I'?

Yes, it is. We have the idea of 'I', and we believe in the 'I-ness' of that 'I'.

Is that why the tradition teaches emptiness, or shunyata?

Even shunyata is a concept we impose on experience. When we negate the existence of something, the negation is still left. There is still a 'from something' or a 'to something'. As long as we project some understanding, nothing really changes. We try to transform our understanding of what actually is: a different appearance, a different world. That may have value, but it is still a projection.

So everything is a projection.

That's a formulation too. If we distinguish between samsara and nirvana, that's another formulation. There are many ways to describe reality.

People often imagine that the scientific worldview is at odds with spirituality, but that's not necessarily so. First of all, the scientific method, with its willingness to question, offers a very good model. But even in terms of what science holds to be real, there may not be a conflict. From what I understand, science tells us that shape and form and qualities and character all trace back to fundamental particles. If we could learn to see that way, it might give us a useful way of understanding the identity of what we call reality. It might help us see that our common concepts, our consciousness, and mind itself are all constructed.

You could also approach it from the other direction, Buddhism teaches six kinds of perception, based on the five senses and the sixth sense of cognition, and it links ordinary experience to the arising of karma and klesha. It asks us to investigate claims of identity and desire, consciousness and perception. Again, that kind of inquiry can have a profound impact. But all of that refers to the ordinary, samsaric level. If we could go to the Buddha's realm, none of that might be there.

If I understand correctly, you're saying that the world that we understand is a construct, that in some sense we create it, and that holds true even for the world understood in accord with Buddhist teachings. But how does that happen, speaking historically? What's the genesis? Why don't we just stay in the realm of the Buddhas, where none of these constructs get set up? I suppose I'm asking how it is that samsara come to be.

The reality we experience now is due to residues of former activity. 'Residue' means that something repeats again and again, like a pendulum that keeps swinging through the same motion, or like a ball that just rolls downhill. No one has to make any effort to get the ball to roll downhill—it just does. The pattern keeps manifesting through its own momentum.

The same is true for the meanings and perceptions and concepts that belong to the mind. They have been established a certain way, and we have been trained in that way. Humans have one way and animals another way, but within the human pattern, to stay with our own experience, there are mostly similarities. It's like dreams: we may find ourselves in a very different world in our dreams, but still the same patterns play themselves out. We like, we dislike, we judge, we perceive. It all unfolds on its own.

The way you describe it all makes sense on one level, but it also completely goes against what we believe about reality. And it's not as though we just make up our beliefs about reality. We accept them because they work; because they seem to give an accurate picture of what's going on.

Yes, there's a difficulty here. If we want to understand anything at all, it has to match up with our usual logic. But when we try to understand on the basis of the prevailing rationality, we are setting ourselves up for wrong views; we are asking for trouble. Rational mind can generate very sophisticated forms of understanding, but the more sophisticated, the more you get stuck in your own view. For instance, you may define a certain reality, or point toward a 'thatness' that is beyond all reality. That's a view. That's how sectarian schools form, and how philosophical debates arise. In that sense, science is based on a particular philosophical view, even if scientists deny that what they are doing has anything to do with philosophy.

146

I don't know about scientists. But I do know that as ordinary human beings we have to know how to live our lives!

Now you're talking about morality, or ethics. But morality arises the same way. "Do this!" "Don't do that!" It all depends on doctrines and schools of thought.

A lot of people would say that they don't need philosophy to know the right thing to do.

Saying that you don't care about philosophy and don't need it doesn't help. It just means that you accept unthinkingly whatever ideas happen to be floating around, whatever ideas you were trained in. You can say you don't care about abstractions and theory, but that just means settling for your own unquestioned views. How likely is it that those views are right, or that they will be of much benefit? How would you know?

It seems I'm always asking this, but let me ask again: what's the alternative?

The highest virtue, the best conduct, is completely free. There are no distractions.

Part Three

Self-Liberation

17

No Borders

We all have our own emotions, our own moods and predispositions. Some are long-lasting themes in our lives, others seem to come and go. They may persist for a few days, a few weeks, or longer, or they may go by too quickly for us to register their passing. We may feel upset, or afraid, or find ourselves acting in destructive ways. We may feel disillusionment, anger, resentment, or disappointment. We may give way to temptation, or find ourselves fascinated by something or someone who appears suddenly in our lives. There may be times when we feel anxious or lost, or times when we lose all interest in our own lives or see no meaning in what we are doing.

Whatever emotions we find ourselves caught in, each one can be transformed into its opposite. The most direct approach is simply to visualize the feeling or emotion—which means letting it become very alive and real—and then instantly switch to the opposite.

That seems almost fraudulent, like trying to trick ourselves. After all, the situation that we say caused the negative feeling is still there, so how can we just pretend that everything has suddenly changed 180 degrees?

That response may sound convincing, but it depends on a whole series of assumptions that can readily be called into question. For our present purposes, however, we do not need to focus on the assumptions. We can take a more direct approach.

Think of your life as being like a fencing match or some other event that requires certain skills or training. When you fall into negativity, it's like making the wrong move or reacting in the wrong way to an opponent. A skilled and experienced coach could probably show you just where you went wrong, what kind of bad habit you are stuck in, and what to do to get the result you want. You can also do that for yourself. The basic move, the one that will mostly work, is simple: whatever is happening, switch to the opposite.

Easier said than done!

Maybe, but suppose for a moment you could do it. If you had that skill, your life would naturally go in a positive direction. You would find meaning in what you did, and you would easily experience happy, joyful feelings. You would be able to shape your actions toward achieving your goals and acting on your own values, and you would experience peace and satisfaction. Your life would be whole and full wherever you turned, 360 degrees in all directions.

It seems important to develop a sense of what it would be like to live in this way. There would be no more anxiety, no distractions that lead you to waste your time with no positive results. There would no waiting around, hoping for a result that you do not know how to bring about. There would be no greedy thoughts, no selfish thoughts, no angry thoughts, and also no disappointment. Without being pulled this way and that, you could see with greater clarity, so that you knew exactly what to do next and where to focus your energy. With greater knowledge, you would not be fooled into confusing the labels you use for reality. You would not be trapped by your own self-image.

All that we need to make this happen is the knowledge that lets us apply antidotes when negativity and neurotic patterns arise. For so long, we have let ourselves be manipulated by our own emotions. We find ourselves taking on certain roles and believing them: "I am lost . . . I am hopeless . . . I am a sinner . . . I am the victim . . . I am a loser." But if we know how to change the patterns that keep bubbling up in our minds, we have the chance for freedom and new opportunities.

Knowledge is the precious key that opens the door to this transformation. With the right knowledge, no obstacle can get in our way for long. Even when it looks like we are losing, we can be winners. Even when the mind is distracted, even when we face big problems, we can use every situation and convert it to our benefit. We know how to invest our resources; we are masters of our own situation. In every circumstance, the choice of what to do, how to react, is in our hands. We know the outcome in advance, and we can support what is positive. Of course, we will still face difficulties, but we know we can meet them in the best possible way.

When we realize that we have this power and gain confidence in our own knowledge and abilities, we can make it our mission to inspire others, to help them to achieve their own goals and live their own lives in more fruitful ways. When a new challenge arises, we can act calmly and with insight, seeing through each blockage and penetrating each obstacle. We will no longer be trapped by our own laziness or fear, our own hesitations and doubts. We can do what needs to be done.

I see the benefit. But how do we do it? And I still wonder if you aren't just asking us to pretend that we're feeling one way when we're feeling the opposite.

Let's look more closely. To start, what can we say about the kinds of mental events that stream through the mind? First are moments of sensing: seeing, hearing, and so on. Then there is the activity of identifying or recognizing what appears in the sensory stream. That seems to be related to knowing or cognizing something to be so. Then there are feelings: liking and disliking, but also emotions of different kinds. There are also thoughts, whether in the form of inner dialog, images, memories, or fantasies. This is not a complete list, but it gives us a direction for where to look and what to do.

Think of each of these events as a focal setting: a way in which we get more clear on a certain aspect of our situation. Somehow a particular event calls out for attention, and we give it: not because we consciously choose to do so, but because something in our mental patterning and the situation at hand leads us in that direction. You might think of it as a dot that shows up in the field of mental activity. Other dots may then coalesce around it.

Now, here is a practice to work with that. Let yourself focus on the middle of the experience: the place your attention naturally goes. Without losing contact with the focal point, gradually expand your attention, so that it grows wider and wider.

What does it mean to grow wider? Is it just bigger in size?

No: it's more than that. It's the surrounding mood; it's past and future; it's associations, and so on. The content, the name or label or the story that we give to what's happening, is the least important part.

At some point, as you widen the field of attention in this way, the initial focal point expands so much that you can no longer find any borders. There is no inside and no outside. There are no directions: no middle, no top or bottom, no edge, no tip, no dimensions. There is nothing to interpret and nowhere to go. You are in the center of the experience, wholly focused on that one experience, which is all-encompassing. At that point, the identity of what you are feeling, and your own identity as well, have become irrelevant.

That's the practice. Simply exercise that borderless point. When you do, you will know how to transform any negative experience whenever it has been activated.

18

Trapped by Zoning

The reason that expanding the focal setting can be effective is that it does away with limits and borders. In order for there to be a problem, there have to be limits. Limits establish identities; you could say that they capture the identity in the act of defining. Once the identity has been established, we apply labels. At that point, problems emerge almost immediately. For instance, it's my house, and the plumbing needs replacing. I have a headache, so I cannot concentrate. I feel depressed, so there is no point in doing anything. This belongs to me and that belongs to you: how does that make me feel? I worry about my relationship to you: are we still friends? It's a pattern that repeats itself over and over.

When you expand the original focal setting enough, the points that define identities disappear. First you focus on the point, then you find that you are inside the point. Then you go out to the edge, to the top or bottom, but as you keep expanding, all those markers and limits cease to operate.

You cannot say where they are or how they are functioning. There are no borders, and without borders, all the limits and concerns simply vanish. They no longer have any meaning.

What happens to problems when borders disappear? If I say, "I have a problem," I am making a claim, and before expanding, I knew very well what I meant by it. But now I cannot point to my problem, cannot identify it. "I have a problem" has become meaningless.

From within this way of seeing, the labels I applied before and the problems they referred to both express a kind of limited perspective, a bias. If I insist on holding on to my problem, I only show myself to be opinionated. If I characterize experience one way, saying that's the truth of the matter, that's just a form of discrimination. Now, after expanding, none of this makes any sense. There is no problem left. There is nothing I need to know and no solution I need to seek.

You make it sound like a wonderful freedom!

Perhaps. But our response may be very different. It may feel as though something has been taken away from us. We may say, "You claim there is nothing I need to know, but I do need to know! That is my right. I have been on a path, and I care about being on the path. I could see new possibilities, new opportunities before me. Now you are trying to take all that away."

That needy, demanding voice is the voice of the seeker, the one who insists on pushing ahead, the one who refuses to let go. But where does the path of the seeker lead? I keep looking for meanings. I push ahead, with great determination. Little by little the way narrows down, leaving me with fewer and fewer choices. In the end, I have no place to go. The way forward is blocked, and there is no way to turn around and go back. I have my meanings, I have my path, I have the labels I use to make sense of it all. The die is cast, and I am stuck. What choice do I have? Perhaps all I can do is cry.

But why should the path inevitably lead to a dead end? Why can't the path open into new possibilities, in the same way you have described?

The reason I find myself facing a dead end is that I am taking a path marked out for me in advance. My intentions are positive, and so I set out with great confidence. But I rely on labels and concepts—the ones I have been taught to apply. Whatever happens, I learn how to give convincing explanations. I look for the 'how' that clarifies the origins of the present situation, the present problem. I am like a carpenter with a hammer: I know how to do fix things that depend on pounding nails, but there are other approaches that I have no access to. I have my label-hammer and my concept-hammer. I rely on thoughts and on the senses, and I grab hold tightly of what they offer. I say, "This is the way it is, and this is what I can do about it."

So that's it! I'm stuck. When pain arises, I can only do my how howls, my "how this" and "how that." I can explain very well how I have been squeezed into a corner. If you ask me about other possibilities or invite me to look in in other directions, I draw a blank. I say, "I am making progress; I almost have it. I just need to know a little more, and then the problem will be solved." But in the end, I have no alternatives.

When we play out this progression, we are only working out limits that have been in operation from the very beginning. So it's natural that we would arrive at a dead end.

I still don't understand why it all gets so hopeless so quickly. Isn't there something besides labels and concepts I can rely on?

Imagine empty space. Somehow thoughts arise, along with limits and labels and feelings and identities. They just show up, like steam rising from a lake on a cold winter day. Each identified entity fills up space, and as it does, it squeezes us in further. We are trapped in a mass of distinctions and differences, labels and names. We may be following a spiritual path, but that doesn't change the basic situation. We crave freedom, but our ways of making sense lead to limits everywhere. Think of a baby that spends its first months confined in the womb, and then when it's born it immediately gets confined in a crib or a carrier. Our situation is like that. We move from one set of limits to another.

What happens to us in that situation? Even if we reach out to others, we are profoundly alone and lonely. We hide what truly matters deep inside, because we have no way to express it. We lose the ability to feel what we are feeling, and whatever we do feel just becomes another kind of limit. Thoughts set limits; feelings set limits. Eventually, we give up, and we go along. We start from the openness of space, but we end up limiting space itself. We turn it into territories, marked out by the borders that give identities. We zone space into domains where only certain kinds of activities or ways of knowing are allowed, and then we live within those zones.

This same pattern repeats on every level. When we look carefully, we see that each thought has its own zone, which is different from the zone established by every other thought. Each thought, each event has its own dimensions. It allows this and prevents that. Within each zone, certain ratios operate. For instance, the zoning determines how much happiness is allowed and how much sadness is inevitable.

Because in this process everything gets measured out, we could speak of this in terms of degrees and angles and points. But the experience itself is much more direct and the impact is immediate. We can only see the images that have been identified and the colors we are accustomed to. We can only think with the symbols we already know how to apply. We can only sense what our ordinary ways of sensing allow. For instance, when I am in the anger zone, I cannot experience joy. When I am feeling greedy, there is no space for compassion. When I am afraid, I cannot be truly generous. When I am worried, I cannot fully appreciate the sounds that reach my ears or the sights that unfold before my eyes. When I am preoccupied with selfish thoughts, I can hardly notice what is going for the person I am speaking to.

It is just this zoning that we need to open up. We are used to living in this way, and we may not think about it, but when we let our lives be regulated by zoning, it makes us small.

So that is why you suggest we expand our attention outward from the original point?

That's right. We want to expand outward from the center of the zone we find ourselves in. First we focus on the center, so that we become aware of how space has been shaped into precise forms, like wrinkles in fabric or ripples in water. Then, instead of trying to smooth out the wrinkles or calm down the ripples, we can expand them. Whatever zone you're in, even if it involves all sorts of negativity, start right there. Keep the feeling, keep the position you are stuck in, but stretch it out. Go to the edge of the edge; go to the edge of that edge; then go further. Go in and out, go to the bottom and the top, then go beyond. At that point you can ask: where is your zoning now? What are you still insisting on? What are you fighting for?

When we are trapped in a zone, we do not necessarily see it as being trapped. If we notice what is going on at all, we may have the sense that we are really focused. Sometimes being focused is helpful: for instance, when we are working on a specific project or maneuvering in a dangerous location. But more often, being focused just means that there is no way out. I have no choice; I can't do anything else. It's like people who feel compelled to wash their hands again and again, even though they know perfectly well that they have scrubbed them clean. In the same way, when we are caught in anxiety or desire, we keep cycling through the same mental reactions again and again. That's what it means to be trapped in a zone.

The image of ripples can help release this kind of fixation. Let whatever you are feeling ripple outward. Just be aware of the ripples. Again, you can focus on the inside or the outside or the edge or on up or down. The results can be dramatic. If you exercise attention, you discover that as soon as the ripples move, the character of the zone is already gone. It might be the zone of anger or pain, worry or tension. It might be positive instead of negative. In each case it works the same way.

So all I have to do is let the ripples expand outward, and I won't be trapped any longer?

You might say it that way. You might say, "I have done this, and now I am not trapped." But that is not entirely accurate. What is accurate is that the zone is no long operative in the same way. The change does not come from outside, based on something you have done. There is no doer. There are just very small variations, instant positions—field changes.

These possibilities can be applied to all negativities, all emotionalities. How you work with them is up to you. As you become more familiar with this approach, you can apply it to states of mind, to thoughts, to feelings, to sensations, to awareness. If you think of it as a technique, you could say it has many applications; it does not operate only in one field or one zone. It is more like an attitude, and you can bring that same attitude to every dimension of experience.

19

The Arising of Experience

If you expand the arising ripples and enter the field in a new way, the field itself may become your environment, undifferentiated, with no 'this' and no 'that'.

Ripples . . . focal settings . . . zones . . . now you're talking about fields. It's a lot to keep in mind. So . . . can you say more about this 'field' that we enter?

We might say that the field is fundamentally spacious and allowing. Beyond that, not much can be said, but we could speculate. For instance, it may be that the sensory inputs that define our usual world derive from this spacious ground. We could ask whether the potential for appearance emerges from this source, through a dynamic we cannot specify.

If we accept the undifferentiated field as the foundation for appearance, our own experience lets us trace out the shapes that emerge. At one level, there is the manifestation of awareness, thoughts, and sense experience. As the whole takes form, there is an interaction of subject and object. It is as though the dynamic of the field generated a force through which conventional experience and the structures that support it take form. Who accomplishes such remarkable creativity? We might think of the subject as the performer of the forms, but that cannot be completely right, because the subject itself is formed through the field dynamic.

Through the emerging dynamic, relationships are established. 'I' as the subject acts on objects. Following the dynamic in the opposite direction, experience happens to 'me'. Identities are assigned and recognition takes place. A power of polarity leads to possession. Within that structure, the 'I' reacts. It tries to grasp 'this' and push away 'that'. It likes or dislikes; it affirms or rejects.

Through such sequences, the undifferentiated field gives way to an established reality. The die is cast; the precise particulars fall into place. Just as moisture in the air will fall as snow or ice or hail depending on the conditions in effect, so different shapes and forms emerge based on the conditions in operation. In turn, their interactions condition other reactions, such as thoughts, feelings, and emotional manifestations. We could think of this as the 'I' relating to what it encounters. On the one hand, it reacts to what appears or what emerges; on the other, it establishes a whole range of further specifications. I may react to what appears with greed or lust or the wish to possess. I may recoil, trying to escape from contact. I may just tune it out, refusing either to acknowledge or engage.

We could think of these dynamics as a kind of gravitational force, pulling us this way or that way. If the dynamic goes one way, we fall victim to a grasping mentality. If it goes another, we react with anger, or willful blindness, or passive acceptance.

I don't think my inner life is that dramatic, at least not most of the time.

"Dramatic" may not be the right word. But consider what goes on when we decide for or against, yes or no. We pronounce our decision, but do we really know why we are deciding? When we see something and react against it, our reaction seems to happen instantly, almost before we have even recognized what we are seeing. But there are certainly stages. First comes the taking of a position, and then we identify with it and acknowledge it as 'mine'. The sense of liking or disliking seems to be part of the position, but what is the basis? We may like to imagine that when we decide one way or another, we are pulling together or summing up our knowledge of the whole situation, but can we really say that is so?

Logically, taking a position seems to depend on some sort of process, whether we think of it as rational or as happening at a more emotional level. But as we experience it, the force of conviction does not seem like an outcome; it seems to come instantly. It is as if someone somewhere had rung a bell, and as the resulting sound reverberates, the echoes shape our mind. We respond, but not at a conscious level. If you ask me why I decided for or against, I may well come up with various factors that went into my decision, but when I look more closely, it often seems I had no real intention, no basis for my reaction.

There are studies in psychology like that. People always tend to give reasons for their choices, even if they have been manipulated into making the choice by factors they are unaware of.

164

When I make an intentional decision, it's because I am aware of what I am saying or doing or thinking. For instance, I might be acting in accord with some plan, following the voice of my conscience, or responding to an argument I have built up in my own mind that convinces me of the right choice. But those kinds of situations are rare. If you look at your own experience, you will probably see that how you react mostly seems to be almost a matter of accident. Sometimes when you are sitting quietly, perhaps waiting for something, you may drum your fingers on the arm of your chair or bite your lip. Our reactions seem more like that. They just happen.

The same thing holds for thoughts. Sometimes when we are thinking, we follow a line of thought, a lineage that leads from one thought to the next. For instance, that might be what happens when we are solving a puzzle. But sometimes thoughts, or memories, just pop up. They seem to come from nowhere at all, with no basis. Perhaps a memory appears suddenly, or perhaps a new idea occurs to me. This is not a process that we seem able to control or even predict. The mind reacts like a guitar string that resonates to a sound in the air. A kind of energy manifests, and we are part of it. That is all there is to say.

Suppose we could learn how this process works. Could we control it? Could we shape the product that emerges? What a useful skill that would be! If we could open the dynamic, starting at the center and going to the edge, we would learn what new elements to introduce and how to do so. We would be like a biochemist who knew how to restore balance in our digestive tract, or an engineer who could determine the right metal brace to preserve the integrity of a bridge. Knowing how different events combine to produce certain mental states, we could apply the antidotes.

Imagine that we could apply such knowledge before concepts and language came into play, before perceptions sealed the identity of what was perceived; in other words, before the process itself, with its labels and cognitions, hijacked our ability to go to the root. Imagine that we could contact a knowledge that inwardly observed as new reactions popped up, not yet related to the structure of subject and object.

Such a knowing would be open to the flow of the elements that combine to make appearance; in fact, it would be a part of it. Knowing the variations, the ups and downs, focusing from the center, we would be like an expert surfer riding the waves of a stormy sea. Like a surfer, we could enjoy our experience as a sport, almost a contest. We could engage the senses without commitment. We could engage the face of thoughts, the dimensions of thoughts, the sense of thoughts, the awareness of thoughts. We could use whatever emerges skillfully and flexibly. We would be living with creative enjoyment: artists of life.

I like the surfer image. You could imagine that some waves would come along and you miss them, either because they are too small or for some reason you're not ready. Other waves would just come crashing in on you, and you would have to do some fancy footwork to keep from being smashed. Then there would be the waves you could ride, perfectly balanced, and it would be as though time was standing still.

I don't know if that's accurate, but it's a nice description. What we can say more definitely is that the approach we're describing would make a different kind of knowledge available. We could deal with thoughts and feelings in a different way. Of course, that's a misleading description, because you don't really 'deal' with thoughts and feelings, as though you were approaching them from outside.

Perhaps that's a problem with the image of the surfer. It's more as though the waves were also the surfer, with no separation.

What matters to me in this image is not the particulars; it's the idea that we could develop a different knowledge. A small child only has available the ways of knowing that her parents teach her: words, labels, and language. But we can develop a more mature way of knowing, one that is more fruitful, more creative, more enjoyable. You can try this out for yourself to see if it's so. It's a kind of skillful means.

Are you referring now to the Skillful Means teachings you've developed?

Not exactly, but there's a connection. What's skillful in this case is that emotionality does not affect us. We are not caught in the usual negative patterns.

This is not just a question of banishing the negativities we don't like: the anxiety, the stress, the craving and all the rest. It's not just about making concepts the enemy, or trying to overcome fear or turn away from our own bad behavior. It's true that neurotic patterns and emotionality are our enemy. If we can't find a way to deal with them, they will rule us and ruin us; they will bankrupt the projects we undertake, whether we do it for ourselves or for others. What we are talking about here, though, is a different approach to working with them.

So you're saying that our minds are not in our control; that unless we develop a different kind of knowledge, we cannot really choose how to live our lives. And you're suggesting how we could develop that knowledge.

When we don't look too closely, our lives seem to have a certain structure and order. We would say that we are headed in directions that we have chosen for ourselves. If circumstances are favorable, we may seem to be making progress. But when we look more closely, we realize that our minds are mostly jumping here and there, pulled one way by our desires, pushed another way by our fears or our emotions, our kleshas. We realize that we are constantly being thrown off balance. It may be very confusing and disorienting, because things seem much more chaotic than we thought.

It is like someone who rents an apartment and brings in nice furniture and puts paintings on the wall, and one day, wholly unexpected, they are evicted and their possessions are put out on the street. Only this is happening repeatedly, literally hundreds of times a day, or maybe hundreds of times an hour. Our attempts to impose order are really just a story we tell ourselves. And if we develop our ability to observe what is going on, the story may no longer be very convincing. It seems more accurate to say that our lives are a chaotic whirl—even if that's a story too.

That reminds me of a quote by the novelist Margaret Atwood. She wrote, "When you are in the middle of a story, it isn't a story at all, but only a confusion, a dark roaring, a wreckage of shattered glass and splintered wood, like a house in a whirlwind, crushed by the icebergs or swept over the rapids, and all aboard powerless to stop it. It's only afterwards that it becomes anything like a story at all, when you are telling it to yourself, or to somebody else."

Yes . . . that's good.

What we are talking about here starts from that realization, from acknowledging the chaos and the confusion. We don't want to turn away from the tricks and trials of the mind—the point is to learn how to make use of them. Nothing that happens in the stream of experience is inherently bad. If we know how to incorporate the mind-senses and the mind-thoughts and the mind-feelings, we can learn to work with all of them, even to enjoy them. After all, they are part of us.

If someone saw their reflection in a mirror or a lake for the first time, they might be very scared. Most animals are like that: if they see their image in a mirror, they think they are seeing an enemy, and they may try to attack. But someone who knows what he or she is seeing realizes there is nothing to be afraid of. It's the same way with mind. Whatever arises in the mind is part of our own expressions or impressions. What we are seeing is the reflections of mind, of self-image. Right alongside whatever appears to the mind, we see our tendency toward possessiveness: the automatic move to make it 'mine'.

This is actually a very interesting area to explore. The various forms and ways of manifesting that appear in the mind express very subtle movements. Can we see what is actually going on?

For instance, the way that language shapes experience?

Yes, that's part of it. Our experience is steadily being manufactured by the language we use for naming, the labels we apply, and the meanings we assign. Our possessiveness is intimately linked to dividing the world up into 'pro' and 'con'.

All of this is based on the workings of samsara. In Buddhism we speak of karma and klesha: our actions and our reactions. Depending on what pattern is most powerful at any time, karma and klesha may create joy or fear, worry or deep satisfaction. The mirror of mind has the potential to reflect all of this.

Just watching these patterns unfold without getting involved in them, without insisting on 'mineness', is already very helpful. But the mind's reflections also open into a dimension of depth. If we can follow them into this depth, we may discover an unknown language and a new way of knowing. This is not mysterious; it just depends on the feedback we receive when we look at what is really happening.

So the key is a different way of knowing.

Yes, but that may be too limiting. The kind of knowledge we're talking about is also a different way of being. It's a master key to being human; it lets us enter the storehouse where vast treasures are found everywhere. We can enjoy those treasures. We can really investigate mind activities and thought activities and sense activities. New knowledge leads to new abilities.

For instance, right now you may think you know what you are feeling, that you have immediate access to your feelings in a way that is accurate and undeniable. But we can learn to understand our feelings more deeply, both the feelings we experience and the feelings that operate unconsciously.

This is really very relevant to our present situation. It's like making an important discovery about your family tree. Suppose that before you did not know where your great grandfather came from, or your ancestors going many generations back. Now you do. You might say, "So what. Does it really matter?" In this case, the answer is yes. When we develop the ability to go into our thoughts and feelings and meanings more deeply, we can discover the ratios that shape our reality.

Engaging the ripples of the mind is potentially very important. Don't take it lightly. It's a way of engaging the whole. A vast knowledge becomes available.

Can you say more? What new knowledge becomes available?

We can ask a whole different set of questions. Where does the language we use come from? What knowledge do we rely on? Can we be sure that it is reliable in the ways we imagine? How do we develop our sense of identity? What is the source of the energy that lets us produce all these mental constructs?

There is so much that we take for granted in the ways we approach the world. For instance, would you say that you have a self? Probably the answer is yes. But are you sure?

I understand some of the reasons to be suspicious, but in terms of my own experience, if I'm honest, it does seem as though the self is really there, and that it's in charge of what I do and think.

Is the self the same as the ego?

I don't know. I suppose it's partly a matter of definition.

Yet you're willing to throw those words around as if you really understood what they meant. The same question holds for the 'I'. Is it the same as the self? The ego?

Then there is the mind. How is the self related to the mind? Does the self control the mind, or does the mind control the self? Do thoughts just arise in the mind, or do I think them? What is going on when I take possession of a thought or a memory, and automatically proclaim it to be mine? How do I carve out the territory that the 'I' seems to inhabit? Are the boundaries of my territory also the boundaries of 'me' or 'mine'?

Those are the kinds of questions we may now be able to investigate. I suppose science would agree that there are many things about self and mind and experience that we have not yet discovered. But the methods of science may not give us very useful ways to explore such questions. Going into the ripples of the mind gives you a way to start on this kind of exploration. You can investigate, and you can describe to yourself what your investigations reveal, even if the descriptions may not depend on language in the usual ways. As you get more clear on what is going on, the investigations themselves give you feedback, which means you get more insight into how the mind is working and how you make sense of things.

One way to think of the exploration we are talking about is as an exploration of the field of space. Within the field, knowledge can become vast. It can engage the time of what we express. It can feed back to our own inquiry the knowingness that makes knowledge possible.

20

Working with Zones

When we are in a zone, we automatically set limits. Specific dimensions and points specify the field. They lead to thoughts and meanings, and they give shape and form to what we experience. In other words, the zoning we accept structures our lives. Of course, we would like the structure to unfold in terms of a life that is happy, healthy, successful, and knowledgeable, but if our knowledge does not extend to understanding the basic structures, we are leaving that to chance. That seems like too much of risk. We can't afford not to question.

I just want to clarify. When you talk about being in a zone, it's not the same as when people say they are 'in the zone', right? That's thought of as very positive, as moving beyond our ordinary experience.

It's not a question of positive or negative. The structures we're talking about go deeper than that. So if 'being in the zone' means something that is always positive, then this is different. Of course, it may just be a question of applying the same word in completely different ways.

OK, thank you.

Now, we've already talked about the way to work with zones. The first step is to realize we are in a zone. We actually move from one zone to another very quickly, so in the beginning we may want to choose a single zone to work with, probably one that recurs often or that seems to be looming large in our experience right now. For instance, if you have been feeling discouraged about some area of your life, that would be a possible zone to work with.

When you focus on the zone, the basic questions are how it arises and how it works.

Does 'how it arises' mean looking for the cause or explanation? Wouldn't that be conceptual?

Yes, it would. We are not looking for the cause. Causality takes place within the zone. It's more seeing how it emerges: the mechanism. Asking 'how it works' is also not meant to be a precise inquiry, like asking how a piece of machinery works. It's more getting a general sense. "Now I'm in this zone: what's going on, what's involved?"

Can you be more specific about working with zones? For instance, could you go through an example of how you would do it?

That would probably be counterproductive. People are so different—you have to work it out for yourself. But it's really not that difficult. Once you know what you're looking for, what it means to be in a zone, you begin to recognize the different elements. Then it's just a question of exploring as fully as you can. In any case, it's not so important what the 'content' of a particular zone is. It's zone-awareness that matters.

So let's move on. Suppose you have been able to explore what it's like to be in a particular zone. The next stage or level is to do the same practice as you move through zones. Engage each zone, one by one.

Isn't there a problem here? You just pointed out that we move through zones very quickly. One moment I'm aware of my breath, the next moment I'm thinking about lunch. If I try to engage each zone, I'll get overwhelmed. Or else I'll just lose track, or get confused. I don't see how to do it.

Don't think in terms of linear time. It's not as though each moment is its own zone. If you have a sense that some thought or experience went by too quickly for you to notice, then that sense itself is the zone. It's not that you missed the chance to investigate; it's that now the focus of your investigation has shifted.

But isn't it true that something slipped away before I could take it in?

Not exactly. Here you are, in the present, which means you're in a zone. A part of the present zone may be a sense that something has been lost. But really, there's no 'thing' that has been lost. Being in the zone means being in immediate experience. You don't need to worry about what's somewhere else; for instance, at some other moment in time. Is that clear?

I think so.

Good, because at this point in working with zones, there's an important shift. As you get more familiar with each arising zone, eventually you can discover within each zone the dimensions of the zoning space.

Dimensions?

Yes. You could also say 'aspects'. For instance, physical space has three dimensions. In the same way, a zone unfolds in various ways: physical, mental, temporal; it's almost like all the constituent parts, but the relationship is not a part/whole relationship.

When you get clear on the various dimensions, that's something like the foundation. From that foundation you can move out again. It's like taking stock of where you are: from within the zone, you extract the operations of the zone. You can see how the different elements manifest, how the principal foundations are conducted forward. You can see how forms manifest and how energy becomes available. You can see how actions take place, how the sequences and consequences reflect each other.

In this way of seeing, there is a kind of equality of whatever arises. You can look in the same way at all thoughts and all sense experience. You can look at your conviction that 'I am the decision-maker', or the sense, 'I have a fixed identity'. Gradually, you can clarify for yourself what it means to say 'I', and how mind and mine, self and awareness relate to each other.

So now you're able to investigate the really fundamental questions, the ones you were naming before?

Yes. For instance, does the mind possess whatever I call mine . . . or is mind itself mine? We usually look for answers to these questions—all questions, really—by relying on meanings we have already constituted and labels we have already assigned. We apply the labels to the various states we experience: happy and sad, negative, positive, and neutral, distracted, chaotic, lost, uninterested, or simply confused. We conduct our activities based on these labels.

All that is not so helpful. We are just conforming to the different dimensions of the zoning mind. As the mind enters different zones, limits are set and points and dimensions are specified. From those basics come character.

You mean my own character?

That's part of it. But more fundamentally, the character of the zone we find ourselves in.

When we begin to sense the character of the zone, we may notice certain interrelationships, or ratios. We need to investigate these ratios forward and backward. How is one aspect related to another? What is the angle of their relation: 60 degrees? 30 degrees? What are the ratios that govern positive, negative, and neutral, or rightness or wrongness? What is the ratio of me to mine, or I to mind?

It sounds like you're not using the idea of ratio in its usual mathematical sense.

Ratios give a way to point out meanings and connections. For instance, there is the ratio of past to present, which manifests in memories and the significance they have for us. Does the ratio of past to present affect our ability to cope with what we are facing now? Does it sustain a fear of losing what we possess? What is the ratio of the present to the future? Do we engage the future in terms of degrees of danger? Do we anticipate future developments as likely to be positive or negative? Exploring these interconnections, we may discover ways to change our situation in positive ways.

Asking questions—whether we think in terms of ratios or not—gives a way to convert the zone we find ourselves in. It allows for a greater flexibility in the dimensions that the zone establishes and the angles of interaction that the zone supports. Usually our projections and our thoughts manifest in characteristic ways that are shaped by the zones we inhabit. Now we can explore the self-projections of such thoughts. Perhaps we can learn something about how the self reveals itself and conceals itself within the zone. Once we can allow for greater flexibility, we have a chance to develop different forms of cognition. We can rely on a different dynamic, a different mode of learning. The feedback that comes through inquiry into the zone can become another useful tool.

With this kind of inquiry, we gradually we become masters of each zone. For each new zone we enter, we can point out what is going on. We discover that we can exercise each point in a spacious way, tasting a special freedom. Don't you think that's a worthy outcome?

I have to ask again: can you give some specific examples? When you start talking about ratios and angles, I feel lost.

Feeling lost is a zone too. You feel you are lost, or confused, or don't know the meaning. Those are all different kinds of zoning, or maybe the same zone approached through different words. Instead of just accepting that reaction, look at it in terms of the field. Can you go there?

Let's agree that you're in a zone. How can you measure that zone? How can you investigate its unfolding, from the beginning to now? Does the zone have a top and a bottom? Are there any directions in the zone at all? Does it have edges? Are there points you can target in the zone? Is there a gravity at work that gives the zone its uniqueness? Within the zone what positions are you holding on to; for instance, 'my problem' or 'my property' or 'my reality'?

You can think of this as an exercise, or you can think of it as an investigation. In a way the two are the same. That's because the investigation itself, the way we are looking, could be the self-reflection of the zone. If we are smart and sharp and fast, the investigation into the zone works like a mirror, reflecting the zone.

When you look for ratios, it's not like looking for the answer to an arithmetic problem, and it's also not like following a recipe. Each investigation is its own exercise. A new situation comes up: what happens? As you enter into it, how can you expand or deepen your inquiry? How do you examine your own situation? How can you apply your inquiry to the past of that situation? How do you plan for the future? Can you come up with your own exercise to look more closely? Can you see how the situation you are in depends on being within a particular zone?

From one perspective, your investigation reflects back the subject who is doing the investigating. In that case the subject is also the reflector. Without the subject, no image can appear.

That is why investigating the zone is so helpful: we need the conditions of the zone to get feedback. The basic environment is like clear crystal, or the depth of the ocean: there is nothing there to reflect. The properties that manifest in the zone are what project back to our inquiry, like an echo. Our investigation needs to accommodate that dynamic. It needs to bring the projection together with the feedback, so that they both show up in the mirror. When we look at them together in that way, it's hard to say which is echo and which is the projector, to say which one is responsible. Does only one of them carry the enduring power of the zone, or is it their interplay? Is the zoning itself a dimension of the way that manifestation reflects itself?

21

No Positions

Let's go back to the practice of starting in the center. First there is development; we talked about that. Eventually, something is labeled: an object. Something is there, the 'ness' of the object. The chair has its chairness, etc.

Is a situation also an object? For instance, the 'here' in 'Here I am': my surroundings.

Yes, it can work that way.

Now, as soon as there is an identified object, the subject responds or reacts. For instance, "I don't like that chair, because it hurts my back when I sit in it. Or, "I have no friends, so I'm upset, I'm sad and lonely."

Notice that the story doesn't matter so much. The story lets you explain to yourself why you are feeling the way you do, but that is a layer that's added on. It's the feeling, the reaction, that's at the center.

Now you are sad: that is the mark of the situation. You might even say it's the 'ness' of the situation; for instance sad-ness or lonely-ness. Once that identity is there, you have to protect it. If someone says, "I don't believe you're sad," you reject that idea. "No, I'm really sad." The reality of the situation has been settled. That is the 'thatness' of the situation.

In the situation we are describing, sadness is in the center. It is not just that you identify what you are feeling from outside, or that your experience is 'about' being sad. The feeling of the sadness is in the center. This means that you don't need to go to the center, because you are already there. Going to the center would not really be going anywhere at all.

Wherever we are, whatever we are experiencing, that is the center. After all, it's *my* center we are talking about—my experience. I am not separate from the center, because I am having that experience, and I am identified with that experience. I feel and see and notice within the experience. The field is the field of my experience, and my identity is not separate from being in that field.

The practice is just to be in the middle of that. Don't let it go. Just sit there. The more you sit, the more you sink into it, the more it opens up. And after a while—it may not take long—it begins to move. It ripples outward, through the whole field. You are still in the center, but now the center is expanding, rippling outward.

When the experience ripples outward like that, there is a real shift. Before, you identified your feeling and you reacted to it, maybe through grasping it or maybe through pushing it away. But when you stay in the center of the feeling, holding it as it is, there is immediately a sense of calm or quiet. The movement of the ripple loosens up. Without the intense grasping, the ripple itself calms, like ripples on the surface of a lake that gradually subside. You are in the center and of the center, and that means it's all a little different than it was before.

That sounds very positive, very healing. I think I've had such experiences. But I often have a problem before I reach that stage. Suppose I'm sad. I may know that I'm sad. I may even realize that because I'm feeling sad, the world seems like a very gray, dark place. But I don't really feel the sadness. It's as though I'm blocking it off. What I feel is more like a dullness. Maybe you could call it depression, because I'm pressing the experience down.

Perhaps what you're describing is one of your standard psychological patterns. But it may also be an example of a typical problem in the West. You think that you have to identify what's going on—give it a label—and that when you do, you know everything there is to know about the situation. So you end up with the label, but you've lost contact with the center.

Westerners are trained in that kind of conceptual or intellectual approach. I don't mean that all Westerners are intellectuals. What I'm referring to is that tendency to substitute the label or concept for the experience in the center. That's what you've learned. It's how you've been trained.

If that is your situation, you can work with it. Just go into the center of your conceptual grabbing. In the center of your experience, you are busy recognizing what's going on, giving it an identity. So let that activity be the center.

When you do that, it can get very interesting. You may notice that there is a disconnect between the identity you assign and the experience. For instance, suppose I come across a barking dog and my reaction is to feel afraid. Now, in fact I know that dog and I know that it is not really angry or vicious; it just likes to bark. But I still feel fear, even when I tell myself I don't have to be afraid. Something in the whole situation, which is the object of my experience, produces my fear reaction. Perhaps it comes from past experiences with dogs. You may think you know or you may not. It doesn't really matter.

This is a different approach from going to the center of the feeling—the fear or sadness, for instance—and feeling it fully, because you are saying that may not be possible. You completely accept the label, and now all you have access to is the label. By applying the label, you give your feeling an identity. Now you react to that identity instead of the feeling.

Yes, that's what is bothering me. You're saying to start from the center of the feeling. But I'm not inside the feeling. I'm still on the outside.

'Inside' and 'outside': what does that distinction really mean? You may not be inside the feeling of sadness, but you are always in the center. There's really no way to get outside the center. If you feel that you are outside the feeling, then be in the center of feeling outside.

What's confusing you is that are taking the position of the commentator, interpreting your experience, projecting your own reaction. You tell yourself that your experience is about this, or about that. That way, you convince yourself that you are not in the center, but it's not true. You are always in the center.

184

But don't we need to say that experience is 'about' something? If we couldn't say that, if we didn't know how to apply labels, we literally wouldn't know what we're talking about. When we say that our experience is about something, we're organizing experience. We're saying, "This belongs over here." And that seems essential. In fact, without that operation, we wouldn't have an identity either. We need to know who we are, where we belong.

OK, let's agree that the mind works that way. Once you understand that this move is inevitable, that you have no choice, then there is no problem. You just need to remember that even while you are busy being the commentator, you are still in the center. Yes, we need to interpret and explain—we need to rely on that kind of knowing. We depend on words and images, on identifying and labeling and projecting and conceptually grasping. Some people rely on that kind of mental operation more, some less.

The problem comes when we think that all this secondary activity is fundamental. It's natural to do that, especially here in the West, because that is how you have been taught. You have learned that this kind of understanding is what lets us make sense of the world. It's what makes our experience meaningful. If something does not have any meaning, it's meaningless, and then why should we care?

If that is how you see things, if you truly believe that your only choice is to rely on your interpretations, you are forgetting that you are in the center. Of course, you might do that deliberately. You may think that somehow not being in the center gets you off the hook. But the motivation is not so important. We all tend to go in this direction. Even if we say that we want to let go of all our interpretations and just rely on direct experience, that is still an interpretation—a pretty popular one!

What we are looking at is very different. Here I am, convinced that I have no choice, that I have to rely on interpretations. I have my own identity, and I assign identities to everything I encounter. In that way, everything is cast in place. My job is to wrestle experience in that mold. OK, fine. That is the place to start. The no-choice one is the center. I can use that; in fact, I have to use that, because that is the center. Each cognition, each observation, each projection and meaning-making can be the center, rippling outward. The interpretation itself is the ripple. The ripple is its own messenger.

I understand that —

Wait! Be careful! If you say you understand, that is an interpretation.

But we're basing ourselves on the idea that interpretations are necessary.

We're accepting that this is your understanding, or a very common understanding. You're saying that interpretations are like your feet, and you need your feet to walk. But that doesn't mean it's so. Walking is all the feet you need.

This is subtle. There are many dimensions, maybe four or five. So we have to go slowly. It's not that it's so difficult, but it goes directly against our usual understanding, our usual way of knowing.

Suppose you say, "I don't want to rely on interpretation and concepts. I'm tired of an intellectual approach. It hasn't got me anywhere. I feel unhappy and incomplete. I want to be more alive." This is good, because it means you understand something about the limits on our standard ways of knowing. But look at what's going on. You have adopted a new position: you're tired of your old approach and you are looking for something different. What are you looking for? You don't know. So you're in the realm of speculation. Speculation has its place, but if you try to build on it, you're very close to delusion.

That doesn't seem fair. You say I can only speculate about other ways of being or experiencing, but that's not true. When I meditate deeply, or when my heart fills with love, or when something beautiful moves me, I get a glimpse of another way of being. I understand that I don't have to stay stuck. That's what I'm aiming for. It's not just a fantasy or speculation.

That's just the problem! The kinds of experiences you describe can be very positive and inspiring. But when you have a glimpse of something higher or deeper or more fulfilling, you automatically reject the rest of your experience. It's just another way to try to move out of the center.

You would like to develop a different way of understanding, but that's not necessary. Even not understanding is useful if you let it be the center. There is no reason to reject the feelings that you label as negative or limiting.

Remember that light depends on dark. That is not just a logical point. The darkness of not understanding manifests the inspiration of light. It's easy to get lost in polarity, but we have the opportunity to see without polarity.

Let's approach this a different way. You are feeling dissatisfied, and the thought comes, "Don't worry; there's a way to change what you're feeling. All you need is different images, or maybe different memories. Here are some suggestions. Give them a try." But that's still just a thought. Is it really useful? If we try to change our interpretations with a different interpretation, we will get stuck in an endless loop. It's not easy to understand that, because it's exactly our lack of understanding that traps us in the loop.

Instead of going through all those complications, which may not lead anywhere, just stay in the center and follow out the ripples. The one who is lost or dissatisfied is the center. Start from there. The one who rejects your own experience or wants to avoid negativity, the one who is afraid of where this might lead: make each one the center.

It might help if you said something about how it feels to be in the center.

When you stay in the center, ripples open and release in very valuable ways. The nature of the field is not what matters: it might be shaped through dimensions of thought or dimensions of mind; it might be the field of sensory awareness or embodiment, or it might be a field of subtle impressions that cannot be put into words. In each and every case, we can open the field. Starting from the center, you can let the ripples expand. As they do, the frozen structures put in place by language and concepts melt away. Whatever arises becomes part of a flawless flow. You enter a spacious, open environment, a kingdom of universal accommodation. Each point—destruction or creation, joy or sadness—becomes the center. Whatever angles emerge from the center become centerless; whatever lines of force emanate also become ripples.

What about the 'I'? Is the 'I' also in the center?

The 'I' has a particular role to play. It is the one who says "yes" to this and "no" to that. That 'I' is in the center. But that does not mean the 'I' is located in a particular place. Like everything else that appears, the 'I' is also nowhere. Being in the center, we begin to see experience in this way.

It is not just the 'I'. That is one dimension, but the same dynamic or rhythm operates in any manifestation, any thought, any minding, any sensation. Every point opens, and every 'open' is interesting and wholly accommodating. Wherever I am, I find myself 'in'.

Part Four

In the Center

21

What it Means to Conquer Samsara

It seems to me that at this point we've conquered samsara, because nothing that appears in samsara is excluded. Are you satisfied?

I don't know about that. Maybe I'm just holding on to my 'I' and my 'mine', but I still have some questions. First, are you saying that since every position and every experience is 'in' the center, there's no point in doing anything or trying to bring about change?

Do you feel that you are always in the center? Is that your sense?

No, it's not. A lot of the time I don't feel like I'm anywhere at all.

Then there's probably something to do. At least, that's how it feels.

At the level we are exploring, nothing is excluded. But that's not the way the world sees it, so until there is a fundamental shift in understanding, there is work to be done. Bringing about that shift is a big project, and we need to go step by step. That is the mission we can be ready to take on.

As human beings, we all go around making our individual claims. We identify one thing as my property and we reject something else as having nothing to do with me. We react to our own impressions and expressions, and we identify entities.

Suppose that instead we understood all these appearances as ripples expanding from the center. As a symbol for this, imagine that each ripple is smiling, relaxed and at home, free from concerns. It would be a remarkable change. Every problem would be automatically solved, not just now but in the past and future as well. We could carry forward an abundance of knowledge as our gift to future generations. It may be that nobody understands this, but again, not understanding is useful. It's a place to start.

Now, you could also do it differently. For instance, you could insist on your own not-understanding and make this your position. That would not be very helpful. Or you might say that what we are talking about is too easy, or meaningless, because it does not involve anything we can grasp or take hold of. But if you approach your not-understanding in a more relaxed way, you see that you are already in the center. You are part of the party, central to the celebration. You are inseparable from an ongoing procession, a rhythm that exhibits what in some systems might be called ultimate reality, the source of all creation.

Mind has its own version of not-understanding. On that basis, mind creates multiples: words, language, concepts, knowledge, philosophy, technology, religion, faith, images,

meanings, labels. But if you are able not to understand all
these creations, you see that nothing is excluded. And if
something *is* excluded, that is included too. That is why we
can say that samsara is bankrupt, that it no longer has any
hold on us.

But nothing has changed!

That's a belief you have. Are you really willing to worship at
the shrine of that belief?

When you say "Nothing has changed," you are excluding
what hasn't changed from the center. You are creating a label,
based on language and conceptual knowledge. Not only that,
but you're naming a nothing that has a shape and form, like
an existing physical object. You are projecting that reality.

You could think of it this way. Your mind says, "Something
needs to change." Or it may say, "I need to change." You
need to focus right there, on the mind that is making that
claim. If you lose that focus, the conversation can never get
started. You have missed the point.

Do you think you haven't taken a position? Then that is your
position. Do you think you did take a position? You never
did. That is what it means to stay in the center. You may not
like it that you have lost your position, so you take an opposite position, pointing out the opposite. That is fine. Stay in
the center of your pointing out. Do not dismiss it or exclude.
Remember, you are the agent of the point-maker.

I don't know what to say.

Right! You have lost your position. That's a new position:
you're the loser.

I'm not just playing games with words here. When I say that you're the loser, I mean that in the kind of transformation I'm describing, you are not getting any benefit. Your investment is lost, because there's nothing for you to grab on to, to take hold of—not even a position. But who told you that you have to have a position? Do you really need another position? You are already carrying so many positions, without realizing it. You are carrying pain and guilt and sorrow; you are carrying confusion and worry and fear; you are carrying projections and ideas and a sense that something is missing. Wherever you look, in every corner, you find another position.

Your problem is that you are not ready to give up your positions. You worry that if you lose your positions, you will have nothing left and no protectors. So you look for protectors, and that leads you to take up other positions. You look to your friends as protectors, or your body, or your little thoughts and fantasies. Even fear and worry and guilt can be your protectors if you approach them a certain way. Your positions are your protectors, and your protectors are positions.

Take fear as an example. When fear is your position, you hold on to it tightly, so tightly that everything is frozen in place and nothing can move. The fear emanates a kind of aura that spreads everywhere, in all directions. The same is true for any position, any protector. With fear, because you are afraid, you cannot act. The same is true of sickness or pain. Because you are sick, or because you are in pain, change is impossible. The position makes that clear.

That is where positions leave you, squeezed into a corner. The voices of your protectors tell you what you need, what is missing: savings, friends, good health, and so on. They point you in the direction you need to go. It all sounds reasonable. But it all stays within the loop. It leaves you with no possibilities for freedom.

All this is happening all the time, 24 hours a day. At night, you take positions in your dreams: shadows, fears, fantasies. During the day, there are concepts and worries and jobs to do. There are positives and negatives, pros and cons. The positions are completely in control. You can't ever breathe freely. There is no room for finding ease, because every position is occupied in advanced. Everywhere you turn, identities close you in: the identity of self, of 'me', of 'me-ness' and 'I-ness'. Behind everything, there is the identity of 'mind-ness', setting it all up, telling you, "Be careful, don't lose that!"

If you could see what was happening, you would be right to complain, because your protectors have become your enemies. The rhythm of ripples becomes the zig-zag of linear time, one moment after the next. Between moments, there are more moments. You are in the middle of all that, but there is nothing in it for you. You have no choice, and no possibility of calling a halt.

But if you are saying we need to go beyond that, it seems as though you are pointing to some grand position, a position beyond all positions, where you could finally find a resting place.

I think you know better than that. This is not about positions. The target, if you want to call it that, is 'behind' all the dimensions within which we assign positions. How do we get to that behind? More important, how can there be communication with what is behind or beyond? Who is the communicator? What is the link between 'here' and

196

'beyond'? It seems that for there to be a link, someone has to be standing with one foot on each side of the divide. But of course, that is only our way of talking. 'Beyond' is not a position, and it doesn't give you a place to stand.

So then is this about taking no positions?

You have to be careful. 'No positions' is also based on position. 'Beyond positions' is not like that. If you look at a map, you might say that to go beyond, you have go somewhere: beyond the river, beyond the ridge, beyond that mountain, beyond every landmark you can name. But we are talking about a different kind of 'beyond': beyond ripples, beyond dimensions.

Think again about the one who communicates from 'beyond'. What does the communicator stand for? Who stands behind the communicator? Who is communicating the presence of the communicator?

Do you see the difficulty? Go back to the image of having one foot on each side of the divide—the position side and the no-position side. For that image to make sense, 'no-position' has to be based on having a position. I say "no position," but when I do that, I am projecting my own position. The mind is thinking about what it means for the mind not to be thinking.

This is exactly what we are doing all the time: always circling in a loop. I take a position and I insist that my position is not a position. I point that out. Of course, when I point it out, I am taking a position.

You're saying that every time I take a position, the result is that I get caught in a loop. But what if I know that I'm taking a position? Doesn't that knowledge let me break out of the loop? If not, how do I ever get free of positions?

The problem is not with taking a position. The problem is with claiming that when I identify my own position, that means I'm not caught in a position. Certainly, when you make a point, you have a right to point. But who is the one who points out the pointing out? Who is making that connection? Who is the translator?

23

Pointing the Center

When you point something out, you are saying you understand something. If you go on to point out that you are pointing out, you are saying that you understand something about your having understood. It doesn't really change anything. You haven't broken out of the loop. There is understanding and not understanding. There is solving the problem and not solving the problem. There is day and night or shadow and light.

We rely on these distinctions. That's just how we think. But how does that whole structure get set up? When the pointer points, it's not pointing at itself, but it's still setting itself up. It's still taking a position at the center. All positions are like that. Every position is the center. Every pointing, every identity, every meaning is the center.

Is this the same as the 'center' you were talking about earlier? Is the pointer who points out also in the center?

That's right. We're always in the center. Your opinion that the pointer is in the center is also in the center.

So it's more accurate to say that there is no pointer, that the pointing out is the pointer?

Yes. And seeing is the pointer, and saying is the pointer, and knowing is the pointer. When feedback specifies the meaning, that is the pointer. Any kind of label or pronouncement is the center. The center is the pointer, and the pointer is the center.

Do you get that?

No!

Then 'no' is the center.

But we're not just playing with words, right?

It's not just a matter of words, or theory, or speculation. How could it be, when any speculation or theory is also the pointer? How could it be, when the watching is also the watcher?

This is not about words. It has real consequences. 'No' in the center makes possible 'yes'. Living your life this way makes a difference. That's the sense in saying that 'no' makes possible 'yes'.

You say 'no', but your 'no' is different. It's still inside the loop. When you are in the loop, there is no going outside the loop. There is nothing that can be added to the loop, because whatever you add will be in the loop too. Even expanding the loop stays within the loop.

So is there anything to do?

Yes and no. The loop itself ripples. Duality ripples. The ripple ripples. The upside of the ripple and the downside of the ripple and the center of the ripple—they all ripple.

Ask yourself, do the distinctions we rely on make any sense? Take 'layers'. If I hand you a glass of water, is there one layer of the water that is 'really' water, and other layers that are not? Or take 'sides'. If I am in space and travel east and look back to the west, is the west empty and the east not? Is there a bottom side of space, or a beginning side? The whole idea of layers or sides doesn't make sense. We can say the same thing for every point or any pointer. They may all have different dimensions or accelerate at different speeds, but they are all within the center. That's why I said in *Time, Space, and Knowledge* that one point is all points.

If all points are in the center, and the center is itself a kind of ripple, it's possible to relax each ripple. When you relax the ripple, it opens up. What happens to those points then? Eventually we realize that 'completely open' is all there is.

Let me ask you: does it make sense to you to say that without space there could be no shape or form?

I think so. I mean, there are lots of philosophical ideas about whether space is even real.

I'm not asking you to think about philosophy. I'm asking you to imagine a reality without space. In that reality, could shape and form ever emerge?

OK, I'm trying to imagine that. . . . I don't know if I really can. . . But my answer would be "No." I don't think you could ever get to shape and form without space.

OK, let's accept that as your answer. It makes a certain sense; it may be true. But perhaps that's just the first level. If you could someday go to another level, you might realize that the question does not make sense at all. Why? Because space is not true, and some kind of emptiness behind space is also not true. In fact, 'from' and 'to' are not true, so 'behind' can't be true either. At this level, the loop is also not true. Now, can you relax a little?

Are you saying that 'true' itself is something we make up?

Saying 'true' is for the sake of convenience. Everything is the center, but we point out. Our pointing out is also the center, but whenever we make a pronouncement about what is being pointed out, we start something in motion. That starting point becomes the ripple. The ripple is also the center, but we have learned to think that it is not. We might say it becomes the edge. So now we begin to establish a 'where', a place we are. We might grasp the top of the ripple, or the side of the ripple, or move beyond the ripple to reach the other side of the ripple. One way or the other, we make the ripple into the basis for zoning. We cast our thoughts into the ripple, and we cast a fixed reality, which we call true. It's just the ripple, though. It's not something else, something more substantial.

This all seems very abstract. Maybe it's the language you're using: ripples and points and zones. I don't know how to think that way.

The one who can't tell what this means is another ripple. But we are not using conceptual language. We are also not aiming at some kind of insight into how things really are. That would all be at the 'truth' level. The target here is more internal, more intrinsic. You could speak of it as a kind of realization or understanding, but of course that's just a description, and it's bound to mislead.

We are not talking here about getting to a deeper understanding, or making progress on a path. There are no stages, no plateaus, no levels. We don't need to find a ladder so that we can climb up higher and see more. We don't need to arrive anywhere.

I think I see: there nowhere to go and nothing to do. But if I look at my own reaction, I'm not feeling more free as a result—I'm feeling more trapped. You have me cornered.

OK, you're in a corner. But you know, there isn't any corner. You're saying you give up, you surrender, but there is nothing to surrender and no one to surrender to. Don't forget what we were saying before: when there's no holding, it's all completely open.

That's why it makes sense to speak of freedom. If there is no holding on, there are no worries or fear, no guilt and no pain. The dualistic mind can't operate. The regime of samsara cannot control you, and the armies of samsara cannot attack you. When the Buddha was sitting under the Bodhi Tree before his enlightenment, the armies of Mara attacked him; they marshalled all their demonic forces. It's really a chilling description: demons taking every imaginable form, everything horrible and fearsome and disgusting. But the Buddha was completely unmoved. He was not holding on, not trying to arrive anywhere. So the demons had nothing to attack.

When the center opens, it's like that. Nothing belongs to you, and so you belong to everything. Everything is expendable. There is not even the arrogance of having no position, or the laziness of nothing to be done. There is not even victory over samsara. There is no one to convince and nothing to demonstrate.

Of course, this may not be your position. But once a while, you may let go of the usual positions. At that time, you may be able to see the heritage of samsara: so much sadness and anger, so much guilt and pain and ignorance. Those are just reflections, but they can be very powerful.

I can almost imagine that kind of experience, but it seems far beyond me.

That's because you're skeptical. 'Skeptical' is also a position: it means that you love to fool yourself.

But wait—'skeptical' means just the opposite: it means you're on guard against being fooled.

Yes, but still you fool yourself. How? By sitting with a concept. You look for what's being pointed instead of looking for the pointer.

Really, you just need to go to the instant 'thatness'. Your problem is that you don't know where 'thatness' comes from. It's not that things 'are' a certain way or have a certain identity. We project those kinds of structures: 'yes' to this and 'no' to that. Can you just let go of all that?

Try seeing whatever appears as ripples, expanding out from the center. That may help you out. Even the appearance of ripples is ripples. Eventually you are drawn into space: space shows space into space.

At that time, can you still find the mind? Not exactly, but you can see the ripple, which means that you can see that

'that' is 'that'. The point pretends there is a point, and instantly 'I am pointing' is established. That's fine, but it's the ripple of the pointer. That is the secret intrinsic. Seeing it as that is very hard, but only because we are committed to a linear way.

How can we undermine the linear way? I know you say it's a kind of instant seeing, but is there some kind of practice that could help? A certain meditation?

Meditation is beside the point. We are not talking about a way of seeing that you develop when you practice sitting in a corner somewhere. We are talking about every corner, every instant, every expression. We are not interested in legends of great practitioners in the past. This is all the time. After all, when did space start? When did time start? How about knowledge? Was there a beginning? Is there a place we need to get to? Those are the questions to ask—at least at one level.

Taking a linear approach, looking for a path, creates all sorts of obstacles. It means we have to use words to explain, even when we know that whatever we say is lies. If we want to have a positive influence on others, it seems we have to do it that way because somehow we need to convince people. But can we ever really convince them? People listen, they reflect, and they say "Yes, yes." They take your meaning. But because they have a linear approach, it's still just based on belief or on principles that they accept. It's based on 'truth'. So they find themselves looking for reality and ultimate truth. That's the only way to be convincing. It's the only way for what's meaningful to 'take place'.

We seem to be back to the same point—there's no way out.

There's no need to get out. That's a prejudice. Getting out may be getting in. It's much more basic than you seem to think. Your responsibility is not to get somewhere. Your responsibility is to free yourself completely. Yes, it sounds like a big job. But it has big value too. That's the way to have an impact. When you understand that, everything is ok.

When you develop knowledge of mind, you see the expressions of the mind as a deeply interesting exhibition. This is what some traditions call "lila." It's a celebration, and the more you understand, the more you celebrate. This is a kind of unique position. From there you can communicate with others. You can lead them, and you can overcome all obstacles.

Is that position real? Yes, if you know 'thatness'; if you know the witness itself. That kind of experience or realization lets you pause. It gives a certain deep security.

24

Ways to Work with Mind

O nce you are inside the circle—in the center—think-ing is part of the process, part of the practice. From inside, you don't really need to separate out different pro-jections. But at the beginning, you are in the zone, so you need to look more carefully. You need to separate out the dimensions of thought, and you need to look carefully at the nature of perception.

Each perception has a very dynamic character. This is so for every sensory field. You could say that each perception has its own specific level, or its own form of expression. That is what the zoning establishes. For instance, in each percep-tion the subject, the one who perceives, has already been produced. Once that's so, the dynamic can take many dif-ferent forms. For instance, there may be a movement toward anger, or toward some other sense of emotionality.

If you look more carefully, you see that every perception has two sides. In perception, something is noticed. What is no-ticed is the object: there is a movement that goes out *to* the object. At the same time, there is the one who is doing the noticing. We usually say that's the 'I', but it doesn't matter; it's enough to know that 'somebody' is doing the noticing. That somebody is involved in a certain set of circumstances, and the perception relates back to those circumstances. For instance, there may be a memory associated with the perception, based on identity and recognition, and that may produce an emotional response.

We sometimes say that this reactive side is the subjective dimension of experience, but that's very misleading. The reaction we have to an object is just as much a part of the object as the identity of the object.

That's not the way I was taught to think about it. In Western philosophy there's a distinction made between the primary qualities of an object, like its shape, and its secondary qualities, like its color, which you and I may see differently. The primary qualities stay the same even when I'm not there to experience them. The secondary qualities depend on my subjective reaction, so they aren't objective in the same way.

That might work for some purposes, but it's actually a strange idea. The idea that there is some object whose qualities don't change even when we aren't there to experience it makes sense conceptually, but it ignores the reality of what it means to perceive something. It's just an abstraction.

It's not that this way of thinking is wrong; it just seems very limiting. Perhaps we could say that approaching an object in that way is one layer of objective reality. It may be that science works best when it sticks with that layer. But there are also other layers, which matter just as much or even more.

For instance, suppose something I see or hear reminds me of someone who has gone away. Memories come up, feeling tones come up. There may be a sense of loss, or a felt impression based on memories of time spent with that person. The perception stimulates emotions. As you get involved with that whole complex, there is a sense of being bonded to the object.

What you are describing is what I would call the subjective side of the experience, not the objective side.

That's the point! As the perception engages the object, the subject manifests too, as the one who reacts. Think back again to the image of steam rising off a lake in winter. The steam and the lake aren't separate. In the same way, the subject and the object arise together. That's why I said they're bonded. The subjective reaction completes the object: it's part of its identity. At the same time, the subject arises and takes on the form that it does through the encounter with the object. Appearance shows up in the form of that polarity. I see the object, so that is one layer of the subject/object polarity. But the object triggers the feeling of loss or emptiness, or gone-ness. On that level, the relation between subject and object is much more subtle. Each shapes the other, and each depends on the other. There is a kind of wholeness.

That wholeness establishes the zoning. The zone operates between the subject and the object, *from* the subject *to* the object. It may operate consciously or unconsciously, but it is that kind of mutual identifying that performs the perception. In that performance, you are on the stage, together with the object. The state of the stage is the point, the center, but that is not how you perceive things. You are caught in the zone, so all you can do is affirm both the subject and the object.

If you had more experience with engaging the zone from the center, you might be able to see other layers of the subject/object polarity. For instance, you could engage the history that the encounter with the object triggers. Perhaps you could see the roots of the attachments that arise. Instead of just being aware of 'from' and 'to', you could engage a vertical dimension.

In the middle of it all, the holder of it all, is the point of the center. But we focus more on the holding than the center. The sense of holding *is* the perception. It gives us the identities we compile and confirm. We perceive, and with the perception comes a feeling: "I feel a great sense of loss;" "I am alone." All the emotions are like that.

I have a question about the way you talk about emotions. If I understand correctly, you would say a feeling like love or joy is not an emotion. You're mostly referring to negative emotions: greed, lust, hatred, anger. That's not how most people use the term.

The word 'emotion' is something of a compromise. Many years ago, when I first started giving talks to my students, I sometimes spoke of 'the emotionals'. That seemed in some ways more accurate. But the Dharma Publishing editors said, "You can't do that. You can't use an adjective as a noun." So we went back to 'emotions'. It's probably better to use the Sanskrit word 'klesha'. It has a broader range than what you would call an emotion in English, but there is no doubt that the kleshas are always negative.

So let's say that all the negative emotions you feel are due to the operation of the kleshas. But why do the kleshas have this kind of power over us? It's because of our commitment to identity. As we move back and forth through our experience, we rely on identity. We create the environment for the kleshas to take hold.

Instead of relying on identity, just stay in the middle of your experience. Hold to the center: stay there. It starts out as a subtle shift, because identity starts in the center. But if you stay in the center, not reacting by establishing identities, the center begins to open up. It dissolves or unravels. You find that you cannot consolidate your experience into one point. Instead, experience ripples outward. It moves toward ridges and rhythms and edges.

What is the relation between ripples and rhythms?

The quality of rhythms works against anything static. The stimulus of the rhythms gives rise to inner impressions, re-printed from the karmic residues that maintain samsara. This is not exactly a fixed perception, because it depends on movement. Consciousness cannot be located in one specific place. The ripple is deposited in the karmic stream, but what was so just a moment before is no longer the same now.

At the same time, there is feedback, which creates the rhythm. You move from A to B, but B also goes back to A. At every step, there is a twofold movement. Ripples feed back, depositing habitual impressions, and there is also a sense of the ripples moving forward into the unknown. It's a specific feeling, not the same as consciousness. Ripples expand in transitional stages.

211

Is there a way to practice with this? Can I understand better if I engage my experience a certain way?

What you need to do is focus each ripple, each point, back toward its own transitions. This means holding the ripples, but not in the sense of trying to stop the movement. The more you penetrate ripples, contemplating them as fully as you can, the more you can stay there. It's like a surfer riding a wave. At that time, there is no 'from' and no 'to'.

Q. Does that mean you give up the sense of identity?

That may happen. You may lose the initial sense of a fixed identity. As you go on, you come to a second identity. It's more open, more allowing, less focused on you and your experience. But as you continue to expand the center, you lose that one too. By the time you get to the third stage, there are just rhythms and ripples.

Imagine that you are holding on to a stick. You start out by trying to focus on one particular place on the stick, the place you are holding on to. Gradually you begin to realize that there is no one place on the stick, that every part of the stick is connected to every other part. If you focus on the point you are holding on to right now, all the other points are there too. The last point goes back to the first point and all the other points. They're all there.

If you contemplate in this way, the rhythm shifts. Before you may have thought that previous ripples were gone, but now you see that you do not need to depend on movement in this sense, where something goes and something new comes. In this rhythm, there are no longer even ripples.

This is a big shift. The regime of mind depends on setting up this and that, but now you are no longer captured by that dynamic. It's just not there. If you think of yourself as swimming in the ocean, and the ripple as a wave in the ocean, you could say that the wave no longer strikes you. You can ride the wave instead of being hit by it. Riding the wave, there is a kind of stillness in the midst of movement.

Q. Is being hit by the wave what happens when an emotion overwhelms you, or you get lost in a thought?

Yes, you could think of it that way. Being hit by the wave, possibly almost drowning in it, is a good image for what happens when you experience a strong emotion. But it doesn't have to be that dramatic. When a thought comes along and carries me away, it's like drowning in the thought, but that doesn't mean that I'm gasping for air or feeling overwhelmed. Drowning in a thought may have a pleasant background feeling. For instance, drowning in a fantasy may feel like that. So why speak of drowning? Because in a sense I've lost consciousness. I no longer have any awareness. I'm just submerged in the thought. The ripple has solidified into a zone: it may be a thought zone, or it may be a feeling zone. Either way, I've lost the chance for freedom.

When the mind is agitated or out of balance, it's like surfing when the waves are high and crashing all around you. At those times surfing the waves, or dissolving the ripples, may be dangerous. One wave may rush in and smash you into the ocean floor. But if you have gained experience in surfing, you know how to keep your balance. There's no danger, even when the waves are really big.

At that point, you can see the impression of the ripples as lila, a simple, playful reflection of what the mind produces. You know how to deal with every situation, like someone who knows how to read the currents in the ocean. Whatever comes up does not affect you. You don't have to try to protect yourself by hiding in quiet shallow pools that turn stagnant or trap you in narrow corners. That's the benefit. It's self-liberation . . . it's freedom.

The Buddha taught that the emotions can support the growth of awareness. Usually we associate that idea with the Vajrayana, but even in the Vinaya, there is a passage that says that while compost is ugly and unpleasant, it helps the sugarcane grow. Emotions are like that, if you know how to apply the right method. The ripples they generate can lead directly to transformation. In fact, this is true for any experience.

How you actually do that is not easy to express in words, because it's a subtle process. If you can touch internally the rhythms of experience, you eventually develop flexibility. That's why the waves of emotionality or the agitation of thoughts won't throw you off-balance or knock you down.

Exercise 17: Inside Emotions

When emotions such as anger, frustration, anxiety, or attachment loom in our mind, they feel very real. Instead of trying to ignore or transform them, in this exercise you can work with that sense of reality. As you proceed be sensitive to your own reaction, and break off the exercise if it starts to seem too intense.

When an emotion or feeling comes up, stay with it and let it intensify, without commentary and without digging into it. Just contemplate what you are feeling. Gradually allow the energy of what you are feeling to take on a specific form and color. Look for the colors red, white, or blue, and let them grow more intense and pervasive. Let the form expand around you in the shape of an egg, with your sense of self in the center. Outside the form there may be waves of energy, while inside it is the feel of the emotion that matters most. Stay within the shape and feeling, holding them as long as you can, not going anywhere else. At some point, you may find that the original emotion transforms. The form that you are inhabiting may change its shape as well.

You can do this exercise with any emotion. You can also do it with positive feelings such as happiness. Each feeling has its own texture, its own field, and its own binding energy or gravity. You can explore each of these elements over time.

There's also a level beyond that, where you recognize that the ripples are a reflection of your own experience. When you contemplate how experience emerges from the center and remains in the center, your understanding of experience shifts. Usually, we think of experience as unfolding in time. We have a particular experience, and we separate that experience out from past experiences. We think of the ripple as starting in the past, but now that past is gone. This is the ordinary way of seeing it. It leads to a certain confusion, because we don't know how to think about that past. Do we divide it up into moments? Do we try to specify what was going on in each nanosecond, a different ripple in each one?

When you engage the rhythm of the ripples differently, you realize that this whole way of seeing is misleading. You are in the present, and that is all: you are simply 'in'. Experience becomes a unity. The ripples are actually gone. Everything is open. You can focus more directly, but there is no more focal setting. There is not even any location: you can no longer say where you are. The dimensions that structure your experience into zones disappear. And since the regime of mind depends on zoning, you realize that you are no longer under the jurisdiction of the authorities that have shaped your life. They cannot compel you; they cannot levy a crushing tax. This is the real self-liberation.

That is why I may sometimes sound critical of meditation. Compared to that kind of self-liberation, the kinds of meditation that most people practice may amount to nothing more than baby-sitting.

25

Beyond Mindfulness

Can you say more about why meditation is not helpful? Many people would say that their meditation helps them a lot. Of course, just using meditation to relax or relieve stress and anxiety is limiting. But can't meditation help you see more clearly what's happening in your own mind?

When we meditate, it's like deciding to spy on our own mind, like putting the FBI or CIA on the case. We take on the role of being the watcher, and we remind ourselves again and again that we have to be mindful, be aware. If we don't, we will lose the opportunity that meditation offers; we'll get lost or go off in the wrong direction.

There's an inherent tension in all this. We are afraid that we may get it wrong, may make a mistake, and then our contemplation will end in failure. So we have to keep the mind on a short leash. This whole way of thinking reinforces the sense that there is a subject who has a specific identity.

As the subject, the one who is meditating, we are traveling a dangerous road, one with many twists and turns and many places where we might go over the edge. That's because our job is to be aware 'of'. Who is aware of? I am—the one holding the leash that controls the mind. I have to be very responsible, very loyal to the job I've taken on. Otherwise I will end my meditation session with that feeling that it has not gone well. So I sit there and I do what needs to be done. I dictate to the mind.

It's useful to practice being aware. But there's a cost, because I'm reinforcing the fundamental structure of dichotomy. There is a subject who is meditating and there is the object of the meditation. Also, either the subject is aware or the subject is not aware. Those kinds of structure—that kind of dichotomy—is exactly what fuels samsara. When we practice that way, we are supporting karmic patterns instead of releasing them. We may be having a good meditation experience, but we are collecting the residues out of which new karma develops. Whatever the positive results, in the end we will have to pay the karma tax.

But there are ways to meditate that don't involve us in that kind of dualistic patterning.

Suppose you do have a meditation experience in which the sense of dichotomy drops away. Then the meditation session ends, and you get up off your cushion or chair feeling very pleased, and perhaps with a sense that you have experienced a different way to be. What happens next? Very soon your habitual patterns begin to manifest. You find yourself acting the way you always act, feeling how you always feel, reacting how you always react. Perhaps the usual patterns have been there all along, operating unconsciously. When the time is right, they will pop back up into consciousness. We all know the results. Soon you are lost once again in streams of thoughts, or you are worrying about something, or feeling guilty or lost.

Now you move on to the next stage: because of your own negativity, you judge yourself to be a failure. "Yes, it's true; I did it wrong again!" It doesn't take very long before your situation is once again cast in stone. The old rhythms of thoughts, perceptions, feelings, and identity operate, and you find yourself back in one of the usual zones.

This is no surprise, because in fact you have no way to leave the zone. Wherever you go, you take the zone with you: the same perceptions and concepts and thoughts. You can't travel somewhere else, because your mind is not free.

Meditation doesn't seem to have the power to help with this, because when you meditate, you are still operating in a familiar zone. You live in a world shaped by 'you-ness' and 'I-ness' and 'self-ness'. You have your property, and you hold on to it tightly because it is part of your identity and you are afraid to let go. Whatever you perceive, whatever image comes to mind reflects back to you your own attachment and fear. There are rules and policies that limit where you can go or what you can build. Even when your meditation experience is good, at some level you are a prisoner.

What we are exploring here is very different. Just stay in the center and expand. Follow out the ripples as they appear, and they will open up on their own. You don't need to spy on yourself or tell yourself what to do.

I think I understand the distinction you are making, but I realize I need to work it out for myself.

219

'Working it out' isn't good enough! That's the pattern you've adopted; it's the system you know how to use. But staying within a system leaves you caught in the same zone. Language tells you what's possible, and you respond. You are emulating the models you were taught, taking on the roles that have been made available.

Here's another way to think about it. In your own mind, you are carrying around the image of some authority and you want their approval. This is not meant to be psychology—the authority might be your father or mother, but it might be your spiritual teacher, or your society, or might be your own concepts, your own feelings, or your self-image. It doesn't matter: the pattern is the same. You need approval because you are lacking fundamental confidence. You don't know how to investigate intrinsically.

That's why you still feel confused. It's why you feel you need to "work something out." You may have a sense that some fundamental shift is possible, but you don't exactly know what it is. So you look at previous models or examples, or you try to analyze through language, or you hope you'll come up with an answer through meditation that lets you make sense of things. Before you had a sense that you understood something, so now you try to emulate that. But you are just relying on old patterns, or on whatever you imagine is possible within the field of your own perceptions.

Sometimes it seems much simpler than that. A different understanding just comes bubbling up.

That may be good. But it's very easy—too easy—to tell yourself that you've had glimpses of something different.

220

That still shows a lack of confidence. You have experience, but you're skeptical about the value of what you experience, so you hold back. Then you're right back into looking for approval, perhaps from your friends or teachers. You imagine that if you could talk to other people about what you've seen, so that they could really understand, they would confirm your own understanding. Or maybe you have dialogs with yourself; you try to give yourself feedback so that you will be convinced.

The problem with all this is that you haven't trained yourself to open up completely. You still have something to protect. That's because you're still outside.

Outside?

From within the center, nothing is left out, and there are no distinctions to make. But if you stay outside, you find yourself looking for the meaning of 'thatness'. Or to put it more simply, you are still putting your experience into a corral. It's like building a wall. The one building the wall is also 'within', but you don't want to acknowledge that. You need to establish your own territory outside the wall. By building the wall, you are building a shelter. But that's something you don't want to talk about, because you still need approval. That's what's most important to you. It matters more than opening the intrinsic.

Building walls is not going to help you. Whatever wall you build is not real; it doesn't do its job. It's really just the imitation of a wall.

So if my own position is also inside the wall, that means there isn't really any wall.

If you could focus on the one who is building the wall, that would be the center. But you aren't willing to make that the focus. You focus on 'thatness'. But how does 'thatness' arise? If you don't include that first arising, that first time, you just get lost in stories. Your experience starts with "Once upon a time." It's still all about patterns and language and perceptions and concepts. You can't just decide. That's why I say you're still looking for approval.

I can at least get a taste of what you're talking about. I know you're going to reject that, and I know that if I ask you a question, you're going to say I'm looking for approval. But I don't see what other choice I have, so I'll ask anyway. Isn't it helpful to get a sense of what it would mean to be completely free?

Getting a glimpse of freedom is like eating baby food. That kind of limited understand is not really helpful. You are still looking for a way to change that lets you stay within samsara, and that won't work. It doesn't do any good to focus on the rest of the universe if you leave yourself out of the picture.

Whatever patterns you identify, whatever reality you name, you are completely above that. You don't need to change anything. You may experience something and call it samsara, or you may call it heaven. Either way, you are the one making the distinctions. That's where freedom comes in. It's like a master chef who can make many wonderful dishes out of the same ingredients. Working in that way means that you are no longer relying on the ordinary rhythms.

There are really countless expressions. It's like an artist who can work with colors to create beautiful art, or a dancer, or a poet. If you understand what is finally going on, any form can be any other form. This world can be another world, another reality. But to do that, it doesn't have to change its shape. There isn't any 'thatness'. It's enough for your understanding to change. Then your view, your perception, your experience can be totally different.

Suppose we invited the Bodhisattva Manjushri to come here. If we accept that he operates with a completely different understanding from you and me, would he see the same reality we do? It doesn't seem likely. When you are not in bondage to your own patterns or controlled by the existing regime, how could the world be the same?

Didn't Jesus say, "My kingdom is not of this world?"

Yes, that's right.

Perhaps he was saying that when the mind is transformed, that is itself a different kingdom. It is not of this world.

When you look at 'this world', it is a world governed by the regime of identity and ego. It is a world where images based on the kleshas are constantly pouring down on us. When that regime is not in control, we enter a different world. The old rules and policies no longer apply. We are free.

This freedom is intrinsic to our being, so it does not depend on radical change. It manifests when we realize that nothing can hold it back. The waves on the surface of the ocean may be agitated and jagged, but the ocean itself remains undisturbed. In the same way, whatever is happening, whatever is going on for us, our experience is completely open.

Sometimes the mind can seem like a cesspool or a swamp, but that is not fundamentally the nature of mind. In the same way, karma can terrorize our lives, but in the center, the claims of samsara and karma lose their power. Because freedom is intrinsic to openness, we are not bound by distinctions such as good and bad or 'here' and 'there'. We do not have to follow rules or make commitments to act one way or another. Thoughts and sensations manifest the nature of mind in various ways, but within that variety, there are no real differences. I am not the same person now that I was when I was little, but my mind now may be the same as my mind when I was a child.

You seem to be talking about a sharp break. Before things were one way, but now they are completely different. But earlier you said that the basic practice was to gradually expand out from the center. Which is it—a gradual change, or a fundamental transformation?

We proceed gradually, because that's how the mind as we know it operates. But once a different understanding is in place, we could say that we don't need that kind of gradual development. We've graduated. Which way we experience it, gradual or sudden, depends on how much experience we have, and what kind.

Maybe this is the same question from a different perspective. You said that there was no distinction between good and bad, or any other dichotomy. But those distinctions do seem very real, and it seems it would be dangerous to pretend that they are not.

Given the rules of samsara, the distinctions are real. Someone could say, "You say that this world is perfect, but that's a lie. My life is hell!" How could I disagree? The only basis for not making distinctions is transformation. But when there is real transformation, distinctions are just gone. They no longer make sense.

'Americans, or Westerners, always depend on the intellect, and the intellect has its way of engaging experience, which depends on the structure of subject and object. In that subject/object structure, the subject always has to improve itself or its position in some way. There is a kind of false humility, where the subject, the self, says, "I'm not good enough." When you operate on that basis, getting a glimpse of some alternative can actually be problematic, because it just shows you that you are ordinarily trapped.

But wouldn't it be a mistake if I tried to fool myself by pretending not to be bound by the subject/object structure? Isn't it important to realize that I have not yet reached the level of transformation?

Yes, but you have to realize that we are not taking about stages in ordinary time. We are talking about instant experience. 'Right now' there is no edge, no position. That's the difference. When there's no edge, there's nowhere to go and nothing to point out. There's no arriving anywhere, no graduation. If you're not there, you can speak of graduation, but that's not really the way things go.

Once you know that directly, you see that 'pointing out' is not a meaningful act. Given the level of mind that operates in our culture, I have to depend on taking that kind of approach, because that is the only way to direct the mind. If I can't rely on that sense of direction, what I see is a blank. In effect, I'm in the dark.

As long as I'm loyal to our habitual way of thinking, I operate with a vision that is grounded in identity. Perception and language are my only tools. If I wanted to communicate in a way that does not depend on perception or on language, I would have no way to go forward.

We may have been operating that way for a long time—30 years, 40 years, 50 years—with no real progress. But at some point, we need to cut that dependence. Imagine that we have the possibility to pass into freedom. How many people have done that? How many people have let go of their commitment to the regime of mind? If we have that opportunity, how can we not act?

The problem seems to be that we want to have an experience of freedom, but we want to turn it into a possession.

Yes, that's right. We want to be able to say, "I am the one who understands. I am above the others." Or perhaps we think to ourselves, "I want to be the one who says to the world, "Don't you see: they are tricking you." But taking on that identity is just another position, another possession.

Really, there is no position to take and no possession to acquire. Since that is so, there is also no difficulty or problem to warn people about. At one level we can say that mind is the problem, but with no positions or possessions, the mind cannot trick you or steal from you. There is a story about the yogi Milarepa: he was meditating in a cave, and some thieves entered, wanting to steal whatever he had. Milarepa said to them, "I don't see anything at all in this cave—there are no possessions here. What is there for you to take?"

That is why we say that wisdom is indestructible. We start with wanting to possess, but when our understanding becomes intrinsically informed knowledge, complete in itself, it all becomes much simpler. Then there are no outside enemies and no internal residues.

Let me go back to Jesus again. Didn't he say something about not collecting treasure?

Yes, he said, "Do not lay up treasures on this earth."

Yes, that's it. But it's not only property like jewels and gold. It may be that you are very compassionate toward others and very generous in giving your possessions away, but internally there may still be grasping at self-image and ego. You have to let go of both worldly activities and worldly attitudes. That may be the inner meaning of that story where Jesus stops people from doing business in the temple.

He threw the money changers out of the temple.

Yes, because they were using the spiritual to make a personal profit. Whatever actions you take, you have to transform your attachment. You have to cut it. There's that story in the Bible about Abraham being ready to sacrifice his son to God. That complete surrender, going beyond the identity of the self to something higher—that is the sign of intrinsic understanding. God asks him to sacrifice his son. It's a test. You could say that Abraham attests to his faith, but the story is also about being completely open, not holding on to any position.

What do you think Abraham was feeling?

I don't know. But in the story, he shows his commitment. He says, "Yes, I'm ready." At that point, he lets go of any grasping and all identity. That is the point of transformation. He manifests a different embodiment, and he frees himself from all obstacles. There is no 'from' and no 'to'.

He had to let go of what he loved most.

Letting go of what you love is still operating within a hierarchy. You need to penetrate that too. It's not complicated. You just allow. You completely accept.

So if I could understand that way of accepting, I could communicate it. That would be important for everyone, anywhere, at all times.

Yes, everyone is similar. Water is water; oxygen is oxygen. The quality of the mind is the same for everyone. The patterns of mind are universal. You may think that you have your own personal qualities, and of course that's true at one level. But a deeper level, that doesn't matter. Everyone agrees on the subject/object polarity. This culture may have a different name for it than another culture, but really it's the same. Different people may wear different clothes, but everyone wears the mind, the senses, and the self. So if you have some level of insight or understanding, it's easily adaptable.

Samsara is the same for everyone.

Yes. The labels are different, but the patterns are universal. You may drive a different model car from other people, but we all use the same roads to get to the same places.

26

No More Obstacles

Can you say more about how the intrinsic way of being relates to rhythms? If I understand you, rhythms are related to time, but they don't involve the linear directionality that we usually associate with time. They are more pervasive than that, and they extend through different zones.

Without rhythms, there would be no experience, but rhythms do not have to do with experience unfolding in time. The movement goes deeper. It's intrinsic to all experience. Eventually, you realize that the movement is in a sense magical, because it doesn't conform to our usual structures. For instance, it may be that beginning, middle, and end are the same unit.

This is not easy to talk about. In a way it's secret, not because someone is keeping it secret, but because there is no way to describe it, so there is no way to know about it. Buddhism and science both speak of cause and effect, but there is a level underneath cause and effect.

For instance, you might tell me you feel unhappy and go on to say what that feels like and why you feel that way. At the underneath level, though, happy and unhappy are expressions of something that remains the same. The same holds true for the point when something begins and the point when something ends, and also for different rhythms or motions. One event occurs at one time, and another event at another time, but in the end everything is uniform.

Would you say that recent developments in science support this kind of understanding?

I have been reading lately about non-locality in quantum physics. I don't claim to understand it all, but the point that struck me is that our usual assumptions about particles being located in a specific place are wrong, and if that's so, the whole idea of identity over time goes out the window. It's tied in to the idea that instead of talking about particles, we should be talking about fields.

That does sound like themes in the TSK Vision. It's connected to the idea of multiple realities.

Let me try to make this more concrete and immediate. You have said that these ideas make possible a kind of self-healing. Can you say more about that?

We are really talking about two or three different levels, or different ways to experience. First is the samsaric way. Then there is what we might call the way of direct experience. Then there is the way of self-healing, which is the most direct way of all. At that level, we don't need teachers or rituals or specific practices. We can transform ourselves.

So that means rejecting traditional religious or spiritual practice?

Not necessarily. It can be valuable and effective to practice devotion, or rely on empowerments, or choose a specific meditative focus, but when you can transform yourself, that is the most powerful way. Other approaches are secondary. When you are free yourself, there are no more karmic obstacles, and the kleshas have no more impact on you. That's what happens at the third level. When you know how to extend and expand, you can exercise that capacity in different ways.

I can't help it—that activates my greedy mind. Are you willing to say more?

In a general way, we could say that the first level is self-observation. That's an approach that anyone can take. Then there's a second level, which had to do with contemplation. It's completely experiential. The third level is above samsara. It is no longer bound to the conceptual frame of mind, so there is no dictator to tell us what is so.

How do you get beyond the conceptual frame of mind?

It's not so easy as long as you think you have to rely on that mind. So let me ask you: do you think you're free from concepts?

Well, I —

You may have some sense that you're free, but really you're still committed to common, conventional language and conventional understanding. Even if you say you've had a glimpse of a way of being beyond concepts, at least 75% that commitment is still there.

When you say you don't understand, that just shows you're operating with concepts. Focus instead on the sense of feeling. That is where transformation comes. Just let yourself be in your own freedom.

At that point are you free from polarity, from subject and object?

Not necessarily. When you understand polarity, it's not an obstacle. It may feel like an obstacle, but the feeling that there is an obstacle can be useful. You are feeding your own experience back to yourself, which means that the obstacle becomes the path to realization. It's magical: whatever is polluted or toxic purifies itself.

For instance, maybe you don't know how to contemplate. Or maybe you are failing to notice what you don't know, or think you know more than you do know. Or perhaps you are skeptical: you have certain kinds of insights but you don't trust them, so then they begin to fade. Or perhaps you are convinced that something is wrong and you need to fix it.

Those do sound like real obstacles. It's not just that I'm committed in advance to a view that involves 'pro' and 'con' or wrong and right; it's that I don't know how to ask different questions or discover a different way of knowing.

Right! Those dimensions of your experience have a very pervasive impact. They influence you at a subtle, profound level. But that's all right as long as you understand them as exhibitions, like works of art.

Perhaps that is what it is like to live in the Garden of Eden. Beauty manifests everywhere. You find it in the ratio of each expression. The exhibition carries with it a perfect confidence. You discover knowingness. Even if what you experience is not knowing, that not knowing is illuminated.

That is why we can say there are no longer obstacles. The obstacle has no subject. Whatever manifests as not knowing feeds back. There is no extra step, no extra job that you have to do. You are not under any obligation and not caught in any system. The mind, as it is, is free. You could say it is almost completely liberated.

When that is your situation, there is no special way you need to act and nothing special you need to do. When you do act, you act in a very normal way. The difference is that whatever is happening, you go inside. Within the time of reacting, within your doing, you just use what's there. You might say it is a kind of exercise, but it doesn't depend on taking any special steps.

So there is nothing I need to do? Everything is fine the way it is?

No—that is a misunderstanding, and it can be dangerous. It's true that you don't need any special situation and you don't need to project some exceptional state. But that does not mean that virtue or understanding is undermined. What matters is to incorporate whatever appears, so that you get the benefit of the feedback.

If someone owns shares in a company and the company performs well, the shareholder gets a dividend. But at this level, you get a dividend that does not depend on performance. You don't have to beat yourself up. You don't have to confront some wrong understanding or challenge the structures of polarity. You don't need to fight against some opponent or discriminate good from bad. Whatever happens, you are already free. Nothing gets frozen in place, and there is no possibility for toxicity to build up, because whatever appears is already open, already flowing. The ice has already melted. That's the dividend that you get from understanding, from knowing how to operate appearance.

So you might say that arguments about wrong and wrong are beside the point.

Arguments can be helpful. They may give you a glimpse of understanding—not because the argument necessarily proves that one point of view is right or wrong, but because in the middle of the argument your own assumptions suddenly become transparent and just melt away. But even if at that point you say, "I understand," you are still relying on a conceptual approach.

From a samsaric understanding, you must take a position. Inevitably, there is separation—you could also call it bias. Your lot is cast. There is a ratio of this to that, and that is who you are and what you believe: You are ignorant, you are Asian, you are an intellectual. And the samsaric way of investigating—arguments and sensations and so on—is based on those same structures. The samsaric approach says, "Do you want to understand? Well then, you have to be rational, you have to observe closely; you have to use the mind to make sense of what is going on. You can't turn your back on all that. That would be nihilism. It would just be wrong."

Well, what's the answer? It sounds pretty convincing.

The answer is that that's not the only way. Yes, I may use that approach, because it can be beneficial. But that way, the samsaric way, is based in the end on the thinking mind. You make sense of things, and that means that first you let thoughts produce appearance and then you confirm the truth of what is produced.

Now, there is no problem with thoughts. But you can also open thoughts. You don't have to simply accept the stories they tell. When you do, you find that thoughts have many different dimensions. Thoughts can have a different feel; they can produce different dichotomies, different outcomes. They can create beauty. They can change the way you relate to time. They can liberate.

It really all comes down to freedom. When you free your-self from the zoning that gets set up within the regime, then whatever arises within a zone—no matter what—is free. Thoughts are free, perceptions are free, feelings are free. Even a glimpse of this freedom can be very impor-tant. When you glimpse a different way of seeing, seeing itself becomes very different. Seeing, hearing—in fact, each quality in experience, each characteristic, can go beyond the samsaric way of operation. The whole human environment changes. You live in a world of beauty, peace, and harmony.

You could think of this in terms of the four immeasurables: love, joy, compassion, and equanimity. Each of those quali-ties manifests naturally. It may be love that comes to the fore, or it may be joy. That depends on the emphasis you cultivate.

But it seems like an impossible dream to live in that way all the time.

At least you can connect with those qualities from time to time. Most people have some experience of that. Once you do, you can extend that experience. You can expand it glob-ally. We are used to going to the edge of each dimension, each zone. But the immeasurables have no edge—that's what it means to say they are immeasurable. Edges set limits, but when you apply the immeasurables to the existing zoning, fixed focal settings give way to ripples that expand outward in rhythms of harmony.

What about distraction. It seems as though I won't be able to get anywhere unless I can focus my attention, or maybe my intention. But when I'm distracted, I'm just lost in a thought or fantasy or memory. I mean, what you're suggesting is still a practice, even if you are saying we don't have to reject anything or distinguish good from bad. If I'm distracted, it doesn't even occur to me to practice. It's what you said before—I'm bonded to whatever distracted me, and there is no possibility for freedom.

Yes, distractions can be an obstacle. But the distraction itself is not the obstacle. It's more accurate to say that when you're distracted, that's the result of having accepted some specific reality. Something comes along and invites you to get involved. For instance, you get an email, or you see a news story on your computer screen. That's not a problem: even when you open the email or read the news story, even when you have an emotional reaction, that's still not a problem. It's when you accept your own reaction as the truth of what is happening, when you enter that zone, that you get distracted.

When you investigate the nature of your experience, there are many dimensions, and each one has different aspects. Thoughts are different from feelings, and feelings are different from perceptions. Positive feelings like joy are different from negative feelings like sadness. Some of those different dimensions don't exercise much gravitational pull on you, even though they might for someone else. Others draw you right in.

That is why traditionally the path is presented as unfolding through many stages, and progress on the path is gradual. But when you reach the situation of openness, with no edges and no zoning, it no longer makes sense to speak of gradual progress. The perfect fruit is already there, and it has always been there. It doesn't emerge from somewhere else through some temporary set of conditions coming together. The system as it is already embodies that openness. You find it within the field or ripples. We can speak of time and transitions, because that's part of the system, but that only makes sense within the system.

When you look at the sky, some days there will be clouds, some days it will be raining, and some days it will be clear and sunny. That's how it looks from our perspective, where we are very sensitive to conditions. But the sky itself is not affected by those conditions: it's always the same. One way of talking emphasizes zones and edges. The other way looks at ripples that are always in the center. We do establish the unique character of this or that situation, but the points we assign when we do that only arise because we treat experience a certain way. We project our experience one way, and that excludes other ways. The situation is cast in stone. Perhaps you could say that we are typecast.

Suppose for a moment that you could give all that up. It's not such a strange thought or impossible achievement. If we know how to extend and expand appearance, wonderful new opportunities open up. It's a new world, a new vision, a new reality. It would truly be sad if we lost such possibilities, especially because we don't need to.

What can we do to prevent those possibilities from being lost? I suppose what I'm really asking is this: are there specific practices that would keep these possibilities alive? But I do understand that you're saying that looking for specific practices is a mistake, because that approach is too closely tied to a particular structure. So what steps can we take?

Right now we need to embody and transmit this other way of being. We don't need specific practices, but we do need to understand that the situation is urgent. We do not have the right models available to follow, and so it's becoming increasingly rare to be able to break through conditions and limits. Time is pushing us in a very different direction. We are losing contact with the inner essence, and we don't know where to turn or what direction to take.

I am saying to focus on the ripples. But we may not know how to do that. We may not have the opportunity to conduct that kind of research.

Yes. You're saying that we automatically pattern our experience in samsaric ways.

That's right. Since we were born, everything has gone in that direction. The total impact is overwhelming. When you're caught in a nightmare, it's not easy to convert it into a peaceful experience. The atmosphere is already toxic, and it's too late to change it.

Who benefits from setting things up in that way? It's not as though there is some evil demon who wants to keep us trapped in our own misery and suffering. . . . Or is there?

A better way to say it might be that the way of reacting we have been trained in is based on looking for security. For instance, I may not want you to suffer—I don't wish you harm. But if you approach experience in a different way, that undermines my way of life and my understanding, and that's not something I'm ready to accept. So yes, I do have a stake in making sure you go along with the automatic patterns that I have learned to accept. That's the only way to guarantee continuity. So I project a certain understanding, and I teach you that same understanding. That's the knowledge we both share.

Then am I just stuck in samsara?

Samsara does not have just a single dimension. We don't have to escape samsara. We just need to engage a different dimension. If we look at the meanings of mind, new possibilities open.

But you just pointed out that we don't know how to do that. Time is pushing us in a different direction. We rush here and there; we try to get some kind of satisfaction while we have the chance. It's a very toxic environment.

Yes, it's a challenge. We don't know where to look or how to project. We don't know how to present our case. All we know is suffering and confusion, and we seem to be the victims of patterns that have been going on since long before we arrived on the scene. Of course we're unhappy—that's the way things are. Not only that, but we don't have the choice to do it differently. So we just make the best of it. We try drugs, or we go into therapy, or we look for new experiences or new relationships.

Of course, all that is ineffective. You can travel to every state in the United States, and in each state different rules apply, but whatever may change, there's much more that stays the same. The tax code may be different, but you're still going to end up paying tax.

Still, that is only one side. We can't see anything else; we can't see the possibility for total freedom. But it's there. There *is* another side.

You keep saying that, and I admit that you have suggested some other ways of looking. But if I just react to what you've been saying now, it all seems pretty hopeless. I may have the idea that things could be different, but if I'm living in a toxic environment, I'm never going to get healthy. So what am I supposed to do?

Think of it this way. Samsara may seem to be in charge, but you are being invited to free yourself from samsara, to see things differently. You just have to accept that invitation. It's up to you to cooperate. When you do, that's enough. Transformation is spontaneous: it serves as its own witness. Your role is just to pledge that you will no longer participate in the regime of samsaric mind.

What's the catch? What do I have to pay to escape from samsara?

Just give everything up. Then you'll be OK.

That sounds like a pretty big price to pay. It sounds like Abraham sacrificing Isaac.

That's not quite right. What do you have to give up? You give up concepts and identities. You give up the way you have been holding on. You give up attachments and grasping, which means you give up pain and fear. What's left? Abundance. Appreciation. Joy. Accommodation. Does that sound so bad?

After all, 'giving up' is a concept. You can frame it to yourself that way if you want, but you don't need to spend your time worrying about what you've given up. When you give up everything, you also give up the fear of giving up.

In the samsaric mind regime, you have all sorts of taxes you have to pay. Now, you've given up your loyalty to the regime, so what you're giving up is your tax burden. There's no authority left to impose a tax. Bondage is gone. Obligation is gone. So you could also say that you are not giving up anything, because now you are the owner of everything.

I'm just free to enjoy myself?

You could say that. But there's another dimension as well. Now that you know that you're free, now that you've given up your bondage, you're ready to share your new wealth with others. You can share your knowledge and your new understanding, your new model for what's going on. Giving *up* means you're ready to give *to*.

Why does that follow?

Because you can see it all so clearly now: how sentient beings hold on to their problems, their doubts, their sense that they are not capable or not qualified. And now you realize you can show them how to give all that up—the skepticism and paranoia, the self-deception, the self-image and identity.

OK, suppose you see in a new way. But if other people are trapped in samsara, how can you possibly communicate to them that it doesn't have to be that way?

It may be easier than you think. When you are free from self-image and all the rest, you may find that you can communicate very directly, that you can share your own experience. It may not even have to be in words. You are living differently, manifesting different qualities, and you can share that with others in an easy, open, effortless way. That's a real gift. It's immeasurable . . . unimaginable.

When you realize the joy that comes with that kind of sharing, you can act with that purpose. Even if you've only had a taste of what's possible, you can pledge to transform yourself for the sake of others. You can manifest your love and caring. You can encourage others who are still trapped.

Once you experience a fundamental freedom, you realize that you have priceless knowledge that you can give to others. You would not be the first to have that kind of realization, but from within the present situation, you can truly say that you have something to offer that has never before appeared in history. You can offer all beings dominated by samsaric cause and effect the possibility of liberation.

When you look at your own life history, now is the time to act, because soon it may be too late. You have this possibility: to communicate what you understand, to help transform, to patiently transmit. This becomes your mission, and the mission itself has a dynamic power. Momentum builds naturally, because each person who understands the truth of freedom will willingly take up the same duty. Samsara has its own momentum, like a snowball gathering more snow as it rolls downhill—now you can set a different dynamic in motion. You can activate it and empower it.

It sounds like a big responsibility.

Not really. Because you are no longer holding on, because you have given up your positions and possessions, you are not afraid. You have nothing to lose, so why not share what you understand? It may not be so noticeable at first, but gradually what you set in motion can become more visible. Ripples of freedom radiate outward, and a few people connect. That is the place to start. Freedom has its own momentum.

27

Movement within Stillness

Let's look at how ripples arise. The ripples are like waves in the ocean, moving, generating their own force. Mind is the ocean—the water—which remains unmoved. There is a movement within stillness.

The foundation for the movement, for the ripples, is mind. From that origin, thoughts and perceptions appear. Something is pointed out, and perceptions are identified. Nothing has been cast or typecast, but a dynamic is underway.

Now comes the identification, the sense of sameness. A perception arises, and I link it to an earlier perception. I say, "Yesterday I was like this, and today I am still the same. I am the same person; I have the same mind and the same attitudes." So first a ripple appears, as though it were coming in sideways, and then I apply a label. The labeling comes at the point where I say, "I did not change." At that point I am affirming identity.

I don't understand. What is the link between identity and the ripple?

The identification has its own instant intrinsic power. When we affirm identity through the label, we are turning away from change.

But why do we turn away from change?

We don't know how to change, and we're afraid to change. Perhaps a gap opens up, which is like making contact with the depths of the ocean, where there are no ripples. That is where the not-knowing comes in. In the face of that not-knowing, I grasp onto identity. That becomes the central focal point—the point of the ripple, based on recognition.

At that point, there is not yet much momentum. You have the possibility of staying in the center, of staying 'in'. If you do, the environment of the ripple—the condition of the field—changes. Experience may still go here and there, but the interpretation of what this means changes. Now you know that a different field is possible, a different experience of a kind you may never have had before. All kinds of difference are possible: different person, different entity, different field, different consciousness.

From within that difference, you may be able to see the dynamics of the ripples, either looking backward at how the present condition arose, or just engaging each arising ripple. The ripples come and you notice the movement, but you see the momentum of the movement as a reflection of the ripple. At the same time, the ripple is not separate from the water. So the momentum of the movement—the drive to identity—reflects the fundamental clarity of the water. We could call this mind itself.

Is this the 'movement within stillness' that you mentioned before? The mind is unmoved, but it generates a momentum, and the momentum points out identity.

When you focus on the momentum, you can see thoughts pointing. Then the question comes, "Who is the pointer?" If it's the mind pointing out, the pointing itself is the pointer. So nothing is really established. You are 'in' the ripple, and a new momentum is developing. You see something new, and that new noticing is itself the ripple. The watcher manifests self-recognition. There is nothing other than that.

There is also another way of describing this. Seeing the momentum is seeing different expressions of clarity and light. Light is disclosed in a cognitive way. A particular expression leads to a certain space and place, a different environment. That is the first stage in the arising of identity.

As that process continues, eventually 'I' and 'me' are established. 'I' is 'I am' and 'me' brings into play the entire objective reality, which becomes 'That is'. But if you stay in the center, you do not need to allocate a place to 'I' or 'me', subject and object. They appear, but there is complete opening, with no placing. The same is true for each recognition. This is not just theoretical. You can experience it.

With this opening, there are no limits. When we enter a zone, there is necessarily an outer edge, so there have to be limits. But the ripples do not need to develop in terms of that kind of environment. There are places, but the places are not established. They are just expressions of the constitution of the ripples.

Usually, we try to answer the question, "Where am I?" by establishing a place. But now we could answer, "I am in the open place." You could say there is identification, but it is an identification that is not established.

That is just a preliminary description of what might be the initial experience of that openness. The more you understand that no place has been established, that there is no basis and no ground to hold on to, the more you can rely on that understanding. You do not need any other foundation.

No foundation . . . nothing established. I know you're described freedom and openness, but to be honest, it seems scary.

Yes, if you are committed to holding on, to having an identity, then this is something to be afraid of. It's like falling into a black hole: you just fall and fall and you never emerge. But what is the hole that you're afraid of falling into? How can there be a hole if there is no 'place'? Is the hole round? Can you fill it?

Your problem is that you are making comparisons. You say, "Once upon a time I was this way, and now I've lost that, now I'm just condemned to wander in empty, unoccupied space." But how can you make that comparison? It only holds if you say that before you were in occupied space. Before you had an identity and now it's been wiped away. Before you could depend on 'me' and 'self' and 'I', and on 'thou' and 'that.' Before you had 'is' and 'on' and 'of'. If none of that applies, what have you lost?

Being afraid, or falling into confusion—those kinds of responses are to be expected. You have no other way to think about things or express things. You understand your own existence as having developed out of certain conditions, and so you are sure you occupy a certain place. If you think about 'open' or 'empty' you can only imagine that before there was something there, and now it's gone. These are fundamental limits. They come from the original conviction that takes the samsaric perspective. Based on that conviction, that commitment, basic conditions have already been set up.

That's why the transformation we are talking about is more fundamental than any foundation, like the sky before any clouds appear. It's as though you have spent your whole life in school, moving from one grade to the next, and now you've graduated. The environment is different. There's nothing to compare it to. If you still think you have to look for the next grade, or wonder where to enroll, you are inevitably going to feel lost.

If we want to describe this in ordinary terms, we have to do it in negative language. It's like being confined in a room where videos are endlessly playing, and one day you discover that the video player has a pause button on it. So you hit the pause button, and then you stay in that new, quiet environment.

And that gives you the opportunity to deeply relax.

Yes, because you release all tensions. But it's more than that. There are no more views or opinions: no right and wrong, no sinner and saint. You can act, but there are no karmic consequences, because karma has nothing to take hold of. There is nothing you need to do and nothing that you did wrong before. You are no longer operating with cause and effect or even with causal sequences.

So you're saying that at this point, staying in the center, we are at peace.

Well, you need to ask: who is the one who is at peace? Is it the one who experiences? The one who has some kind of intellectual insight into what we are describing? That's not good enough. It's still based on a conditional understanding.

When you base your understanding on a view in which everything is constructed, you set limits before you even get started. Openness, Beingness, selflessness—it doesn't matter; those are conditional too. You may say that whatever was there before is not there now, but there is still a place where that 'nothing there' comes from. Whatever I say now will become part of what has previously been recorded. My present expressions and impressions become an aspect of what there is to experience. I may have a good experience; I may have feelings of joy and pleasure that I can try to hold on to. But all this goes along with the samsaric way.

And so does all language and all descriptions. So there's really nothing left to say.

What we can say is that ripples continue to expand. If I insist on identifying carriers of the ripples, I will just be relying on impressions in the mind.

Can we do it differently?

Do what? There isn't anything to do. Just let the rhythms or ripples of the mind exhibit. That's enough.

28

Ripples in the Rhythms of Time

Mind is primary. Buddhism says we have six senses: the five sense faculties and the faculty that receives mental impressions. All of them, all of our direct experience, come from the mind, like bubbles that pop into being in the middle of the ocean waves. Different impressions emerge, and then interpretations follow. Without the mind, the sense faculties could not operate.

That's the Buddhist understanding. Would you say Westerners think this way?

Yes, that seems right. Without the mind, there could be no sense experience.

The words sound the same. But the Western view is that the source of experience is the internal mind, the subjective, personal mind. They don't have the idea of expansive mind, invisible mind.

If you understand all experience as coming from the center, you need to analyze it in a way that can be useful. Is there a way to gain access to the center? A question to start with is to ask where ripples come from. Can you trace them to any direction—east, west, north, south, top, bottom? We know that directions are related to positions and to zones. Does mind depend on those structures? Or is mind itself the center of each zone and all directions, the source of all sense impressions?

We do believe very strongly that the mind exists. But if that's so, we need to be able to ask how it exists. Is there a ripple of awareness that gives rise to mind? Is mind part of our zoning? How does it appear? If it doesn't arrive from a particular direction, does it come from all directions at once? Does mind have shape and form and identity, in the same way as other things that exist?

Mind seems in some ways mysterious. Can we touch it or feel it? Can we see it, or trace its operations, or measure it? Those are the typical opportunities we have in the zone, but they don't seem to apply to the mind. Still, mind is so important, so powerful—we can't just pretend we understand it when we don't. Is there a way we can understand it from within the zone? If it doesn't have any shape or form or size or character or place; if it doesn't come from any direction, is there anything about mind we can identify? If it doesn't fit within the zone, how can we make sense of it?

Maybe we could say that it doesn't fit in any zone because we are just making it up. Maybe there isn't any such thing as mind.

But who is making it up?

If the zone is the mind, then we could say the maker comes from the mind, but the mind doesn't come from anywhere.

Is that mind limited or not? Do we need mind to point out mind? Let's stay concrete. If I'm angry, where does the anger come from if it doesn't come from mind? Is it just that it's indescribable?

Maybe we should say that mind is just a theory, an explanation for how things like anger arise.

That doesn't seem very satisfying. We depend on mind so much: fear mind, lustful mind, longing mind. If mind is just a theory, then what about all our mental states? You can't deny the states we experience—they are so strong that sometimes they are almost visible. Go back to the image of surfing: when a surfer is riding the crest of a wave, that's all there is. Emotions are like that. When you are really angry, that defines your whole experience. It gives shape, identity, meaning. The same thing is true when you're feeling unhappy. Who is it that's not happy? We have to blame the mind. It's mind that's not happy.

Exercise 18: Following out Negativity

Negative feelings eventually dissipate or lighten. As much as you can, contemplate that process. Where did the feeling go? What's left of it? What replaced it? How real was it in the first place? What is it like to have the memory of having had that feeling? What conclusions can you distill from this contemplation?

That's not how we say it. We don't refer to mind at all. We say, "I am not happy."

But 'I' is the owner of the mind. And the relationship runs both ways. Without mind, there would be no 'I' as owner of mind. 'Mine' and mind are given together. The owner of mind grabs the ripples of seeing and hearing and so on, and at the same time grabs the identity of 'I am' and 'me' and 'mine'. On the one side, 'I am' is the creator, the artist—or perhaps we could say the manufacturer or the engineer. But who recognized the 'I am' that is the owner? Who recognized 'me'? Who is it that says 'mine'?

You cannot really separate 'I' out from mind. Mind is the principal, and the labels given by language are the support. Otherwise, there could be no language and no assigning meanings. Without sound, you cannot form the rhythms of speech, and without words, the voice cannot communicate—it's like that. The foundation is mind; after that words and labels create meanings and establish governing rules. Based on mind, a structure is set in place, and I accept it: 'A' is 'A' and 'B' and 'B'.

But as you say, mind does not appear. It seems to be hidden. So how can we say anything at all about mind?

That's exactly what we need to trace. How are the matters of mind set up? Could we be greedy without mind? Could we be sad or happy? It's hard to imagine how. So the place to look is the zoning. We can ask where the zoning originates: from what direction does it appear? And we can ask how the zoning is taken up. Where does it fit? Who is there to receive it? Who recognizes it, who knows it, and who accepts it? Who is the one that traces out the zoning and identifies the nature of mind on that basis? Who is the one who decides the right place to look, and what to look for? If there is no 'where' to look and no 'who' to do the looking, can we even say what we are doing?

Exercise 19: Ripples in the Mind

Trace out the widening sequence of ripples in the flow of mental events. For instance, a perception comes, followed by a judgment. Then there may be a judgment on the fact of having reacted with a judgment, as noted in Exercise 13. Other ripples emerge at various points in this linear sequence, such as cognition, recognition, feeling tone, etc. Still other ripples may go off at different angles: associations, memories, body sensations, concerns, and so forth. Investigate these dimensions in a leisurely way.

I'm still not convinced that we can establish the mind based on that kind of inquiry. But if I understand correctly, you're saying that mind is a story that we depend on. I can accept that.

OK, that seems like enough for us to proceed. Even if I just believe because everybody believes, that's the truth of where we are. Perhaps we don't know, and perhaps we even know that we don't know, but that doesn't matter. We still have to go forward.

But ordinarily, we don't necessarily want to go forward. We may not want to do anything: perhaps we are afraid to know, or perhaps we would rather be lazy. So we hold tightly to what we are used to, and we carry on the same way we have been up to then. Even if we have the sense that we have been mistreated or misunderstood, we still we want to go on the same way. It's as though the old, established way exerts a gravitational pull on us and we align with it. In fact, we use our own stubbornness, our own will power, to hold on. Even if we realize there is something fundamental we don't understand, we are willing to pay that price. That's why we say ignorance is bliss.

At the same time, that's only half the story. We also take a contradictory view. We don't like the negative spaces we find ourselves squeezed into: the pain, the disillusionment, the uneasiness. We don't like feeling lonely, or feeling that we are pretending. We don't want to feel sad or agitated, or worry all the time about failing, or wonder if we are really loved.

Still, what choice do we have? We're convinced there is really no solution. We wish things were different, and we may try to change our situation in some way to bring about improvements. But most of the time we just have to swallow it. Whatever the source of our unhappiness, however we describe it to ourselves, we don't really know how to get away from it.

It does happen sometimes that we feel better. It may be that something good happens to us, and we are excited and happy. Or it may be that we just start feeling better, as though whatever was bothering us had run its course. But before too long, the negativity starts to build up again, even if we do our best to avoid it or ignore it or change it.

If we have the sense at some fundamental level that our lives have meaning, that can help us deal with the negative times and the frustrations and irritations.

If you were a thoroughgoing skeptic, you might question that. Do our lives really have meaning? Maybe the sense of meaning that we discover is produced by mind. How could we tell?

Still, I am not trying to make everything sound negative. I am just saying that often a big shadow seems to fall on our lives, and whatever solutions or alternatives we try, we cannot get out from under that shadow. More important, we don't want to, because we are afraid of the price we may have to pay. We would rather stay with our not knowing, despite the gloom, the misery, the doubt and uncertainty. We know that the old patterns will automatically repeat themselves, and we accept that.

It's almost like a slave who is offered the chance at freedom and decides against it, or a prisoner who is let out of jail after many years and just sits in his room, staring blankly. The gravity of what we know crushes us, and we cannot move. We are squeezed into a corner. There is no place to go, no alternative. Just pain, numbness, darkness. We don't know, and we don't want to. In a strange way, we want the idea of the shadow: gloom, despair, sadness, again and again. Repeat automatically . . . repeat . . . repeat.

And you say you're not trying to make everything sound negative! It sounds bleak to me. How can you square that with what you've said about finding absolute freedom?

In one way, it's bleak. But it's also familiar, so we like to go there. We may almost find it entertaining.

Entertaining!!?? It doesn't sound that way to me. Listening to you, I just shudder. Now you present it as though it were no big deal—like deciding to go see some depressing art movie one Saturday night because we have nothing better to do. If the best we can hope for is feeling numb, how can you call that entertaining?

It may be a very realistic reaction, because we have no choice. The mind is in control, and the mind has its patterns, which we cannot change. It's not like operating to remove a malignancy: we can't operate on the mind to remove the negative patterns. We can't ignore or forget the painful realities. Even if we taste the bitterness and sadness, we may just have to learn to live with. It's like someone who lives where the water is polluted and makes him sick, but there's no other place to go, so he drinks the water.

I know this strikes you as a too pessimistic and too one-sided. But even if you wouldn't describe your own life in those terms, think of the past history of humanity. There are still people alive who remember the atrocities of World War II, when many millions of people were killed, not to mention the civil wars and genocide of more recent times, which have produced suffering few of us can even begin to imagine. Then there is the suffering of animals, both domestic and in the wild. All these things are well known, and there are certainly many people who try to prevent this kind of suffering, or at least reduce it, but it still goes on.

Is it possible to change this? We can say for certain that when it comes to people killing each other, the cause is anger, hatred, greed, and other forms of negativity. If we were all Bodhisattvas, these kinds of things would just not happen. They start as ripples of mind, but they harden into positions and identities, and we see the consequences.

The path of the Bodhisattva is an important ideal, but for the most part that is not how people operate. So whether we look at history or at the world today, this kind of pain and suffering is undeniable, and we can predict that it will go on the same way in the future. So many people have wished that it could be different, and have tried to do something about it, but no one has ever found a method that is completely successful.

People are driven by revenge and resentment and pride and all the rest. So there will always be people who attack each other, who vow to wipe out the other side, who look for ways to kill better and kill faster. If that seems grim, it's an accurate reflection of how our minds work. The mind is set up to feed back cycles of anger and agitation and negativity. It's strange, because when we act on those patterns, we are trying to find a source of ultimate refuge. The point is to show that we have the power to get our way; that the other side has to surrender, that our way of thinking or believing is right. The witness wants to bear witness to its own victory.

If you push people hard enough, that may be accurate. But most of the time, we live more peacefully. What you describe is what happens when people go to extremes.

In terms of how we act, this may be extreme. But these are the patterns that push our minds, even when we are just going about our ordinary business. We are driven by the concerns of identity, self-image, and ego. The ego wants power and it looks for protection. Even more basic, the ego is always worried, already afraid. If it loses its position, it has nothing left. For the ego, that is the big danger. It wants to be someone, or be something. It wants to have a special 'be', a noticeable 'be'.

We may tell ourselves that all we want is to get along and not be bothered, but that's not really how we engage the world. The truth is much more that we insist to ourselves that we are unique. If we are not unique, not special, then it is almost as though we are nobody at all.

That is how the mind gets its power. It responds to the ego's fears. It says, "Yes, don't worry. I will support you. I understand that you have needs—self, identity, image. I will protect you. I will protect what protects you." We are deeply grateful. That is how the mind establishes its regime.

All this is set up before we even know it. So naturally, we never question; we never ask "Who is telling me this story? How do I know it's true?" If we began to question it, there could be some very fundamental changes, because the rules and policies that the mind puts in place only function if I accept them. But I do accept them. I become a loyal follower of the regime, and I behave accordingly. I have no other way to manifest. That is why we say that mind and the thoughts that it generates are so important. They set things up a certain way, and we go along.

For myself, I don't want to be someone special. Or at least, that's not my main motivation. I understand what you're saying about the nature of the mind, but that just makes me want to develop inner peace or peace of mind.

I don't doubt that you are sincere when you say that. But really, you have no choice. You can't tell the mind, "All I want is peace of mind." It won't listen. It's already moving in a different direction, and it doesn't know any other way to operate. It's like a factory where the assembly line can only produce one kind of product.

That is why it's so important to develop a different approach, which is what we've been talking about. Whatever the focal setting, whatever points come up, we need to directly follow out the ripples of mind. When the zoning is established, we shouldn't just accept it. We should try to survey the lay of the land.

259

If we don't do that, we literally don't know what we are talking about. We have a sense that there are connections between 'me' and mind or between 'I' and mind or self and mind, but we don't know how those connections operate. If we look, we can see how we rely on 'my' consciousness and 'my' identity, and how we link those to the mind. But do we really understand how this whole structure came about? Do we know the parenthood?

In a way, the difficulty is that we don't how to do this kind of research. We don't know the right questions to ask. We can't really point to mind, or see the shape of mind, so how can we question it? What kinds of tests can we devise? There is no microscope that will let us investigate the subtle structures of the mind and map them out. The mind is invisible.

Still, we can't seriously deny that mind exists—we talked about that before. Our experience is based completely on mind interactions, on sensing and feeling. Without the mind how could perception even arise? It's not enough to say that perceptions depend on mind. You have to say that they manifest mind. Without water, there can be no ripples. So the nature of mind is a part of every experience—an unknown part.

There are various ways to talk about this. The Abhidharma puts it one way and Madhyamaka puts it another. It's no so important how you describe it: the basic point is that without mind, none of the faculties we rely on can function. When you dream at night, that's mind in operation. If you accept that there is a bardo after death, that's mind also. When your eyes are closed, you may still see images. That's mind too.

29

Shelterless Mind

I'm sorry if we keep going around in circles. I appreciate your being patient. I think I'm beginning to see how it's possible to explore in the way you've been saying.

Good! But you have to ask if 'beginning to see' is good enough. You are still operating according to the rules of samsara—you're a good student, an obedient child. Maybe not in every way, but in this way you respect your father and mother and what they taught you. You have learned very well the right ways of seeing and the right wording to describe what you see. You have the right opinions, you know how to be a good intellectual. You can do what society asks you to do.

That's all fine, but now you need to let go of it. All of it. Go to the ripple of the point. If you don't hit the target, it will slip away.

What is the target?

The target is words; the target is the conceptual frame of mind. But not just words and concepts—the target is an outlook based on perceptions and stimulated by the products of mind and the meanings given by language. The target is whatever is not real.

What's real? Is it the ripples? Is it the rhythms of time?

"Rhythms of time" is good. But it might be confusing, if it leads you to think that time moves forward, like when you shoot an arrow. Ripples do not move forward. You could say that rhythms express.

We haven't talked very much about time. There is something magical about points in time, because as soon as you have recognized a point in time, it has already changed—it's already gone. Every instant is gone as soon as it arises. It's not like saying the fruit is here, but the tree that bore the fruit is gone. It's more fundamental than that.

Usually when we describe experience, we say that experience requires time to happen. Theoretically, that's true. But I'm not so sure. My feeling is that something shows up 'inside' time. You could speak in terms of the appearance of dots. The dots themselves may be external to time; perhaps you could say that they manifest in space. Those dots are what produce labels and guarantee concrete manifestations. Timing may be a part of that reality, but time itself is not involved in bringing it into being. There are particles, and form takes shape, and there are external transitions. Timing is a part of the calculation. But it is based on names and labels, not on a timing dynamic.

Think of a sundial. The pointer on the sundial doesn't move; it's the shadows that move. And the shadows move because of the ratio between the position of the sun and the position of the earth. That changing ratio is like the rhythms of the ripples. You could describe it in terms of a temporal dynamic, and it seems natural to do so. But the shifting ratio expresses a ripple, and if we stay within that ripple, movement simply becomes an aspect of the ratio. Only when we designate points and assign locations can we calculate the hours of the day and confirm the linear progression of time.

Now, focus instead on the focal setting. The ripple shows itself at a point. That point of showing is the center. We need to make that center intrinsic rather than relating to it externally. If we station ourselves in the immediate experiencing of the instant, the psychological environment changes, and so does the environment that shapes the operation of the sense faculties. The ongoing conversation about what is so is transformed. The identity that gives 'mineness' becomes something very different. Our usual experience is no longer the measure.

If we can penetrate there, it is like opening a door to a different realm. You might want to say that that in this new realm, time and space are different, but that is not necessarily true. It might be better to say that time and space no longer apply.

Can you say something about what that feels like? How can we recognize when we have made that shift?

At first, experience may seem very calm, very peaceful. If you want to apply labels, you could label it as joy, or freedom. Samsaric memories dissolve; samsaric problems are gone. The case is closed. It is as though a new generation has come on the scene, and new possibilities open.

Now a new problem may arise. We find ourselves in this new place, and we would like to own it.

Why is that the response? If it's that wonderful, why can't we just let it be?

Because 'ownership' is our usual model. That's what we are familiar with. When a positive change comes, we want to own it. We find ourselves in heaven, and we want to make sure we stay there.

Think about what it's like when you see something really beautiful. Even while you're enjoying it, you are also trying in a subtle way to hold on to it. Or think about entering into a very pure meditative state. As soon as you realize what is happening, you start imagining that now you will always be able to have that same meditative experience—which of course is not true. The act of holding on, the possessiveness, changes the experience.

I understand why this is a problem. But let me play devil's advocate. If I can't hold on to the experience, if it's not mine, what use is it to me? Don't I somehow have to get the benefit? If it just comes and then goes again, and there is no lasting impact, it's as though the experience never happened at all.

It's exactly at that point that the problem emerges. Instead of staying in the center, we take a position. We identify 'me' and 'my' concerns. As soon as I start operating in this environment, I begin to worry about my own security, and from there, I move instantly into samsaric ways of thought. I have been taught how to accept and reject, how to say yes or no, and that is how I respond. Here too you could say we are operating in a different space and time. In this time and this place, the patterns of ownership dominate.

In that environment, your question is the right one to ask: what is this good for if I can't own it? Just suppose, though, that we did not focus on ownership. Then we could say: it's good for everybody! Total freedom is not just for me—how could it be! Total freedom means there is space for everybody.

The Bodhisattvas live in that kind of space. As long as there are beings that have a problem, the Bodhisattvas have a job. Wherever samsara operates, wherever there are beings in the hell realms, they have work to do. It's not enough for me to be secure. That's almost a contradiction.

So Bodhisattvas have their work cut out for them.

They still have a lot to do. And if we follow that path, that's true for us too. Whatever my understanding, my situation, my environment, I have to look also at my friends, my neighbors. I have to look at what has happened in the past and I have to look at tomorrow. What are my friends going to do? Do they have a solution for their problems? They may not know how to protect themselves. In fact, I can see that this is true. Even if they try to pretend otherwise, if I know how to look, I can see that they are in trouble. On the outside, people may smile. On the inside, there are lots of tears.

Still, it's not so easy to share, to be helpful. People don't want to know; they don't want to acknowledge the truth of their situation. If you approach them with the wish to be helpful, they may turn away. If you are confident that you have something of great value to share and you say, "Here, you can have what I have," they may not want it.

This is a situation that takes patience. The right response may unfold slowly, across several levels. Right now, we are talking about the first level. At this level, the right response is to focus on mind. How can the mind transform itself? What are the benefits when it does?

Exercise 20: Relax and Release

For this exercise, set aside 20 minutes or so in a place you do not know. Go for a walk, or just sit quietly. Let yourself appreciate the newness, the unknownness. Anything could happen—but maybe nothing at all will happen. Either way, you don't need to have any expectations. Just relax and re-lease. Let go.

It seems discouraging not to know what to do and not even know what to do so that you can know what to do.

Not if you recognize that you have a great opportunity. You are investing in yourself, and you are getting remarkable feedback, for your sake and the sake of others. We are talking about self-liberation, about knowledge that leads to freedom.

There are many ways to challenge samsara, but what we are talking about here is special. You can meditate or engage in ritual and offer prayers, you can study the nature of reality, you can uproot your personal patterns through psychotherapy—none of that reliably leads to self-liberation. You can develop theories and find new forms of language, and that won't do it either. So this is a rare opportunity. Yes, it may mean going through several stages. It may mean going very deep. Should that stop us?

It may not sound so special, but contacting the mind in the way we are talking about is the real thing. That's how we can learn to know the self. There are paths that tell you what you have to do, but that is not what's going on here. This is a very direct approach. Once you discover intrinsic realization, there is nowhere else to go, no higher realm to reach. You become partners with knowledge, and you discover the kingdom within. This is immeasurable bliss, joyful, free from all obstacles. Even if you penetrate the truth of impermanence, you might not detect this joyful truth. In ancient times they might have put it this way: space to space, with no separation.

And no separation means no separation from others too?

Usually we only know how to measure out, internally and also externally. Now you embody what is immeasurable. Of course you want to share it with others. That is the meaning of the four immeasurables.

In this perfect freedom, you find your task and duty and mission. The benefits are too great to name, but the path is easy. Knowledge itself accommodates what we are looking for: freedom, peace, joy. It's a simple, direct approach. I don't think anything quite like it has been introduced before.

And the difference with this approach?

Pain and suffering become ripples, and the ripples open. Obstacles disappear, and you can take the profit. This is the learning process, the graduation process, the expression process. At a higher level, you may not even label what is happening or notice it, but you can still teach other people. You can give them the tool they already have. You can let them examine for themselves. You can graduate into complete freedom.

30

From Ripples to Freedom

Ripples spread out. If you think of them as rivers, there are valleys between them, a little like the space between planets. We could say that the ripples rally in the valley: they spread out, and they take form.

This is the place to loosen up or open up. It happens naturally; you don't need specific instructions and you don't need to make a special effort. Once the ripples rally, you may think that you need to do something specific: concentrate in some way, or think about what is happening in a different way. But that only happens because of the rallies. You can open that up too.

You say there is nothing we need to do, and then you describe the results. But if we do something 'in order to' get some result, that's not doing nothing.

There is a dualism in being focused and also in not being focused, in doing the practice and not doing the practice. But the dualism can be overcome if you are fully present and fully allowing. Our situation is that we start with zoning, and we have to loosen that up. We start with locations and boundaries and identities. There's a lot to let go of.

When a ripple rallies, hard edges form. The edges depend on the transition provided by memories that 'account for' how the present situation comes up. So that is another way to open your situation. You can open those memory transitions. All you need to do is look back. Here you are: how did you get to be here? How did this situation arise; where did it come from? How is it constructed as its own closed environment? The intention here is not to give an explanation; rather, by opening the ripple 'backwardly', you loosen its claims.

It seems like you are making a lot depend on this image of the ripple in the valley. But is it really accurate? It's hard for me to connect it to my immediate experience.

The exact image is not that important. Perhaps your sense is that when you open a ripple, you enter a space that is flat and empty. But when you make that characterization, you have again set up a point, from which more points can be established. Tensions, thoughts, or ordinary sense projections could all develop in this way. If you can open the ripples, no tension or projections are needed. The image or metaphor is secondary.

Opening in this way is a question of attitude. Our ordinary attitudes are the basis of holding on. They provide the power that sustains our perceptions and tensions. First come the manifestations of thoughts; then we notice a basic tension, which arises together with the one who notices—the outcast. We enter a flat world, the world of the rally and the valley. But if we can open ripples into other dimensions, not just accepting a two-dimensional flatness, the depth we discover transforms the rallies and restores the open.

Tell me, have you been working with this understanding?

Yes, I have. I am letting experience just be 'in'. Or you could say, I am staying 'in' experience.

What differences do you notice?

When I do that, there are really no problems.

Yes, that's true. 'No problems' is really the best. That seems good for this culture. Isn't that what Westerners are looking for: to be free of problems?

For example, I have been feeling sad. But when I am in the sadness, it is not a problem. It's just a way I feel.

It would be good for you to explore this in your own thoughts, to use your own questioning. After all, it's your journey. Just develop an easy attitude toward your own mind. That's the easiest way.

Let me ask you a question. When you say 'mind', what do you mean by it?

I think of it as being a space—a mental space, where mental events appear.

What about when we say, "What's on your mind?" We seem to mean something specific by that. What would you say?

When we use 'mind' in that way, it seems to refer to something like a general attitude.

A general attitude. Good. My suggestion is that you try to take that attitude differently.

So that's "the easiest way?"

Yes. 'Easy' means that you don't treat the attitude as a general attitude. Let me ask another question: What does it mean to you if I say, "shelterless mind?"

It sounds scary. I'm always trying to protect my mind. I want there to be a shelter.

That's right. Now, can you see what it would be like not to build a shelter for mind? It doesn't have to be a problem. When I have something in mind or on my mind, I build a shelter. But when I don't have an attitude in mind, I don't need to build a shelter. Why don't you give that a try? See what happens if you don't talk or think that way.

You may feel that if you don't build a shelter for the mind, you're taking on a burden, because it's risky. But it's not a burden, at least not for you. You could say it's a burden for your view or attitude, or a burden for the ego, or a burden for language. It doesn't have to be a concern for you.

We always assume that we have something in mind. That's the general attitude. When you think that way, you establish that something is there. Then there will be a burden. Can you ease that? That's what I mean by a shelterless mind.

We are always insisting: "This is how it is."

Right. That's the attitude. So look at the attitude, the foundation for thinking 'this' or 'that'. That's the attitude you need to ease.

But it's not attitude that says, "I have a mind"

No. The attitude is thinking that when you say "I have a mind" or "This is that," there is something there. Attitude generates tension, and that's the source of problems.

Operating without a 'something there' seems to be difficult for Westerners, almost impossible. It's so simple, so easy, but you can never think that way.

For instance, if I say, "Don't think; don't even think about thinking," you might say that was impossible. That's the attitude you need to ease. It's the same attitude that says, "I have a mind." From there, a whole environment emerges. It's just a ripple, but it's a label-ripple, and it makes a claim that our attitude supports.

If you cannot ease that, you are caught in the regime; you're under the rule of a dictator. You're following the dictator's policies; you're the carrier of what the dictator proclaims. That's the real burden. You really don't need to make it that hard for yourself. Can you see that?

31

Blessings

Is what you're presenting here another way of explaining Buddhism?

I wouldn't say that. What's being presented here has its own integrity, and it won't help to make comparisons. But you should definitely approach what's said here with respect. You may have had opportunities to study and practice very important approaches to knowledge, but it would be helpful to set those aside. Of course, it's fine to question or challenge what is said here, but you will get the most benefit if you take the attitude that something deeply important is being presented. Just say to yourself that this is a special chance—you have the possibility now to be completely free.

You may think of yourself as special in one way or another—most people do. But really we are all fundamentally alike. In particular, we are all getting old. Our time is running out, and the opportunities we have today will not last forever. You have the opportunity to investigate these teachings, here and now. So please, take them seriously.

I do . . . I truly do. But still, can you say what makes this teaching special?

Other teachings, including Buddhism, give a monopoly to the conceptual frame of mind. The same holds for science and for philosophy. They always make use of the patterns of mind.

Can you really say that? It seems that a spiritual or meditative tradition like Buddhism doesn't just rely on concepts. In fact, there are many teachers in different traditions who say that you have to let go of concepts. They say you should rely on experience instead. How is that different from what you're saying?

Well, we've already talked quite a bit about experience. There is a problem with emphasizing certain kinds of experience or certain ways of experiencing. For instance, if people learn meditation practices that let them experience bliss, they may become attached to that experience. In itself, that's not very valuable. It's a temporary technique for dealing with the suffering and dissatisfaction of samsara. It's like patching a puncture on a bald tire, or putting a band aid on a deep wound. Even if you say that you are going beyond bliss to a state where the mind is completely blank, or where you stop all mental activity, you are just choosing a kind of black hole. In the end, it's a stagnant situation.

There is certainly a place for cultivating practices that help you deal with psychological problems such as stress, or depression, or anxiety. Sometimes if the mind is very agitated, that may be the best you can hope for—you just don't want to feel crazy! But you are still not free. There are many ways to affect the nature of your experience, but even the most sublime experience does not necessarily go beyond the regime of mind.

That reminds me of something that Freud said. He wrote that the goal of psychotherapy was to cure neurosis, so that you could go back to dealing with normal unhappiness.

I don't know much about psychotherapy, but I agree that there is nothing wrong with being normal. You don't need extraordinary experiences. At the same time, being normal is not the goal. Normal means having the same thoughts that you always have, the same feelings, the same identity, the same self-image. Normal means going along with 'mineness' and 'me-ness'. Maybe that was enough for Freud, but it's not what seems important to me.

Why are we talking about these things? Because we have a chance to get more profit from our being alive. And we can do it without great effort. For instance, it does not depend on getting rid of the ego or self-image. You can operate within that set of concepts, as long as you are not trapped by your own possessiveness. That's where the toxicity comes in.

We are always putting limits on our situation and our possibilities, but we can go beyond those limits. Think again about the four immeasurables. 'Immeasurable' means bigger than anything; it is pervasive. It means full understanding. It goes beyond 'my' situation. It includes all sentient beings.

That's what the Bodhisattvas understand and practice. They feel deep compassion. There is nothing else there: not emotionality, not obligations, not demanding or commanding. Their practice is responding naturally, the way the sun shines. We spoke before about the job of the Bodhisattva, but it's not really accurate to say they have a job to do, and if they don't accomplish it they have to feel guilty because they have failed. The Bodhisattva just responds to every situation, fully and without effort.

We can do that too. We think that to get things done, we have to organize our activities or make a superhuman effort. We tell ourselves that that is where the power to succeed comes from. Or we may go to the other side and say that we have no power to do anything, that it all depends on the power of blessings, or on grace, which comes from beyond us. But the reality is that we don't have to depend on anything outside ourselves.

It can be helpful to speak of blessings, because blessings do have power. There is an ancient image of the wish-fulfilling jewel. If you somehow come into possession of that jewel, then whatever you pray for will spontaneously manifest. But it's possible to misunderstand this. It has nothing to do with praying for long life, or getting rich, or getting a good job or entering into a wonderful relationship. Blessings are not about fulfilling 'my' desires. That would be like a shadow hoping that it can cross over into the world of substance by accumulating lots and lots of shadows. Blessings operate at a different level. They have their own power and their own dynamic.

Blessings are also not a measure of your faith. Sometimes people say that if you pray with real faith and devotion, you will receive blessings. But blessings do not just come to the person who prays. They do not just manifest in one place. The power of blessings does not discriminate in that way. Blessings are like sunlight, shining equally on everyone.

When blessings flow, the heart opens. The same applies to higher knowledge. In both cases, there is no more 'belonging to' and no more 'arriving at'. When the spirit is open, you no longer need to focus on doing it that way—one thing after another.

I don't understand the distinction.

Here's an example. One way to develop compassion is to start with your loved ones, your family and friends, and then expand the focus of your feeling to your neighbors, people you interact with, strangers, and then perhaps people in your community or your country. From there you can go on to human beings everywhere in the whole world, or to dogs and horses, birds, insects, and so on. In the end you encompass every living being. But there is also another way to do it, in which you simply expand the feeling of compassion in all directions, so that it pervades the whole world. That is similar to blessings. Any being anywhere has the opportunity to share in those compassionate feelings. You don't have to take it one step at a time.

Our responsibility is to open to the rich opportunities we have available to us. That is the direct way to cultivate transformation. As we open ourselves, we give more, and we also receive more. It simply depends on being ready. We can speak of freedom, or blessings, or knowledge: the words are not so important. It may be better just to say what we are releasing: releasing worries, releasing entanglements, releasing all the basic emotions. When there is no 'belonging to', we can heal fear, anger or greed. These kinds of patterns open easily.

Does this depend on letting go of concepts?

The conceptual mind depends on applying labels. We have specific names that refer to specific things. Once we have identified something as belonging to a particular category that has a specific name, we make the assumption that what we have identified truly exists. But the kind of knowledge we generate that way is inevitably limited, because the labels are arbitrary. For instance, we learn the alphabet when we are very young, so we know 'A' and 'B' and 'C'. But we don't know why A comes before B, or why Z comes at the end.

The same not-knowing operates at every level. We have available the label 'mind', and so we are sure there is a mind. If we investigate, we may say that mind depends on the operation of the senses and our ability to use concepts. We can say the mind is happy or unhappy, agitated or calm; we can identify cultural or social patterns or trace out events in our personal history that shape the way the mind operates. But do we really know the meaning of mind or the operations of mind? Do we know the form and shape of mind? Do we know how the mind is activated, or what happens when the mind seems to fall silent? Many people today say the mind is produced by the brain. Maybe so, but do we know for sure? Can we find the mind in the brain?

There are many questions like that; we have been looking at them all along. Once we look, we realize we actually have very few answers, but somehow our not-knowing doesn't bother us. Despite our ignorance, we act as though we can rely on the mind. In fact, we make it the boss of our experience.

Really, our ignorance is quite striking. For instance, there is the one who is asking questions about mind: the searcher. Is the searcher part of mind, or generated by mind? Is it acting on behalf of mind? Or what about perception? When we perceive our environment through the senses or notice the inner workings of the mind, how much can we say about what is going on? Can we trace the backward and forward of perception? Can we see how certain zonings are established, or how they interact with one another?

We may talk a lot about all these things, but really we are just manipulating different concepts and thoughts. We name names, and think we have gotten closer to reality, or at least to the meaning of reality. We investigate the instrumentality of mind, but that is not the same as investigating mind itself. Our knowledge does not seem to extend that far.

It seems surprising that we are willing to settle for this limited form of knowledge. From the moment we are born to the time we die, we are partners of the mind. Don't we want to understand more fully? Don't we want to get closer? Whenever and however mind manifests, don't we want to go to the center, the central point? Don't we want to stay with the ripples?

What do you think? When we talk about ripples and staying in the center and getting closer to mind, does all that make sense to you?

As I understand it, we take positions, but whatever position we take, it's exactly that—a position. So it's limited. Instead, we want to go to the center.

OK, but that doesn't tell me what you really understand. 'Center' means face to face, point to point. It's not something you have to dictate. You just need to *be* that. That's what 'to be' means: to be that point.

Don't dismiss this as just theory, or make a note that you will try to practice this way the next time you have the chance. It's present now, not somewhere else or at some other time. It's not a something to practice! Just be 'in' . . . be 'on'.

I don't know if I am really doing it right now. How can I know?

The problem is that you don't trust yourself. The regime has its spies, and they are very sharp. They know what to say; they know where to step in. They tell you yes or they tell you no. Most important, they tell you that it depends on choosing yes or no. They want you to commit to your perceptions.

You need to learn to pin down experience, to expose it. Just open up. Later the tendency will come to name or interpret or separate, but when that happens, it's important not to lose the point. When you come to the point where you don't even know what experience is, you can ask: "What is the meaning of mind? What is 'I'" That is the place to look.

Open up completely—that's the crucial point. At that point the impression of the impression applies. If you want shelter, that is where you can find shelter.

So is that the path? A path that is not a path, because there is nowhere to go?

A super path! A higher path! It's not just a path for walking. You could say it's a rocket path. It's a path without a goal and without a direction or directionality. It's not located, and it doesn't depend on there being places. It doesn't involve specific possession—not possession of wisdom, or knowledge, or blessings. There are no fruits to enjoy and no points to own.

Can you follow along with this, right now? You need confidence; you need to be secure. Otherwise doubts will come, and that is when concepts start. "What do you mean? What are you saying? I'd better go back and check."

You don't need to go back and check! You are in it. Whatever thoughts and manifestations you can generate, whatever shape and form you can name—everything is in it, just popping up like bubbles. Why go back and check, or make plans to go ahead and obtain? We don't have time for that. We don't need that kind of feedback. As you are, you are completely free. You don't need to exhibit some attainment, and you don't need to report to yourself on your experience.

32

The Taste of 'In'

*I feel that if I understood directly what you are saying, immediately
here and now, we could stop. There would be no need to say anything
more. But even though what you say is stirring, something is missing.
Somehow there is a gap.*

That's because of the spies. It's the CIA at work in your own
mind.

This is not just your problem, or even a problem that's specific to this culture. Buddhism would say that it's due to
the residues of past experience. The tradition says that we
have been accumulating residues for at least thirty-two kal-
pas—an incredibly long period of time. So of course there
are consequences, and that is what we experience. When
moisture rises up into the air and cools, rain falls. That just
the way conditions cooperate. The same thing is true in our
experience. Because there are residues, our concepts have
power over us.

That's what I mean by gravity. Gravity is not a part of nature—it's the product of causal conditions. For instance, it's through causes and conditions that polarities arise: 'from' and 'to' and 'pro' and 'con' and 'subject' and 'object'.

I know what you're going to say: "I don't understand." But your "don't understand" is based on referring back to some previous condition. Instead of an understanding 'to', cultivate an understanding 'in'.

I'm trying to do that.

'Trying' is still pointing. You are not in it. You are 'pointing out to'. That 'to' has a particular aim. And that is not the point.

It's natural for this to be confusing, because we don't know how to live with these possibilities. Think about gravity. We rely on gravity to operate in the world—if you find yourself in a gravity-free zone, it's literally 'disorienting'. What we are talking about is something like living free of gravity. But the analogy doesn't fully work, because there isn't really any disorientation. It just seems that way as long as you keep trying desperately to generate some gravitational force.

In the ordinary world we all live in, everything and everybody cooperates to make sure that gravity continues to operate. Your friends and your allies will jump in to tell you your ordinary understanding is correct, that nothing else makes sense. They approve your usual ways of thinking and acting, because they share with you the same conceptual framework.

If you were a politician competing for office, that would

be good, because you would have their vote. In a sense, that's our situation, because we are looking for approval and acceptance. The problem, of course, is that this makes us dependent. We are not free, and when we are not free, we cannot be 'in it' completely. If we were in it, none of these concerns would come up, but we're not. At best you could say we are 'on' it. That's a problem, because 'it' does not even have a place.

So even relying on 'it' is wrong.

Right. But that is where we are, or at least where we start from. There is always a boss, located at a point, or an agent who is the actor. Conceptually we may understand that being 'at' a point is what keeps us from being free, but that is not enough to change our fundamental commitment.

If I'm the one who understands, or the one who wants to reach some other situation, that seems self-defeating. How can I get started? I see the target, but I don't have an arrow or a bullet to take aim and hit it. I can't even send a signal that would bounce off the target and give me feedback.

When you think that way, you've already accepted a certain zoning. You assume there is somewhere you have to go, and one specific direction that you have to take to get there. Why not start where you are? Just stay at the beginning, the very first 'place' That may be the point.

When we lose the connection to where we are, we set ourselves up for failure. Now we need a path, and we need a map to make sure we stay on the path, and we always risk going off on the wrong track. I worry that I may not concentrate the right way, or meditate the right way, or develop the right style or approach. That's how people normally live their lives.

Why not just forget about all that? We're fine exactly where we are, without any 'there' or any 'it'. Have you seen the story I wrote about the Prince? It's a simple story, a fairy tale really, but it makes this point. There is no need to go anywhere. In fact, when you leave the starting point, when you are no longer 'in' it, you inevitably get lost. Wandering here and there, you won't even realize that you are lost.

Of course, when we talk about the starting point, we also risk getting lost, because conventionally we think of the starting point in terms of history and linear time. Language points us in that direction, and we have no other tool than language to communicate. So we come from that level, and we get lost. But even in the midst of being lost, we can be 'in' our being lost.

When I get closer to being 'in', I can use conventional language and accept conventional situations, because I am not depending on conventional history to establish a conventional zone. The ripple itself opens. The point becomes the carrier of the ripple, the carrier of time, the carrier of perceptions. The word we have for that is 'mind'.

The conventional is inescapable. Without any vehicle, we have no possibility to act or to understand. Without sensory perception, identity, judgments, or concepts, how can there be knowledge? Without that, we only have, "I don't understand." Right?

But this 'don't understand' is not like a baby that doesn't understand.

The vehicle is still there. We have been trained to drive it; we know how to implement the program. Those are our tools. We need them to act.

At the same time, you have to recognize that we are using this familiar language in a new way. We say we are acting conventionally, but we are not doing the same thing we did before. We are not repeating or emulating the past. We are not trying to retrace or renew history. We are not insisting on answers or commanding ourselves to act in a certain way. We have been doing that for far too long.

Now we have reached the point, and we can stop. We see more closely, and we can ask new questions. What is going on? What is happening? We find a self. Is projection going on? Is there a projector? Is the self there? Is there knowing there? Is there 'there' there? Is 'there' not there?

Whenever we find ourselves in a particular place, or headed in certain direction at a certain time, we can apply knowing. There seems to be an agent, or someone judging. Apply knowing: is there someone doing the knowing?

We answer, "Yes. Someone is knowing." Immediately we depend on that answer. We go in that direction, and at once we are repeating the past, repeating our perceptions. We are demanding answers.

Now we can do it differently. That's important, because if we just do it the same way, we will never find security. There will be no real change, no progress. The samsara wheel will continue turning, and we will have no choice other than delusion or suffering. We are where we are, and there is no other place to go, so we might as well just settle down and

286

make the best of it. There can be no new time and space, no new home, no new vision. There are no new places to journey to, and no possibility to celebrate the unknown beyond what we know.

Is the point clear now?

Yes, because you keep hammering on it. But I have to be honest. I still hesitate. I would like to go there, even if there is no 'there' there, but something holds me back.

Sure! The FBI has its agents, its informers. They are embedded in you perception. The forces that keep samsara operating are very powerful. We can speak of karma or karmic residues, or habitual patterns. It's all on automatic: you have no way to control it and no other access.

So it's the same question. How is it possible to overcome all that? I understand enough at this point to say I don't want to just give up.

You may have the wrong picture. It's not as though there is some part of you that really wants to be free, but you are overwhelmed by karmic residues, or whatever you want to call it. You have to accept responsibility too. There is a part of you that refuses to change, that doesn't want to participate. You do have power, but you use that power to hold on. You're stubborn. You are convinced that you can't let go, you're afraid to let go, but the bottom line is that you don't want to let go. Why? Because you could lose everything. You could lose your identity, and there would be nothing to put in its place. Disaster!

Of course, that's all an intellectual projection. And it operates below the conscious level. There is a voice in your head that says, "Don't do that," but you have been hearing that voice for so long that you don't hear it at all. And then there are other voices in your head, the voices of your friends and the voices of your teachers, and they agree; they say, "Don't even think of doing that." You don't hear those voices either, but they're powerful. If you don't know how to thoughtfully investigate, how to become familiar with the ripples, there's no possibility of change.

In a way, this is the fundamental issue for Buddhism in the West. What we are talking about is related to the teachings of the Prajnaparamita or the Madhyamaka. Can Westerners receive this kind of teaching? Are they ready to really investigate the mind and transform it?

Every culture has its gatekeepers. Their job is to keep out ideas that are truly new, that could undermine the traditional understanding. So how do you get past the gatekeepers? You can't do it in a conceptual vehicle. Just criticizing the existing understanding is not going to work. You can present new ideas, but all you get in response is a shrug: "That's not relevant. It doesn't apply."

But now we're going in circles, because the very idea that there is a problem is already based on conceptual understanding. You can look at the past history of this culture and the tremendous momentum it has created, and decide that there is no way to overcome it, that you can't leave behind the ways you know of walking and talking and acting.

That makes sense, but it's wrong. You need to learn that transformation is easy, not difficult. The not-understanding or misunderstanding *is* the understanding. The ripple opens by itself. Its nature is self-opening, self-accepting. Then there are no more ripples.

So again, nothing to do.

Right. It may help to have some suggestions, so we could put it this way: Cultivate acceptance. Cultivate ease of perception, ease of consciousness, ease of thoughts, ease of timing. Whatever conditions arise, cultivate ease.

When you have nothing to do, you may be 'in'. There is a certain taste to 'in', so you will know. You may say, "I got it." It doesn't matter what you say. The point opens up, and there is no longer operation of the ordinary mind, the conceptual frame of mind. Any formulations are irrelevant, and no effort is needed. If you still find that confusing, there are further instructions that can help clarify what this means and how to put it into practice. But really, you don't need instructions.

Your difficulties will disappear when you realize that you have no difficulties. When you don't understand what to do, it is because you are projecting not understanding. You are not in it.

One way the Buddha described this situation was in terms of the marayas, demons who oppose our efforts at realization. You say to yourself that you want to know, but the marayas discourage you from knowing. One by one, they undermine you, speaking softly or threatening loudly:

> "You are not ready."

> "You have to stay loyal to your own ego, your own image.

"You belong to samsara. That's your realm, your
birthplace, your territory. Don't mess up."

"Who do you think you are? You have a different
job to do."

The Buddha showed the way to cut through all this negativity. But let's be honest. Even the Bodhisattvas may not
cut through completely. The Bodhisattva vows to release all
sentient beings from suffering, but if you look from a certain angle, by taking this position the Bodhisattva is just
creating job security.

Why not free all beings right now? "Well, because they're
not ready. I need to do it gradually." But in the meantime,
the hell realms fill up again and again with beings that suffer in agony.

The Buddha was not prepared to accept that. That is why he
transformed into Dharmakaya. In the Dharmakaya, global
healing is possible. Enlightenment can manifest in consciousness directly. All beings can receive universal blessings and know the truth of holiness. All beings can share in
the embodiment of all knowledge.

The Mahayana offers ways to do this. The teachings of the
Bodhisattva path present in a very clear and detailed way the
ten bhumis and the stages of the path, which remove karma
and klesha. But even on the path, the karmic residues are
very powerful. You may take hold of the residues in order
to overcome them, but in fact you are just grasping at their
shadows, so it takes a lot of effort. There are fish in the sea
that catch birds by following their shadows and anticipating
where they will land in the water, but it takes a lot of skill to

operate at that level. Asanga presented this clearly: perhaps his approach will prove the best for the West.

In the Tantras, there are teachings that can penetrate all this directly in this lifetime. They are very rare. They were not taught in Tibet until King Trisong Detsen asked Padmasambhava for them directly. Then the Great Guru gave him some of these teachings, aspects of the 84,000 tantras. Lochen Vairotsana and Vimalamitra made them available as well. So what can we say? The possibilities are there.

291

Afterword

The subject projects the object.

The object projects the subject.

The subject encompasses the object.

The object feeds back to the subject.

On the mind and in the mind—
each acts on behalf of the other.

This interplay, this variation—
the radiant nature of light manifests, reflecting itself.

The reflective reflector itself reflects, reflecting itself.

Self-reflection repeats itself.

The continuity of identity projects to the subject and to the object. They interact. We cannot say and do not know who is actively engaging in the interaction, but still we speak, calling out separately the subject orientation and the object orientation, the subject mind and the object—one, or the other.

As these points are made, the unique opportunity arises to present characters, qualities, natures. They show and share mind itself. We do not know how, but we can question. It seems we know one point, but not the second. We seem both to know the known and not know the known. The not known has been known. 'Known or not-known' project the knowing or not-knowing. The unknown itself shares itself, repeats itself.

This repetitious way is magical. The magician actively engages. Beginning and ending seem almost the same transmission. Not much changes, but for points and variations. But points and variations seem to have the nature of the mind. What is that nature? It is not necessarily specific to one time or one unique situation. It does not occur as reality or as absolute experience.

When we look more analytically, penetrating the selfness point directly, we can analyze many parts: conditions, causals, reflections, past and present and future. When we look now, it becomes puzzling. Even knowing the mind is puzzling. Any mental activity seems to show and share and shift within the regime of mind. The moment we identify becomes the transmission place for the next.

The transmission transaction is difficult to say. Can we say water waves, or liquid ripples; can we say light shining lightness? Can we say space, or translucence? Can we say there is no interference?

The mind is like that. All opportunities can manifest; all processes can develop. Knowledge and wisdom, compassion and love, karma and klesha, delusion and confusion, ignorance and not knowing. Clear and not clear, positivity and negativity. They all have to do with our mind. Mind manifests, and we actively engage. Mind accommodates, positive or negatively. All could understand.

Knowing can produce the impossibility of knowledge wisdom; it can produce equally emotionalities and negativities. Everything seems to operate by or for or to, or in or at. We are capable of creating this. Yet understanding and reflecting, we can learn—better than through reading books, better than through meditation or blocking thoughts, better than through concepts.

We seem to need to make the journey: through nature, action, and environment. We need to begin to see the importance. But we do not know that mind is the whole embodiment. We do not know the dimensions of mind.

This may be a useful way to think about knowledge of mind—knowingness mind. Entering the mind of the known, entering the realm of mind, entering knowing, we complete what we could call external progressions—an ongoing transmitting.

These are dynamic manifestations. They show or share within reflections. We can label it all; we can specify all the subjects and all the objects. But it seems to have to do with the essence of our being, with our transmission on this planet, with our part. It all has to do with our mind.

Knowing this mystery of the mind, we enter the journey toward knowledge of the mind, understanding of the mind. May we expand in the future our search, our investigation.

May there be thinkers.

Talking, inviting, knowledge comes. If we take the opportunity, we can let go of the baggage we carry, the confusion we hold. Mind can be our kidnapper, our jailer, but it can also be our friend. That possibility is there. We can prevent suffering.

These are all experiences, arising through mind. Knowing the causal of mind can become a knowingness that overcomes all toxic concepts and thoughts. We can learn from them all. Reflections of mind, they can become our teaching. Uniquely, they can express the echo of mind.

Appendix A

The 20 Upakleshas

1. Krodha   khro ba   rage/fury; indignation

2. Upanāha   khon du 'dzin pa   resentment

3. Mrakśa   'chab pa   concealment, slyness

4. Pradāśa   'tshig pa   spite

5. irśya   phrag dog   envy, jealousy

6. matsārya   ser sna   avarice, stinginess

7. māyā   sgyu   pretense, deceit

8. Śāṭhya   g.yo   dishonesty, hypocrisy

9. Mada   rgyags pa   self-infatuation, mental inflation, self-satisfaction

10. Vihiṃsā	rnam par 'tshe ba	malice, hostility, cruelty, intention to harm
11. Āhrīkya	ngo tsha med pa	shamelessness, lack of conscience
12. Anapatāpya	khrel med pa	lack of propriety, disregard
13. Styāna	rmugs pa	lethargy, gloominess
14. Auddhatya	rgod pa	ebullience, excitement
15. Āśraddhya	ma dad pa	lack of faith, lack of trust
16. Kausīdya	le lo	laziness
17. Pramāda	bag med	heedlessness, carelessness, unconcern
18. Muṣitasmṛtitā	brjed ngas pa	forgetfulness
19. Asaṃprajanya	shes pa bzhin ma yin	inattentiveness, non-alertness
20. Vikṣepa	rnam par g.yeng ba	distraction, desultoriness

Appendix B:

Dialog of I, Me, and Mind

I: I'm worried. I don't have enough time. The things I want to do aren't done. There are things I want to do. My mind is pressuring me. It's confusing. It's very scary.

Me: Yes . . . the pressure.

I: I worry I may be lost. I'm trapped in confusion. There's so much I haven't accomplished. And there's nothing I can rely on.

Me: That means a lot to me. My dear friend is not there.

I: I care about so many things that are mine: my family, my best friend, my property, my position, my body, my mind, my feelings. I care about my sense of me-ness.

Me: Without you, without my companion, there's a terrible fear. It's threatening; it's lonely. Nothing has much meaning for me. Thinking this way is totally devastating. What does 'I' stand for? What is its meaning? You could always recognize 'my' position, 'my' thoughts, 'my' knowledge. But if my companion is not reliable, if 'mine' doesn't belong to me anymore . . . .

I: It's like I've lost my mind. Who am I? I thought there would always be an 'I am', but now . . . .

Me: Yes . . . your 'I am' has been my best friend, the one who would always be with me. But if 'I am' is gone, what is the meaning of 'me' or 'to me'?

I: Mind is still there! It makes all kinds of decisions; it expresses itself.

Me: But who knows mind? If you don't know 'I', you can't be a reliable knower. But if no one knows 'I', then no one knows me either. And then how can there be 'mine'? What belongs to what? There's a great longing, but the longing has to attach to something and someone. There has to be a 'mine'. But what does 'mine' depend on? 'I' goes to 'me', and 'me' goes to mind.

Mind: YES, YOU ARE MINE!

I: But who owns 'mine'? Is the owner 'I'? Is it 'me'? Is it 'mine'? Is it mind?

Mind: EVERYTHING IS MINE, BECAUSE I MAKE YOU 'I'.

I: But you have been given to me. I am the owner. But now I don't know anymore: is that really so? If I don't know 'I', what does it mean to say 'owner'? Is the owner 'I' or 'me'? Or does 'I' belong to mind? Mind, you say, "You are mine." But who owns 'mine'? My recognition of 'I' makes 'I' mine, so maybe 'I' belongs to 'mine'.

Me: But 'mine' means 'my property'. So then 'I' belongs to me.

I: When I look to see who the real owner is, I have an image of being the owner, and I present that image to you.

Me: But who is 'you'? 'You' seems to be 'I'. Does 'I' own the image? Does the image own 'me'? It seems that mind is the one who gives the answer, who says what is so.

I: Do I have to be obedient to what mind says? Or is mind obedient to what I say? How could mind know how to operate without the 'I'? At least, *I* wouldn't know how to operate it.

Me: Mind seems to be intimate with 'I'. 'I' projects an image, but the image is projected by mind.

I: So which one is it? Right now I'm worried. It's my worry, and my thoughts. It's 'my' mind.

Me: Where does 'my' come from? Who makes all these decisions?

I: I have no clue.

Me: You mean you can't tell me? But wait! Who is 'you'? Can you tell me who you are?

I: I am knowledge of what's so.

Me: Now we're back to 'I am.'

I: Yes, that's so. 'I am' is the source, the decision maker, the one who dictates to mind. I say, "I am right," or "I am wrong." I say, "I am lonely . . . I am in love . . . I am enjoying . . . I feel good . . . I know . . . I get it." I am the one doing it all, the operator. I am responsible for each transition. What is there without 'I am'? Nothing at all.

Me: So why do you need me? Why do you need mind? No, it all seems very shaky. Tell me: Where is 'I'? Have you ever met 'I'? Have you ever even had a glimpse of 'I'? If you have, give me a description. Can you do that? Yes, you can tell me how you feel or what kinds of experiences you have. But what's underneath that?

Experience comes from mind, or so we're taught. But you are telling me that 'I' is the one making decisions. At least, that's your image of 'I'. So what's really happening? Who is following whom? Wouldn't we like to know?

I: For me, what matters is my experience. The most important experience is, "I am happy." But mind sets limits on whether I am happy or not, on whether I'm secure or prepared for what happens. Maybe it happens that I lose my best friend, or my job, or my money, or I lose my country. So I've lost what is mine.

It's very hard for mind to cope with that. It goes to my sense of self. There were things that were mine, and now they're not there anymore. My 'self', my own one, is lost. So of course there is despair and confusion. I have to get back what is mine. That's my identity. I am the owner—that's who I am.

Me: That's how it is for me too. 'Mine' is my partner. I need that 'belonging to'. Without that, how can there be peace or calm for me; how can there be relaxation and enjoyment? What does it mean if it's not mine? It's unbearable.

I: But maybe it's the other way round. Maybe 'me' belongs to what's mine.

Mind: THAT'S RIGHT. YOU NEED TO THINK ABOUT THAT.

I: I don't know if I can. It's really up to mind. Yes, I can respond to you, but it's all based on the meanings operated by mind. Mind gives feedback, and then I know what it means, or what it means to me. My understanding depends on mind. Even my not understanding is still mine. But is there a way to go to understanding directly, without relying on 'my' understanding as a bridge?

Mind: YOU NEED TO THINK ABOUT THAT.

I: I've already made my decisions. I've already thought it out.

Me: Right! You're already in the realm of mind. Even when you're thinking, you need to go through the mind operator. Mind seems instrumental. It's always introducing 'me' to 'I' and 'I' to mine—all the time. Mind portions experience out; it assigns roles.

Tell me: how do the senses arrive at each situation? How do they make points and determine directions? How do they allocate different experiences? How do we get an understanding of what's where? Are we aware of these operations? Each time a new experience comes, there are already situations and entanglements. How can we not be skeptical? We're automatically caught up in something unknown. We can make projections, but we can never arrive at conclusions. It's beyond our power to control: not 'me', not 'I', not even 'mind'.

I: So again I ask: Is there any other way of operating? It's a genius way of operating really. But who put it together? How do the connections hold? How do the operations interconnect? Is there some all-powerful magician who makes it all happen?

If I look at the connections, what I see is prepositions: 'from' and 'to' and 'before' and 'after'. All these polarities, leading to continuity. Everything flows together: all my activities. That's how I operate; that's how I aim for well-being.

Me: Can you offer me any other way? Can we question the whole structure of 'I' and 'me' and mine and mind?

Do you have any ideas?